Immigration, 'race' and ethnicity in contemporary France

Alec G. Hargreaves

London and New York

First published 1995
by Routledge
11 New Fetter Lane, London EC4P 4EE

Simultaneously published in the USA and Canada
by Routledge
29 West 35th Street, New York, NY 10001

Typeset in Times by
Ponting–Green Publishing Services, Chesham, Bucks
Printed and bound in Great Britain by
T.J. Press (Padstow) Ltd, Padstow, Cornwall

British Library Cataloguing in Publication Data
A catalogue record for this book is available from the
British Library

Library of Congress Cataloguing in Publication Data
A catalogue record for this book has been requested

ISBN   0–415–11816–6
ISBN   0–415–11817–4 (pbk)

For Margaret Hargreaves, to whom Robert and Alec
owe so much

Contents

Figures and tables

Abbreviations and acronyms

AIF	Association Islamique en France
CFRES	Centre de Formation et de Recherche de l'Education Surveillée
CNF	Code de la Nationalité Française
CNLI	Commission Nationale pour le Logement des Immigrés
CNPI	Conseil National des Populations Immigrées
CORIF	Conseil de Réflexion sur l'Avenir de l'Islam en France
CRE	Commission for Racial Equality
CRMF	Conseil Représentatif des Musulmans de France
CSA	Conseil Supérieur de l'Audiovisuel
DOM-TOM	Départements d'Outre-Mer et Territoires d'Outre-Mer
FAS	Fonds d'Action Sociale pour les Travailleurs Immigrés et leurs Familles
FIS	Front Islamique du Salut
FN	Front National
FNMF	Fédération Nationale des Musulmans de France
HCI	Haut Conseil à l'Intégration
HLM	Habitation à Loyer Modéré
IGAS	Inspection Générale des Affaires Sociales
INED	Institut National d'Etudes Démographiques
INSEE	Institut National de la Statistique et des Etudes Economiques
JALB	Jeunes Arabes de Lyon et sa Banlieue
LCO	Langues et Cultures d'Origine
MRAP	Mouvement contre le racisme et pour l'amitié entre les peuples

OMI	Office des Migrations Internationales
ONI	Office National d'Immigration
PCF	Parti Communiste Français
PS	Parti Socialiste
RPR	Rassemblement pour la République
SONACOTRA	Société Nationale de Construction pour le Logement des Travailleurs
UDF	Union pour la Démocratie Française
ZAC	Zone d'Aménagement Concerté
ZUP	Zone à Urbaniser en Priorité

Preface

It is now twenty years since France officially halted inward labour migration. Yet immigration continues apace, and the phenomena associated with it have become a central concern in French public life. The purpose of this book is to present a wide-ranging analysis of these developments and to confront the question which, more than any other, has come to dominate the public debate over immigration: how effectively are recent immigrants and their descendants being incorporated into French society?

This is a complex issue, embracing politics and culture as much as economic and social structures, and the attitudes of social actors are often as significant as – and sometimes at odds with – *de facto* developments on the ground. These tensions are reflected in the analytical framework of my study, which attempts to delineate and chart the interaction of three main dynamics: the attitudes and aspirations of the majority population, those of immigrants and their descendants, and the empirically observable pattern of social intercourse between majority and minority groups. Precisely because they are in a constant process of interaction, it is impossible wholly to separate any one of these strands from the others. For analytical purposes, the main focus of each chapter (except the first) falls on one or other strand, but it is important not to lose sight of the fact that they are bound together in a dialectical rather than a linear relationship. Chapter 1 presents an overview of the problematic; Chapters 2 and 3 focus on the experiences and attitudes of minority groups, with particular reference to economic and cultural issues; while Chapters 4 and 5 deal mainly with the majority population, focusing particularly on the political mediation of attitudes towards immigrants and their descendants.

Because it hinges on a complex mixture of behavioural, discursive and attitudinal factors, the question of how far immigrants and their descendants may be said to 'belong' to French society traverses many disciplinary boundaries. In the course of my study, I have drawn not only on my own research in the cultural and political spheres but also on the findings of specialists in many fields ranging from political science, sociology, history and economics to anthropology, social psychology and geography. As there is no up-to-date multi-disciplinary study available in English devoted to the contemporary scene in France,[1] I hope that my analysis will be of interest to a wide audience. It aims to serve both students who have little prior knowledge of ethnic relations *per se*, although they may have some familiarity with contemporary France, and anglophone scholars active in the field of ethnic relations seeking a more comprehensive survey of developments in France than has hitherto been available in English.

While French perceptions and policies in the field of immigration are the subject of a number of specialist studies by anglophone researchers – notably those of Freeman (1979), Grillo (1985), Schain (1985, 1987), Brubaker (1992), Hollifield (1992) and Silverman (1992)[2] – very little scholarly literature is available in English on the minority side of ethnic relations in France.[3] I hope that my own study will help to correct this imbalance. It deals essentially with the period since 1974, and more particularly since the early 1980s, when what the French call 'immigration' – a large part of which would more commonly be known in the English-speaking world as 'race' or ethnic relations – became a major preoccupation in French public life.

Where appropriate, I have tried to relate developments in France to the theoretical frameworks within which similar experiences have been analysed in English-speaking countries, while at the same time seeking to convey the specificity of the French experience and the particular terms in which it has been articulated by francophone scholars, politicians and ordinary members of the public. Without an understanding of the terms in which the French debate has been constructed, it is impossible fully to comprehend the way in which minority groups have fared in French society.[4]

Immigrants originating in Africa and Asia, and particularly those from Islamic countries, are at the heart of this debate. It has become commonplace to assert that unlike earlier minority groups, who came mainly from Europe, those of Third World origin are difficult if not impossible to incorporate into French society. Claims of this kind are not only advanced by extreme right-wing politicians such as Jean-Marie Le Pen (1984: 99–114) and apparently swallowed whole by the general public (see, for example, the Indice-Opinion poll in *Le Magazine-Hebdo*, April 1984, and the BVA poll in *Paris-Match*, 14 December 1989), but are also given credence by mainstream politicians on both the Left and the Right (on the emergence of this consensus, see Silverman 1992: 70–94). Similar ideas have also become influential among academics. Safran (1986), for example, suggests that Muslims of North African origin in France are less socio-economically adaptable and far more resistant to cultural change than were earlier waves of Jewish immigrants from Eastern Europe;[5] Fitzpatrick (1993) presents a similar view. Heisler and Heisler have argued that this sort of pattern obtains not only in France but across Western Europe as a whole, with 'large numbers of culturally essentially alien migrants' leading to 'the emergence of a socioeconomic and political underclass' (Heisler and Heisler 1986: 12, 19).

I am not in general convinced by these arguments. While I agree with Heisler and Heisler (1986: 16) that the state plays a central role in cultural reproduction and other aspects of social experience, there is overwhelming evidence to show that the receiving state far outstrips in economic resources and political authority anything that can be mustered by the majority of sending states. It is certainly true that today's immigrants are often reluctant to abandon the cultural codes that they internalized in their countries of origin, but there is nothing new in this. Few adults seek to annihilate the culture that they learnt during their formative years. Most seek to transmit what they inherited to their own children. Only in exceptional circumstances, however, do international migrants succeed in inculcating in their descendants a level of attachment to pre-migratory cultural codes which is in any way comparable to their own. In most cases, the necessary precondition for this has been a degree of political control amounting to colonial or quasi-colonial authority. Europeans who migrated to colonial Africa and Asia succeeded in maintaining their cultural heritage despite being numerically weak, because they were politically and economically strong. To a lesser extent, the privileged status enjoyed by German settlers in Russia and neighbouring lands enabled them to achieve something similar.

The experience of immigrants from former colonies in France and other parts of Europe has been directly the opposite of this. Economically weak and politically excluded, they have found the odds stacked heavily against them in the struggle to sustain their cultural inheritance across succeeding generations. As is shown in Chapters 3 and 5, after a mild flirtation with notions of cultural diversity during the late 1970s and early 1980s, the French state has returned to the well-worn and still successful tradition of acculturating as fully as possible second-generation members of minority groups through the public educational system. Television has done the rest. The cultural norms internalized in this way are, of course, by no means purely French. The essential point, however, is that immigrant-born youths share through the mass media and state education in the cultural system of their French-born peers.

This is not to say that minorities of recent immigrant origin are being successfully incorporated into the fabric of social and economic life in France. Contrary to the claims advanced by Safran, the high rates of unemployment, the low levels of social mobility and the poor-quality housing to which many second-generation members of minority ethnic groups find themselves condemned cannot be convincingly attributed to 'the inability of their unassimilated parents to provide role-models for cultural adaptation' (Safran 1985: 55). The principal obstacles to the incorporation of Third World immigrants and their descendants into French society lie not in cultural differences but in the radical restructuring of the labour market since the mid-1970s, greatly reducing the opportunities open to minority groups, and in the discriminatory treatment which they have suffered in the competition for jobs and scarce resources. These socio-economic developments are the subject of Chapter 2, while the factors contributing to the hierarchical ethnicization of immigrants and their descendants are examined in Chapter 4.

Minorities originating in the Maghreb (i.e. former French North Africa) have been both quantitatively dominant and qualitatively hardest hit in these difficult decades. It would be impossible to understand public perceptions and political responses to immigration in France, dealt with in Chapters 4 and 5, without giving due weight to the role of Maghrebis as objects of debate. The fact that they also occupy a central position in the first three chapters should not, however, be interpreted as a sign that they are of interest only as a function of that debate. The demographic fact of the matter is that because Maghrebis dominated migratory inflows from the 1950s onwards, with a clear pattern of family settlement emerging during the 1960s, they and their descendants have been the most dynamic element in the pattern of ethnic relations which has unfolded in France since the mid-1970s. Other groups of Third World origin –

particularly sub-Saharan Africans and South-East Asians – have gained in importance among immigrants entering France during the 1980s and 1990s, but as the overall inflows are now much lower than before, Maghrebis are still by far the largest single group among the population of immigrant origin. No less importantly, the relatively recent arrival of most sub-Saharan and South-East Asian immigrants means that they have yet to produce a large second generation of young adults socialized more or less entirely in France. Among Maghrebis, the second and third generations now far outnumber immigrants in the true sense. Their role in the mobilization of minority groups was one of the most striking features of the 1980s.

Wherever ethnic relations are analysed and debated, there are fierce arguments over terminology. The conceptual framework for my own study is outlined in Chapter 1, where definitions of key terms are outlined in the context of a historical survey of immigration in France. Most of the terms adopted here will be familiar to specialists in the field of ethnic relations, and while my own usage of them will not necessarily command universal assent, it is, I hope, clearly explained and internally coherent. Several less standard expressions require a preliminary word of explanation. As used here, 'people of immigrant origin' encompasses immigrants (i.e. people born in a country other than that in which they now live) together with their children and grandchildren. 'Immigrant-born' people are to be understood as second-generation members of minority ethnic groups, i.e. people born in the receiving country to immigrant parents or, while born abroad, brought to the receiving country while still children. The defining feature of those whom I describe as immigrant-born lies in the fact that, by contrast to their parents, who spent their formative years in the sending country, they are socialized largely, if not exclusively, in the receiving country. This distinction is important for understanding the long-term development of ethnic relations, for patterns of socialization play a fundamental role in shaping inter-generational trends.

Many scholars distinguish between immigrants and their descendants on the one hand and the 'native' or 'indigenous' population on the other. The latter terms are best used sparingly, not least because the distinction between natives and people of immigrant origin is in practice far less clear-cut than it might appear at first sight. Basing her analysis on a span of three generations, Tribalat (1991: 43, 65–71) estimates that about a quarter of the people living in France today are either immigrants themselves or have at least one immigrant parent or grandparent. If the analysis of ancestral origins were pushed back a further generation or two, the population of immigrant origin would appear larger still. Yet if a quarter or even less of a person's ancestry is foreign, of what significance is that compared to the three-quarters or more that is 'native' to France? If the succeeding generations have all been socialized in the receiving country, what does it matter if all four grandparents were foreign? In their everyday lives, many people descended from immigrants are quite ignorant of their foreign origins or attach little or no importance to them. They are apt to consider themselves – and to be regarded by others – as part of France's indigenous population, especially if they are white. By contrast, second- and even third-generation non-whites are less likely to be treated as part of the indigenous population, despite the fact that all those born in a given country, including the children or grandchildren of immigrants, are, in the literal sense of the term, natives of that territory.

Because of its contamination by socially constructed hierarchical differences of this kind, the word 'native' is generally avoided in the present study, except in a limited number of contexts where its literal meaning is appropriate. More commonly, I distinguish between majority and minority groups. The latter consist of people of immigrant origin (as defined above), while the former encompasses that part of the population which was born in France with no immediate immigrant ancestry (i.e. immigrant parents or grandparents). Because of gaps in official statistics and family memories, discussed in Chapter 1, it is not always clear whether particular individuals should be formally ascribed to one side or the other of the majority/minority divide. It should also be remembered that the relatively high level of social acceptance enjoyed by most second- or third-generation whites means that their formal minority status (as defined here) is of little significance when compared with the stigmatization experienced by many of the children and grandchildren of African or Asian immigrants.

Valuable comments and suggestions were made in the formative stages of this book by Martin Schain, Claire Duchen, Peter Morris, Brian Jenkins, Philip Ogden, Beverley Adab and Gary Freeman. Several of these early advisers were kind enough to offer more detailed comments on drafts of various chapters. Patrick Weil and Wendelin Guentner also made extremely helpful comments on the typescript. At Loughborough, I benefited from the advice of Jeremy

Leaman and Paul Byrne, while Louisa Fulbrook prepared the tables and graphs. I drafted parts of the book while holding visiting fellowships at the Centre for Research in Ethnic Relations at the University of Warwick and at the Institute for European Studies at Cornell University, where I am particularly grateful to Zig Layton-Henry and Susan Tarrow respectively for the warmth of their hospitality. It is also a pleasure to acknowledge the assistance given by Catherine Wihtol de Wenden, Michèle Tribalat, Véronique de Rudder, Jacques Denantes, Moncef El Bahri and Françoise Lorcerie. Patricia, Kate and Rose Hargreaves provided vital support on the home front and generously tolerated my absences while I was absorbed in the preparation of the book. Patricia's unfailing eye for detail strengthened the typescript in many ways. For any errors or inadequacies which remain I am of course solely responsible.

AGH
Loughborough, December 1994

Chapter 1

Overview

INTRODUCTION

In June 1993, French Interior Minister Charles Pasqua announced that one of the prime objectives of the centre-right government which had just taken office was 'zero immigration' (*Le Monde*, 2 June 1993). Although Pasqua later qualified this statement, saying his objective was 'zero illegal immigration' (*Le Monde*, 8 June 1993), his remarks were deeply symbolic of the acute sensitivity attaching to the field of immigration in French public life. Far from being an overstatement, accidentally slipping beyond the narrow target of illegal migratory inflows, Pasqua's comments carried at a subliminal level a much wider resonance. In its everyday usage in France, the word 'immigration' has come to denote not simply the process of movement from one country to another, but everything associated with the permanent settlement of people of foreign origin within the receiving society (Tribalat 1993: 1911). Understood thus, 'zero immigration' is an impossible but hugely appealing objective in the eyes of many ordinary French men and women, for it carries the promise of somehow ridding the country of all the problems linked in the public mind with people of immigrant origin. In a word, it encapsulates the notion that immigrants and their descendants are fundamentally out of place in French society.

The use of the word 'immigration' to encompass what are in many respects post-migratory processes is itself symptomatic of the difficulties experienced by the French in coming to terms – both literally and ontologically – with the settlement of people of immigrant origin. In the English-speaking world, such people are commonly referred to as 'ethnic minorities' or 'minority ethnic groups', and a large part of what the French call 'immigration' is commonly known as 'race relations'. In France, such terms are taboo (Lloyd 1991; Rudder and Goodwin 1993) except among a small but growing number of academics, particularly in urban sociology and anthropology, who, inspired in many cases by the Chicago school of sociology (which pioneered the study of relations between blacks and whites in the US), are adapting the Anglo-American problematics of 'race', and more particularly 'ethnic relations', to their own field of study (Rudder 1990; Battegay 1992).

A key reason for the general rejection of these terms in France lies in the fear of giving even verbal recognition to the settlement of people seen as enduringly different from the indigenous majority. Fearful that the use of such terms might encourage the entrenchment of ethnic differentiation within French society, Schnapper (1990: 88–92), for example, argues that the notion of 'ethnic groups' is an unacceptable Americanism. Like most of France's intellectual and political elite, she prefers to speak of 'integration', a term which in recent years has been officially adopted by the state as a means of designating the incorporation within French society of people who originate outside it. As such, the notion of 'integration' has become the functional equivalent in France of 'race' or 'ethnic relations' in Britain or the US. Whereas the concept of 'race relations' appears to imply the recognition of permanently distinct groups, 'integration' is predicated on the assumption that social differentiation is or should be in the process of being reduced (Weil and Crowley 1994: 113–20). Thus even when the social heterogeneity resulting from immigration is implicitly recognized, as in the discourse of integration, the terms of that recognition presuppose its actual or future effacement.

Two state-of-the-art surveys of research in this field were published in France in 1989. The central term in the title of both (Dubet 1989; *Babylone* 1989) is 'immigration(s)', yet the analyses themselves focus not on population movements but on the social processes consequent upon the permanent settlement of immigrants. The pivotal term which informs the whole of Dubet's analysis is in fact 'integration'. In surveying scholarly and government research, Dubet's primary concern is to evaluate the extent to which it indicates that immigrants and their descendants are being effectively 'integrated' into French society (Dubet 1989: 5). If the title of his survey reflects the generic sweep of the semantic field now covered by French usage of the word 'immigration', the centrality of 'integration' in the main substance of his analysis exemplifies the conceptual framework within which the social consequences of immigration are most commonly articulated by academics as well as by policy-makers in France.

These conceptual considerations are important because they shape not only the terms in which the policy debate over 'immigration' takes place but also the forms in which knowledge itself is constructed. Academics often rely for much of their data on information collected by state agencies such as census authorities. In countries like Britain and the US, it is standard practice to categorize the population into groups defined by racial or ethnic origins. Census and other data collected in this way are used to pinpoint problems requiring public intervention and to monitor the effects of such initiatives. In France, the state refuses to collect nationwide information of this kind and, through its data protection laws, makes it difficult for others to do so.[1]

France does publish statistics on what are known in migration studies as population *flows* (i.e. the number of people entering, and to a lesser extent those leaving, the country over a given period of time), but only fragmentary data are available on migration *stocks* (i.e. people born outside France and now resident there), and still less information is compiled on their descendants. Deficiencies in records of immigrants who have died or left the country make it impossible to calculate those stocks simply on the basis of recorded inward and outward flows. The body responsible for conducting censuses, the Institut National de la Statistique et des Etudes Economiques (INSEE), does record the birthplace of every resident. However, very little of the census data released by INSEE makes any reference to place of birth, and no information at all is collected on the birthplace of people's parents. Only very recently has a limited amount of data on countries of birth been exploited in important studies by Michèle Tribalat and her colleagues at the Institut National d'Etudes Démographiques (INED) (Tribalat 1991, 1993). For most practical purposes, the closest one can get to official information on the ethnic origins of the population – and it is a very rough approximation indeed – is through the data which are published on the nationality status of residents.

The 'common-sense' equation which is often drawn between foreigners and immigrants is seriously flawed. Not all immigrants are foreigners; nor are all foreigners immigrants; significant numbers of people are neither foreigners nor immigrants but are often perceived and treated as such. By focusing on nationality to the exclusion of immigration status or ethnic origins, official data make it extremely difficult to conduct reliable analyses of the impact of immigration on French society at large. The statistical lacunae generated by the state reflect once again an unwillingness at the highest level officially to recognize immigrants and their descendants as structurally identifiable groups within French society.

It is true that most immigrants are foreigners. Foreigners stand, by definition, outside the national community and are formally identifiable on this basis. However, foreigners who fulfil certain residence requirements may apply for naturalization. Others become entitled to citizenship if they marry a French national. All those who acquire French nationality disappear from the official ranks of the foreign population. Censuses do record the previous nationalities of people officially classified as *Français par acquisition* (i.e. individuals born without French nationality who have since acquired it), but published information of this kind is seldom sufficiently disaggregated to facilitate detailed socio-economic or spatial analyses. Most of the children born to immigrants have until now automatically become French nationals on reaching adulthood, or in some cases at birth, without having to go through any formal application procedures. The grandchildren of immigrants are all automatically French from birth. Strictly speaking, children of foreign birth who become French nationals on reaching the age of majority are *Français par acquisition*; in practice, the great majority are declared in census returns as having been born French (Tribalat 1991: 28). By the same token, they, like all the children and grandchildren of immigrants born with French nationality, are in statistical terms lost without trace. Thus in the official mind of the state, the formal integration of immigrants and their descendants goes hand in hand with their obliteration as a distinct component of French society.

IMMIGRATION IN FRENCH HISTORY

This official disappearing act has been matched until very recently by a sustained bout of collective amnesia. There has been very little awareness among the public at large of the contribution of immigrants to the historical development of France (Noiriel 1992b). This forgetfulness is due in part to the paucity of historical research in this field. State formation reached an advanced stage in France at a much earlier point than in many other parts of Europe. The founding myths of the French state were created over many hundreds of years under the centralizing monarchical system which prevailed until the end of the eighteenth century, when they were recast by the French Revolution into the modern forms associated with the ideal of a unified nation-state. The central myths of national identity were thus in place before the rise of large-scale immigration into France during the nineteenth century. Entranced by the spell of those myths, historians in France continued to pay little if any attention to the contribution of immigrants to the national experience even when, by the middle of the twentieth century, sustained migratory inflows had for several generations been an integral part of French society. By contrast, in countries like the US, immigration and nation-building were intimately intertwined. The overwhelming majority of present-day Americans are descended from immigrants who entered the US after its official establishment as an independent state at the end of the eighteenth century. Immigration is in this sense an integral part of American national identity, and it is recognized as such in American historiography (Noiriel 1988; Green 1991).

It was not until the 1980s that the preoccupation with immigration in contemporary France brought an upsurge of interest in historical studies of this phenomenon over a much longer period (Citron 1987; Noiriel 1988; Lequin 1988; Ogden and White 1989). Such studies were long overdue, for it is an important matter of historical fact that during the greater part of the last two centuries France has received more immigrants than any other country in Europe (Dignan 1981). Indeed, for much of the twentieth century, after the US imposed tight quotas in the 1920s, France was the most important country of immigration in the industrialized world. By 1930, foreigners accounted for a larger share of the population in France than they did in the US (Noiriel 1988: 21).

As formally defined by French demographers (Tribalat 1991: 6), immigrants are people born abroad without the nationality of the country in which they now live. On this basis, there are today over 4 million immigrants in France, almost one-third of whom have acquired French nationality. In addition, it is estimated that about 5 million people (the great majority of whom are French nationals) are the children of immigrants, and a similar number have at least one immigrant grandparent. Thus, in all, about 14 million people living in France today – a quarter of the national population of nearly 57 million – are either immigrants or the children or grandchildren of immigrants (Tribalat 1991: 43, 65–71).

In explaining migratory flows, a distinction is usually drawn between 'push' and 'pull' factors. Industrialization, and the country's relatively low rates of natural population growth compared with most of her neighbours, were the principal 'pull' factors inclining France to accept and in some cases actively recruit inflows of foreigners. Heavy population losses suffered during the First World War and to a lesser extent during the Second World War gave an additional impetus to pro-immigration policies. Those who migrated to France felt 'pushed' from their home countries by a variety of factors. Most commonly, these were of an economic nature. When they compared their present circumstances with those they hoped to find elsewhere, migrants motivated by economic considerations calculated that by moving to another country they would have a higher chance of improved living standards. In some cases, political pressures weighed more heavily than purely economic concerns. State persecution of individuals or groups, pursued sometimes to the point of genocide, induced many of those targeted in this way to seek refuge elsewhere. Ever since the revolution of 1789, France has cultivated an international reputation as a country committed to the defence of human rights, making it a natural destination for would-be refugees (Noiriel 1991).

Three further general points should be made concerning the pattern of migratory flows. First, it would be a mistake to view those flows as a mechanical outcome of impersonal forces. While substantial numbers of people have sometimes been forcibly transported from one country to another (as slaves or convicts, for example), most international migrants have themselves made the decision to move. Often, of course, the choice has been made in circumstances in which they would have preferred not to find themselves (such as poverty or persecution), but in each case the decision to migrate has nevertheless depended on an act of personal volition, without which 'push' and 'pull' factors would have been no more than analytical abstractions. One place does not push or pull against or towards another. Places have the power to attract or repel only to the extent that they are perceived positively or negatively within the personal projects constructed by individual human beings (Begag 1989).

Second, the relative weight of push and pull factors may be perceived differently in the sending and receiving states. If unemployment or inter-ethnic tensions rise in a receiving country, voters and politicians may seek to halt or even reverse migratory flows. If, at the same time, the situation worsens or simply remains stable within a sending country where people already consider their lot to be intolerable, they may seek to enter the other country in spite of the barriers placed in their way. Contradictions of this kind have become increasingly visible since the mid-1970s, when most West European states declared a formal halt to inward labour migration. As living standards and political conditions have stagnated or worsened in many African and Asian countries since then, would-be migrants have turned increasingly to illegal modes of entry into European labour markets.

Third, the choice of a particular destination on the part of an individual migrant is always conditioned by a complex set of calculations in which immediate opportunities and constraints are weighed against the chances of securing long-term objectives. Thus countries with less than ideal conditions but relatively low barriers may pull in more migrants than states that are perceived as highly attractive but to which access is tightly policed. Geographical proximity, transport systems and social networks based on friends or relatives who have already migrated may also play a role.

During a large part of the nineteenth and twentieth centuries, French perceptions of the need for immigrants, and more particularly immigrant workers, dovetailed more or less closely with the calculations made by would-be or actual migrants in nearby countries. There have, however, been important exceptions to this pattern. An economic downturn in the late nineteenth century was marked by growing antagonism towards foreign workers in some sections of French society, particularly those who feared for their jobs. Anti-Italian sentiments became especially strong in southern France, where a number of violent attacks took place. The most serious of these occurred in 1893 at Aigues-Mortes, where at least eight Italians were killed and dozens more were injured. During the slump of the 1930s, the French authorities organized the forcible repatriation of trainloads of Poles (Ponty 1988: 309–18).

Until the First World War, France exercised only weak immigration controls, effectively leaving most population movements to the free play of market forces. Even after official controls were instituted,[2] these were often circumvented with the more-or-less open connivance of the state. For example, the majority of immigrant workers who entered the French labour market during the economic boom of the 1960s did so illegally, but the state was happy to 'regularize' their situation *ex post facto* by issuing residence and work permits to foreigners who, by taking up jobs, were helping to ease labour shortages. Even today, when the state appears to be more earnest in its opposition to illegal immigrants, many find jobs (usually of a precarious and poorly paid nature) because their employers calculate that their own interests are well served by the recruitment of undocumented workers. In this way, employers bypass and yet at the same time benefit from the regulatory intervention of the state, for the fear of deportation prevents undocumented workers from complaining about poor wages or working conditions.

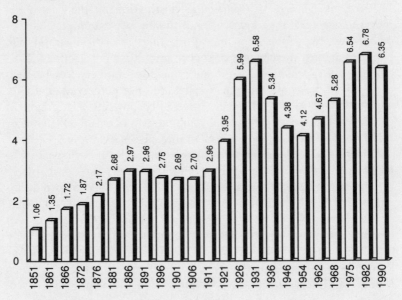

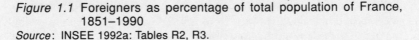

Figure 1.1 Foreigners as percentage of total population of France, 1851–1990
Source: INSEE 1992a: Tables R2, R3.

During the nineteenth century, labour shortages in France's expanding industrial sector induced considerable internal migration from rural to urban areas. However, these internal population flows proved insufficient to meet the demand for labour, and foreign workers came in increasing numbers. Census data on the foreign population were first collected in 1851. Figure 1.1 shows the number of foreigners, expressed as a percentage of the total population, at every census conducted since then. It shows a steady rise in the foreign population from one per cent of the national total in 1851 to almost 3 per cent in the 1880s, when economic circumstances entered

a more difficult phase. The figure then stabilized until after the First
World War, when it more than doubled, to 6 per cent, by the time of
the 1931 census. The economic slump of the 1930s saw a sizeable
fall in the foreign population, though it remained at a higher level
than that seen prior to the First World War. The strong growth rates
achieved during what the French call *les trente glorieuses* (i.e. the
thirty years immediately following the Second World War) brought
the figure back up to above 6 per cent, where it has remained since
the mid-1970s despite the much weaker economic growth and higher
rates of unemployment which have prevailed since then.[3]

Until as recently as 1968, the majority of the foreign population
in France came from neighbouring countries. Prior to the 1920s,
Belgium and Italy alone accounted for over half of all foreign
residents. Belgians, attracted by job opportunities in the coal, steel
and textile industries just over the border in north-east France,
outnumbered Italians until the beginning of the twentieth century.
Italians, who were traditionally concentrated in unskilled jobs in
south-eastern France, then took over as the single largest national
group, which they remained until being overtaken by the Spaniards
when their numbers peaked in 1968. Spanish immigrants were
particularly numerous in south-western France, where many worked
as agricultural labourers (Dreyfus and Milza 1987; *Cahier de
l'Observatoire de l'Intégration* 1994).

Between the wars, a large Polish community had also developed.
Most Polish immigrants took jobs on the land or in the mines. They
quickly became the largest expatriate community originating in a
country without a shared border with France, second only in size to
that of the Italians. By 1931, they accounted for half of all foreign
workers in the mining industry. The slump hit this sector particularly
hard, forcing tens of thousands of Poles to return home. Up to
100,000 more followed them immediately after the Second World
War. When the Iron Curtain sealed Poland's borders shortly afterwards, the remaining community in France stagnated and then
declined rapidly in importance (Ponty 1988).

While economic motives were to the fore among the four main
national communities which dominated migratory flows to France
until the middle of the twentieth century, political factors also played
a significant role in two of them. Throughout the nineteenth century,
political exiles from Italy had found a refuge in France, and their
numbers were swollen following Mussolini's accession to power in
1922. Political refugees began leaving Spain almost as soon as the

Civil War began in 1936. When it ended three years later with the defeat of the Republicans, almost half a million Spaniards crossed into France; though many later returned home, at least half of them stayed.

A number of smaller immigrant communities were formed mainly as a result of political persecution. Armenians, for example, regrouped in France during the 1920s after fleeing a campaign of genocide instigated by Turkey. At about the same time, more than 100,000 Russians hostile to the Bolshevik Revolution settled in France, mainly in the Paris area. Before the First World War, about 40,000 Jews had fled to France from the Russian Empire, where they were threatened by widespread pogroms. With the rise of Fascism during the 1930s, well over 100,000 Jews from Germany and Eastern Europe sought refuge in France. During the Second World War foreigners – particularly those who had come to France because of political persecution – were to play a vigorous role in the Resistance, thereby contributing to the liberation from Nazi occupation (Courtois 1989).

After the war, plans drawn up by the French government foresaw a need for substantial numbers of immigrants to assist in reconstruction work and to compensate for the country's weak demographic growth. In the debate over the orientation of immigration policy, there were two main camps: economists such as Jean Monnet, who were mainly concerned to remedy immediate labour shortages, and demographers such as Alfred Sauvy and Georges Mauco, who favoured permanent immigration by families to compensate for France's low population growth. There was also considerable debate over whether or not to impose ethnic quotas similar to those operated by the US until 1965. While there was widespread agreement that Africans and Asians were less desirable than Europeans, those whose main concern was the labour market were less anxious to formalize an ethnic hierarchy than were those who saw immigration as vital for France's demographic future. A compromise eventually emerged when the foundations of France's post-war immigration policy were laid in a government ordinance issued on 2 November 1945 (Weil 1991: 53–62).

One of the most important aspects of the regulations laid out in this ordinance was the separation of residence and work permits. Although it was expected that most immigrants would in the first instance be foreign workers, the right to live in France was not made conditional on being in employment. Thus while labour recruitment

quickly outpaced demographic considerations as the dominant concern shaping immigration policy (Tapinos 1975), the regulatory
framework readily permitted family settlement, and would later
make it difficult for the state to subordinate residence rights to
narrowly economic criteria.

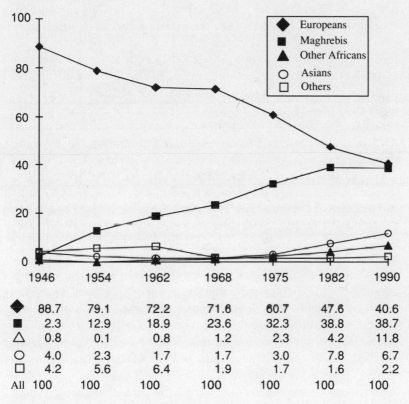

	1946	1954	1962	1968	1975	1982	1990
◆	88.7	79.1	72.2	71.6	60.7	47.6	40.6
■	2.3	12.9	18.9	23.6	32.3	38.8	38.7
△	0.8	0.1	0.8	1.2	2.3	4.2	11.8
○	4.0	2.3	1.7	1.7	3.0	7.8	6.7
□	4.2	5.6	6.4	1.9	1.7	1.6	2.2
All	100	100	100	100	100	100	100

Figure 1.2 Main nationality groups as percentage of France's foreign
              population, 1946–90
Source: INSEE 1992a: Table R6.

No ethnic quotas were laid down in the 1945 ordinance, but in
implementing these formal regulations, successive governments
sought as far as possible to encourage European rather than African
or Asian immigrants. Thus the Office National d'Immigration
(ONI),[4] a state-run agency established under the 1945 ordinance with
the task of regulating migratory inflows, immediately opened recruiting offices in Italy while leaving other countries untouched. The

pattern of inflows which subsequently developed was, however, very different from what had been expected. Italians and other Europeans were less attracted to France than had been hoped. As Figure 1.2 shows, the share of Europeans in the foreign population of France has declined steadily throughout the post-war period, falling from 89 per cent in 1946 to 41 per cent in 1990. The fastest-growing groups originated in the Maghreb (i.e. the western part of North Africa, consisting of Algeria, Morocco and Tunisia). Their share of the foreign population leapt from just 2 per cent in 1946 to 39 per cent in 1982. This shift is in part a reflection of the fact that differences in living standards between different parts of Western Europe have generally lessened during the post-war period, particularly since the creation of the European Economic Community in 1957, and this has reduced the incentives for intra-European migration. At the same time, the gap in living standards between European and Third World countries has grown, making migration towards the rich north an increasingly attractive prospect to those in the impoverished south.

The countries commonly labelled as belonging to the Third World lie primarily in or close to the southern hemisphere. While they include parts of Latin America and Oceania, those with which France has been most closely associated are in Africa and Asia. All these states are characterized by relatively low levels of economic development; most are also former colonies of richer 'northern' countries. After the Second World War, France's overseas empire, which was second in size only to that of Britain, was gradually decolonized. The last major step in this process came with the independence of Algeria in 1962. Until then, Algeria had been officially regarded as an integral part of French territory, and all its inhabitants – including those of non-European descent – had the formal status of French nationals. Neighbouring Morocco and Tunisia were also under French rule until 1956, but as these states had the juridical status of protectorates (implying a milder type of colonial domination than that obtaining in Algeria) their citizens were not officially classed as French. The formal equality enjoyed by Algerians under a new statute applied to their country in 1947 gave them complete freedom of movement in and out of metropolitan France (i.e. France as commonly understood, as distinct from overseas territories under French sovereignty), and they retained this right for several years after independence. They were by the same token exempt from the regulatory powers of the ONI. From a mere 22,000 in 1946, their numbers grew to 805,000 in 1982, making Algerians the largest national group among the foreign population in France.

If immigrants are defined without regard for nationality as people living in a country other than that in which they were born, one of the largest groups of immigrants in France consists of people of European descent who left the Maghreb at the time of independence. Because they are French by both nationality and culture and generally indistinguishable in their somatic (i.e. bodily) appearance from the majority of the French population, they are never referred to as immigrants in official or popular discourse, but are instead known as *rapatriés* ('repatriated citizens') or, more popularly, as *pieds-noirs*. France still retains a few overseas possessions, known as the DOM-TOM (Départements d'Outre-Mer and Territoires d'Outre-Mer, i.e. overseas departments and territories). The most important of these possessions are the four Départements d'Outre-Mer: Guadeloupe, Martinique and French Guyana (in the Caribbean) and Réunion (in the Indian Ocean). As French nationals, their inhabitants are exempt from French immigration controls and do not feature in official statistics on the foreign population. Even Tribalat, one of the few demographers to have attempted an analysis of France's immigrant population based on birthplace rather than nationality, excludes people originating in the DOM-TOM from her study (Tribalat 1993). However, as they are mainly of African or Asian descent and easily recognizable by virtue of their somatic features as originating outside France, at a popular level they are often treated as 'immigrants' in a way that the *rapatriés* are not.

At the time of the 1990 census, 340,000 people born in the DOM-TOM were living in metropolitan France. If, excluding the *rapatriés*, we define immigrants as people born outside the territory in which they now live, regardless of their nationality status, those originating in the DOM-TOM at present constitute the sixth largest immigrant group in metropolitan France (Figure 1.3). If nationality alone is taken as the defining criterion, the DOM-TOM group disappears from the picture, and the rank order of the others is modified as a consequence of different rates of naturalization (Figure 1.4).

The Iberian peninsula has provided the only major exception to the post-war decline of Europeans among France's foreign population. The number of Spaniards in France grew from 302,000 in 1946 to a peak of 607,000 in 1968, falling back to 216,000 in 1990. The rise of the Portuguese community was the most rapid of all. During the 1960s, under the dictatorship of Antonio de Oliviera

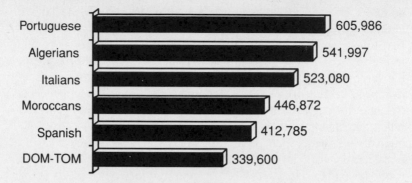

Figure 1.3 Immigrants (excluding *rapatriés*), by main countries of
       origin, living in metropolitan France in 1990
Source: INSEE 1992a: Tables 11, 12; Marie 1993a: Table 1.

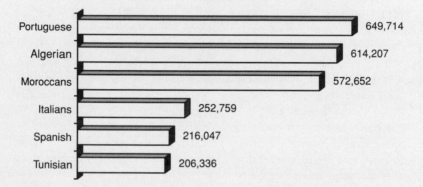

Figure 1.4 Main nationalities among France's foreign population in
       1990
Source: INSEE 1992a: Table 4.

Salazar, Portugal became engaged in a series of wars designed to
prevent its African colonies from becoming independent. Rather than
fight, hundreds of thousands of young Portuguese men fled the
country, and most of them headed for France, where the authorities
unofficially waived normal entry regulations (Weil 1991: 68). Unlike
the Spanish, they had no previous tradition of mass migration to
France. Between the 1962 and 1968 censuses, the number of
Portuguese expatriates in France rose from a mere 50,000 to 296,000.
By the time of the following census, in 1975, the figure stood at
758,000, the largest for any national group in France.

While the size of the the Portuguese population has remained
fairly stable since then, the number of non-Europeans has continued
to rise. Maghrebis have contributed significantly to this, but the
fastest rates of growth during the last twenty years have been
recorded among other Africans (up from 2 per cent of the foreign
population in 1975 to 7 per cent in 1990) and even more strikingly
among Asians (up from 3 to 12 per cent during the same period).
Third World countries are thus by far the most dynamic components
in current migratory inflows.

Before the Second World War, when most of these countries were
under colonial rule, relatively few of their inhabitants migrated to
France. During the First World War over half a million 'native'
troops were enlisted in the French armed forces, and more than
200,000 'colonial workers', mainly from the Maghreb and Indo-
china, were brought over to ease civilian labour shortages in
France, but as there was a deliberate policy of repatriation as soon
as the conflict ended only about 6,000 remained by 1920 (*Hommes
et migrations* 1991b). Small numbers of Algerians had begun
migrating to France before the First World War, and these flows
resumed during the inter-war period. Unlike European migrants,
many of whom settled permanently in France with their families, the
overwhelming majority of Maghrebis came to France alone, worked
there for a few years and then returned to their families in their
countries of origin. Often, they were replaced by a relative or
sometimes a neighbour from the same village, in what became known
as the 'rotation' system. In all, it is estimated that as many as 500,000
Algerians may have migrated temporarily to France during the inter-
war period, though the number present at any one time was very much
smaller than this (Gillette and Sayad 1984).

Immediately after the Second World War, the French government
had encouraged family immigration from Italy and other European
countries (Weil 1991: 63). Family reunification was also rapidly
facilitated for the Portuguese migrants who arrived during the 1960s
and early 1970s (Rogers 1986: 45; Amar and Milza 1990: 263). A
very different attitude was taken towards immigrants from Africa
and Asia. In 1956, faced with large numbers of Algerian immigrants
living in extremely poor housing, the government set up a state-run
agency to provide them with hostel accommodation; while the
initiative was in some respects clearly beneficial, it was hoped that,
as the accommodation was unsuitable for families, this would
discourage the wives and children of Algerians from coming to join

them in France (Weil 1991: 60). After independence, the authorities in Algeria and other Third World sending countries concurred with their counterparts in France in seeking to discourage permanent family settlement, partly because it reduced the flow of remittances sent home by expatriate workers (Weil 1991: 70–1). However, they were to prove increasingly unsuccessful in this.

Table 1.1 Females as percentage of selected nationalities in France, 1946–90

	1946	1954	1962	1968	1975	1982	1990
French	53.1	52.6	51.9	51.8	51.8	51.8	51.8
Italians	45.2	42.7	42.7	44.0	43.7	43.0	42.8
Polish	48.5	47.9	47.8	50.2	54.0	58.5	61.3
Portuguese	24.8	27.0	30.0	35.5	46.2	46.0	46.8
Spanish	39.7	42.1	44.1	46.8	47.3	47.3	48.0
Algerians	2.3	6.5	16.0	26.7	32.0	38.3	41.3
Moroccans	1.7	9.3	16.2	21.8	26.7	38.9	43.8
Tunisians	8.5	24.6	31.5	33.3	30.9	38.2	41.1

Source: INSEE 1986: Table 8, and 1992a: Table 10.

The trend towards family settlement is clearly visible in Table 1.1. Within the French population, there is a roughly equal balance between the sexes, with the longer life-expectancy of women reflected in the slight numerical superiority of females over males. Among foreign nationals, men usually outnumber women. This is because most (but not all) immigrant workers have been men; spouses and children have usually joined them at a later stage, while some have remained in the country of origin. The current imbalance in favour of females among the Polish community reflects the unusual age pyramid of this group, more than half of whom are aged 65 or over; the longer life-expectancy of women consequently weighs particularly heavily here. The general imbalance in favour of men is far less pronounced among Europeans than among Maghrebis. Throughout the post-war period, family settlement has been the norm among Italians and Spaniards. While the few Portuguese in France during the early post-war period were mainly men, as soon as mass migration began in the mid-1960s families quickly followed, and within a decade a gender balance similar to that of other European groups was achieved.

Family reunification was much slower among Maghrebis. Although Algerians far outnumbered the Portuguese during the early post-war decades, it was not until the mid-1960s that a trend towards family settlement began to gather pace among Algerian immigrants. Even today, almost half a century after the rise of mass Algerian migration, Algerians have still not achieved quite the gender balance attained by the Portuguese in little less than a decade. During the last twenty years, family settlement has nevertheless become the norm among all three Maghrebi groups, with a female-to-male ratio approaching that of Europeans. A similar pattern is also apparent among other groups of Third World origin. According to the 1990 census, 41.3 per cent of nationals from francophone sub-Saharan states were female; among Asians the figure was 45 per cent (INSEE 1992a: Table 10).

IMMIGRATION AFTER THE 'END' OF IMMIGRATION

Charles Pasqua is by no means the first government minister to have promised the French public zero immigration. Successive governments have been doing much the same since 1974, when France officially halted further inward migration. This was one of the most important early policy decisions taken under the centre-right presidency of Valéry Giscard d'Estaing, who was head of state from 1974 to 1981. The halt – formally termed a 'suspension' – of immigration was not all that it seemed. It has in one sense become a classic example of what the French call *le provisoire qui dure* ('a lasting temporary measure'), for twenty years later the 'suspension' (a seemingly interim arrangement) still has not been lifted. At another level, however, the moratorium was never as sweeping as it appeared. From the start, there were several important gaps in the seemingly blanket interdiction on inward migration; other blindspots later became apparent.

The decision to suspend immigration came in the aftermath of the Middle East War of 1973, when a sharp rise in oil prices sparked widespread fears over the prospects for economic growth throughout Western Europe. France, like other labour-importing countries, decided to close her borders to fresh inflows of immigrant workers because of fears of rising unemployment. As a member of the European Community, however, she was not allowed to impede the entry of EC nationals. Nor did the ban on labour migration apply to asylum-seekers, who were covered by entirely different legal and procedural arrangements. Certain categories of professional and highly skilled personnel were also exempt, and there were provisions for making other exceptions if the need arose in particular sectors of the economy.

If these exceptions did not appear to cut across the principle of a ban on 'immigration', this was in part because of unstated but nonetheless powerful stereotypes attaching to that term in everyday discourse. Because of the dominance of the labour market in shaping the basic thrust of migratory flows, *immigrés* (immigrants) had come to be regarded as synonymous with *travailleurs immigrés* (immigrant workers), who were in turn equated with unskilled workers rather than professionally qualified personnel (Sayad 1979). As the victims of political persecution, asylum-seekers and refugees stood outside this economic matrix, and were consequently not associated with popular notions of immigrants. Because most unskilled foreign workers were non-Europeans, immigrants as a whole had come to be seen essentially as people of Third World origin, whereas European and other Western residents were more commonly referred to as *étrangers* (foreigners). The degree to which the 1974 ban on immigration was perceived to have taken effect would therefore depend on the extent to which people of Third World origin became less visible to the general public. In the event, exactly the opposite was to happen. Far from tapering off, the presence of Third World immigrants and their descendants has become ever more visible in virtually every sphere of French society.

This increased visibility has been partly a consequence of growing numbers, despite the formal ban on immigration. One of the main reasons for this lies in a complex web of domestic and international law which has prevented the state from subordinating the rights of foreigners to the crude dictates of the labour market (Hollifield 1992). A crucial instance was the failure of the government's attempts to impose a ban on family reunifications. Such a ban was announced as part of the 1974 freeze on immigration, but it soon proved unworkable and in 1978 the *Conseil d'Etat*, France's highest administrative court, declared it to be unlawful. While procedural obstacles have continued to hamper dependants wishing to join family heads in France, the principle of their right to do so overrides the ban on new labour migrants, and family reunifications have been the single most important element in documented migratory inflows during the last twenty years.

This has helped to bring about a major structural change in the population of Third World origin. Whereas men of working age had been dominant until the early 1970s, families subsequently became the norm. Before family reunification, many immigrant workers had been housed in hostels and other forms of accommodation which kept them apart from the majority of French nationals. The arrival of families led to a much deeper penetration into the mainstream housing market. At the same time, the children of immigrants were enrolled as a matter of course in French schools. In this way, immigrant groups which had seldom been encountered outside the workplace became visible on a daily basis in a growing number of neighbourhoods. Their increased visibility would not, of course, have been so marked had it not been for one other crucial point: far more than earlier generations of immigrants, those originating in Third World countries were instantly recognizable because of their skin colour and other somatic features.

By 1977, the government had reached the view not only that the temporary suspension of immigration announced three years earlier should become permanent, but also that the existing immigrant population should, if possible, be reduced. This task was entrusted to Lionel Stoléru, Minister of State for Immigrant Workers from 1977 to 1981, who focused his efforts on inducing non-EC, essentially Maghrebi, immigrants to return home. Financial incentives designed to encourage voluntary repatriation under a system known as *l'aide au retour* (repatriation assistance) launched in 1977, met with little success. Most of those who took up the offer were Spanish or Portuguese immigrants who had probably decided to return home in any case, partly because the political climate there had recently improved with the end of the Franco and Salazar dictatorships; very few Maghrebis, at whom the programme was primarily aimed, took advantage of it.

In collaboration with the Interior Minister, Christian Bonnet, Stoléru therefore devised a scheme under which immigrant workers and their families could be forcibly repatriated if they were deemed to be surplus to current labour requirements. Such a system would require a radical overhaul of the regulations governing work and residence permits, but legislative proposals brought forward in 1979–80 to facilitate mass expulsions of this kind failed to command the necessary parliamentary majority. The Interior Ministry used discretionary powers to expel as many invidual foreigners as possible, but the numbers involved − on average, about 5,000 a year between 1978 and 1981, most of them young Maghrebis − were far smaller than the hundreds of thousands explicitly targeted in Stoléru's mass repatriation plans (Weil 1991: 107–38).

With hindsight, it seems clear that these strong-arm tactics were counter-productive. Precisely because they feared losing access to the French labour market if they returned home – as Maghrebis had traditionally done under the rotation system – many decided to remain in France, and to bring in their families, thereby increasing the population of Third World origin. That population was further swollen in two other main ways: by a rise in the number of asylum-seekers, and by inflows of illegal immigrants.

Under the Constitution adopted in 1946, France committed herself to granting asylum (i.e. formal refugee status, including full residence rights) to anyone persecuted for acting to uphold liberty. The grounds for entitlement to refugee status were widened by France's signature of the 1951 Geneva Convention (subsequently updated by the New York Protocol of 1967), which applies to people fleeing their country out of a well-founded fear of persecution because of their race, religion, nationality, membership of a particular social group, or political opinions. Today, almost 200,000 people in France have the formal status of refugees (OFPRA 1994). Most are of Third World origin, and more than half are from former French territories in South-East Asia. The formal decolonization of French Indo-China was completed in 1954, when, after terminating her protectorates over Laos and Cambodia, France granted independence to Vietnam. The Vietnam War, between the Communist North and a US-backed regime in the South, ended with a Communist victory in 1975. This was followed by an exodus of asylum-seekers who became known as 'boat people' because of the small craft in which many of them fled. Vietnamese exiles were soon joined by Cambodians fleeing the authoritarian regime of Pol Pot, and by Laotians who feared for their safety because they had assisted the US during the Vietnam War. Most went to the US, but about 100,000 – divided more or less evenly between Vietnamese, Cambodians and Laotians – entered France; several thousand Chinese nationals, who had a long history of commercial activity in the region, came with them.

Because they were clearly perceived as victims of political intolerance and because Vietnamese nationals in particular were held to have valuable entrepreneurial skills (many fled their country following the blanket nationalization of the private sector in 1978), asylum-seekers from South-East Asia aroused relatively little hostility in France. During the 1980s, however, when asylum-seekers from other Third World countries grew in number, with Africans eventually outstripping Asians, a less welcoming attitude developed. During this period, requests for asylum grew sharply across the whole of Western Europe, and there were widespread suspicions that many applicants were really economic migrants attempting to circumvent the ban on labour migration imposed in the mid-1970s. In France, the number of applicants rose from fewer than 20,000 in 1981 to 61,000 in 1989; at the same time, the rate of rejection grew from 22 to 72 per cent (OFPRA 1994), a clear indication that the authorities were increasingly inclined to view claims of political persecution as a cover for economic motives.

Many of those to whom asylum was refused remained in the country illegally, partly because the often lengthy procedures involved in asylum cases were such that by the time a decision was reached applicants had in practice become settled in France. By 1990, about 100,000 rejected aslyum-seekers were estimated to be living illegally in France. That year, the government sought to reduce cases of this kind by speeding up decision-making procedures, reducing the average length from three years to six months. This, combined with the high rate of rejections, appears to have acted as a disincentive to new asylum-seekers, for the number of applications fell steadily each year from a peak of 61,000 in 1989 to 27,000 in 1993 (OFPRA 1994: 2; Wihtol de Wenden 1994b).

For many years prior to the 1974 suspension of labour migration, most foreign workers had technically broken the law by taking up employment without the required residence and work permits. Because of labour shortages, the government had willingly acquiesced in this, issuing the necessary documents *a posteriori* under a procedure known as 'regularization'. When the 1974 suspension was announced, many thousands of undocumented workers found themselves trapped without papers; others later joined them, often in the belief that the freeze was only a temporary measure. When the Left came to power in 1981, it declared an amnesty for illegal immigrants, provided they had entered France before 1 January and provided they had proof of employment. In all, 132,000 illegal immigrants were regularized in this way during the winter of 1981–2 (Marie 1988). Since then, the best available estimates suggest that undocumented immigrants have been growing at the rate of about 30,000 a year, making a total of perhaps 300,000 by the early 1990s (*L'Expansion*, 19 March 1992).

While the numbers and origins of undocumented residents cannot, by definition, be known with certainty, it is likely that most are of Third World origin. This was certainly the case with those regularized in 1981–2, some 61 per cent of whom were Africans, with Maghrebis alone accounting for 46 per cent (Marie 1988). When a partial amnesty for rejected asylum-seekers was declared in 1991, 49,000 came out of clandestinity in the hope of securing residence permits; a similar number is thought to have remained in hiding. Africans and Asians accounted for 90 per cent of the 12,000 whose applications were successful (Lebon 1993: 104).

Besides undocumented additions to France's immigrant population, over 100, 000 foreigners currently take up residence each year under recognized procedures. As can be seen from Table 1.2, Africans and Asians account for almost two-thirds of the annual total. Half of all new entrants are family members of people already living in France. Most relatives joining foreign residents are either children or wives. Among the spouses joining French nationals, however, men and women are more evenly represented, and in some cases (Turks, for example) men are in the majority. Some 9 per cent of new residence permits went to asylum-seekers who were granted refugee status in 1992; applicants whose cases had not yet been ruled upon are excluded from the figures. Well over one-third of all entrants – mainly skilled personnel and other categories exempted from the 1974 freeze on labour recruitment (HCI 1993a: 41) – came to take up jobs. This was the only group among which Europeans were the dominant element.

Despite regular inflows of the kind detailed in Table 1.2, the total size of the foreign population of France has changed very little during the last twenty years. In the 1975 census the foreign population totalled 3.4 million. A small rise was recorded in 1982, when the figure stood at 3.7 million; it fell slightly to 3.6 million in 1990. While the overall picture may appear stable, major changes have in fact taken place. In 1975, a year after the freeze on labour migration was imposed, Europeans accounted for 61 per cent of France's foreign population. By 1990 the figure had fallen to 41 per cent. In the migratory flows contributing to this shift, those of Third World origin have been dominant.

Additions to foreign population stocks during this period have been counterbalanced by reductions resulting from other mechanisms. As the age profile of the foreign population is much younger than that of the population as a whole, deaths account for no more than about 21,000 losses each year (INSEE 1992a: 133). More

Table 1.2 Foreign entrants granted French residence permits in 1992 (excluding seasonal and other short-term permits)

	Salaried workers	Self-employed	Family members of foreign residents	Family members of French nationals	Refugees	Others	Total	%
Europeans (inc. ex-USSR)	25,178	66	1,823	2,542	642	2,477	32,728	28.3
of which EC	*23,768*	*–*	*23*	*399*	*–*	*1,674*	*25,864*	*22.2*
Africans	8,396	1,098	21,804	15,175	1,820	2,212	50,505	43.3
of which Maghrebis	*1,406*	*1,070*	*18,939*	*9,700*	*95*	*1,479*	*32,689*	*28.0*
Asians	5,922	58	7,263	2,793	7,540	978	24,554	21.1
of which Turks	*2075*	*28*	*4,661*	*819*	*1,429*	*157*	*9,169*	*7.9*
*S.-E. Asians**	*287*	*2*	*74*	*215*	*2,178*	*29*	*2,785*	*2.4*
Others	2,759	60	1,775	2,537	817	853	8,801	7.6
All nationalities	42,255	1,282	32,665	23,047	10,819	6,520	116,588	100
%	36.2	1.1	28.0	19.8	9.3	5.6	100	

Source: Lebon 1993: 85–7.
* Ex-French Indo-China

significant is the departure of foreign residents who have decided to leave France permanently. According to the best available estimates, departures of this kind were running at between 65,000 and 88,000 a year between 1975 and 1982 (Zamora and Lebon 1985); by the early 1990s, the annual rate was believed to have slowed to about 40,000 (*Le Monde*, 31 January 1993). However, the single most important factor contributing to the apparent overall stability of the foreign population has been the acquisition of French nationality by a steady flow of foreign residents.

Table1.3 Naturalizations in 1992 (excluding persons born to foreign parents and acquiring French nationality automatically)

		%
Europeans (inc. ex-USSR)	13,105	22.1
of which EC	9,059	15.3
Africans	32,094	54.2
of which Maghrebis	24,693	41.7
Asians	11,243	19.0
of which S.- E. Asians*	4,894	8.3
Others	2,800	4.7
Total	59,242	100

Source: Decouflé and Tétaud 1993: Tables 3, 5.
* Ex-French Indo-China.

Before the 1993 reform of the French nationality code (CNF), which may lead to a modest reduction in the number of people acquiring French nationality, about 100,000 foreigners became French each year. About 60,000 of these – roughly three-quarters of whom originated in Africa or Asia – were individually documented under naturalization procedures, initiated by a formal request on the part of those concerned (Table 1.3). In addition, until the 1993 reform, children born in France to foreign parents automatically acquired French nationality on reaching the age of majority without going through naturalization procedures. In the early 1990s, around 24,000 young men and women – most of whose parents were of Third World origin – were estimated to be acquiring French nationality in this way each year under Article 44 of the CNF. A further 12,000 children acquired French nationality each year without any formal act of registration when one of their parents became French (Decouflé and Tétaud 1993: 7–8; *Le Monde*, 11 May 1993).

In addition, more than 17,000 children born each year to foreign parents, mainly Algerians and sub-Saharan Africans, were French from birth under Article 23 of the CNF, which conferred French nationality automatically on anyone born in France having at least one parent who was also born on French territory. Because Algeria and certain other former colonies, principally in West and Central Africa, were deemed to be part of French territory prior to independence, the children of immigrants originating in those countries were not included among the ranks of foreigners acquiring French nationality, for they were by law French from birth. While the 1993 reform amended Article 23 so that it no longer applies to children born since then to sub-Saharan Africans, it is still valid for the vast majority of children born to Algerian immigrants and remains in force for anyone born in metropolitan France or territories still administered by France overseas (i.e. the DOM-TOM), provided at least one of their parents was also born there.

It follows from all this that statistics on nationality, even when combined with data on naturalizations, provide no more than a very rough guide to the number of immigrants living in France, and they offer an even poorer index of the population of immigrant origin, i.e. immigrants together with their descendants. At the time of the 1990 census, some 5.9 million people living in metropolitan France (i.e. France including Corsica, but excluding the DOM-TOM) were born elsewhere (Figure 1.5). Of these, 1.7 million – mainly *rapatriés* and people originating in the DOM-TOM – were French nationals from birth. If we define immigrants as people living in France who were born abroad as foreign nationals, 4.2 million residents of this kind were recorded in the 1990 census. Almost one-third of these – some 1.3 million – had acquired French nationality. At the same time, there were 740,000 second-generation foreigners in France who, having been born there, were not immigrants; despite the 1993 reform of the CNF, most were likely to become French on reaching the age of majority. As the core of Article 23 of the CNF was not affected by the 1993 reform, the third generation (i.e. children born in France of parents who were themselves born there to immigrants) will all be French from birth.

A similar pattern has been at work throughout the twentieth century. About 10 million people living in France today are either the children or the grandchildren of immigrants. As the vast majority were born in France and have French nationality, fewer than 1 million of them – consisting essentially of the 740,000 immigrant-born children who have not yet acquired French citizenship – appear

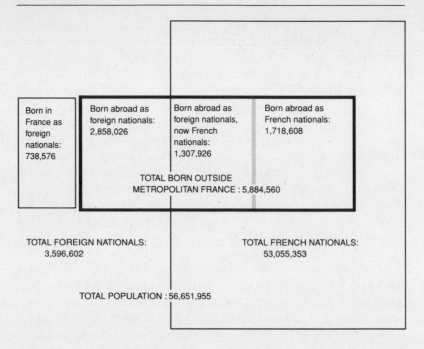

Figure 1.5 Population of metropolitan France in 1990, by place of birth
    and nationality
Source: Based on data in INSEE 1992a: Tables 1, 2.

in Figure 1.5. As noted earlier, the absorption of people of foreign
origin into the national community has left relatively few monuments
in the collective memory of France. The seeming invisibility of past
generations of immigrants and of those who are today descended
from them is often regarded as proof of the success with which they
have been incorporated into French society. Immigrants who have
settled in France during the post-war period, and more particularly
those who have come to the fore during the last twenty years, are
often felt to threaten this tradition. It is widely claimed that people
of Third World origin are much harder to 'integrate' than Europeans.
Far from disappearing without trace, they have actually increased in
visibility at a time when successive governments have been claiming
that immigration is at an end. While there is a marked reluctance to
speak of them as ethnic minorities – as if the very use of the term
might somehow make a reality of the spectre which now haunts
French public debate – the fear is that immigration is leading

remorselessly to the formation of permanently distinct minorities within French society.

ETHNICITY AND INTEGRATION

Ethnicity and a range of associated concepts play a central role in migration studies in the English-speaking world. They are often mistrusted in France (Rudder and Goodwin 1993), and it should be said that certain aspects of British and American usage may justify some of these misgivings. The French preference for a discourse of integration is regarded with equal mistrust in Britain, again often for understandable reasons. It would be a mistake to side uncritically with either camp. No less importantly, it would be foolish to disregard potentially valuable insights derived from one or other approach. Understanding of this kind is possible only if terms are defined and applied with care. Unfortunately, both the discourse of integration and that of ethnicity have been characterized by enormous diversity and not a little confusion.

There is fairly general agreement that the core of ethnicity lies in a sense of group belonging. Theorists and practitioners of ethnic studies disagree, however, over the types of groups involved and the criteria by which belonging is established.[5] Even when – as is the case in the present study – the field of ethnic relations is confined to phenomena associated with international migration, there are many variations in the approaches adopted. A first difficulty concerns the relationship between subjectively felt identities and groups delineated on the basis of empirically observed criteria. Are ethnic groups the subjective creations of social actors, or should they be defined through empirical procedures devised by outside investigators? Bearing in mind that a group of people stigmatized by others may not *ipso facto* share a sense of community, if scholars accept that ethnic groups are the creations of social actors, what should be the relative importance accorded to exclusionary as compared with self-inclusionary practices? The specific criteria by which ethnic groups may be subjectively or objectively delineated are very diverse. Three main strands may be usefully distinguished: biological, politico-territorial, and cultural. Few if any conceptions of ethnicity rest on just one of these components. Most involve a complex hierarchy of elements.

In the US, the most common notion of ethnicity has been based on the relatively objective criterion of national origins. A person may be said to belong to a particular ethnic group to the extent that he or she comes from or is descended from someone originating in a particular country. While territorial origins are the prime element in this view of ethnicity, a biological dimension is also involved via the question of ancestry. Biological ancestry is fundamental to another form of inter-group analysis pioneered in the US, that of 'race relations'. Here somatic features, notably skin colour, serve to delineate different groups, above all 'blacks' and 'whites'. In recent years the fairly neat distinction between these two approaches has become blurred (Yinger 1985: 153; Lee 1993: 86), partly because it has been recognized that both involve more subjective constructions than may at first meet the eye. For a person whose ancestors come from a variety of countries, there is a large element of subjectivity involved in identifying with one ethnic group rather than with another. Similarly, the seemingly objective fact of somatic difference becomes significant only when human beings make it so in their social dealings. Bearing in mind that the majority of blacks in the US have at least one white among their ancestors, it is impossible to draw a purely biological line between blacks and whites. 'Blacks' were constructed as such by 'whites' as part of a process of social domination and exclusion.

In British academic and political discourse, which has drawn on and adapted American models, ethnic minorities are conventionally defined as groups subjected to discriminatory behaviour by members of the majority population. Because carefully controlled tests have shown that people who are somatically different from the 'white' majority suffer from particularly severe discrimination, until very recently they alone were officially recognized as ethnic minorities by bodies such as the Commission for Racial Equality (CRE). As the CRE's name implies, its main purpose is to fight against 'racial' discrimination. The inverted commas are necessary because there is now broad agreement among scholars that the idea of biologically distinct races of human beings has no scientific foundation. 'Racial' categories are not, as the expression may unfortunately be taken to imply, objective facts but products of racialization, i.e. patterns of meaning in which 'social relations between people have been structured by the signification of human biological characteristics in such a way as to define and construct differentiated social collectivities' (Miles 1989: 75). The socially constructed nature of 'racial' differences is regrettably obscured by the British and American habit of talking about 'race relations', a phrase which misleadingly suggests that objectively distinguishable 'races' exist and inter-relate.[6] Somatic differences between individuals do of course exist, but the relationships at the heart of 'race relations' are between social actors who view each other through the lenses of invented – and often pernicious – notions of racialized group boundaries.

For scholars working within the race-relations paradigm, racial and ethnic minorities are one and the same the thing (Jones 1993) and are generically defined by skin colour: ethnic minorities are that part of the national population which is not classified as 'white'. It is significant, however, that within the CRE's current classification system, minority groups are sub-divided by regions of origin, all of which lie outside Britain. This reflects the fact that the stigmatization of somatic features is a consequence of their association with distant territorial origins: dark skins have served to mark ethnic groups treated by members of the majority population as not belonging fully or legitimately to the national society in which they live. These biological and territorial factors are often implicitly linked in turn with cultural assumptions: people originating outside Britain have often been felt not to 'fit in' because of linguistic, religious or other cultural traditions associated with foreign countries. The recent recognition by the CRE of Irish people as a group suffering significant levels of discrimination in Britain confirms that distinct-ive somatic features are not a necessary precondition for attracting exclusionary behaviour, though the point is somewhat blurred by the bizarre legal requirement that in order to qualify for protection the Irish must be formally regarded as a 'racial' category.

A differently structured combination of biological, territorial and cultural criteria characterizes the notion of 'ethnic Germans'. This is the standard English translation of *Volksdeutsche* and *deutsche Volkszugehörigen*, terms denoting individuals who are formally recognized as belonging to the German people. The legal foundation of this concept is a 1913 law basing German citizenship on *jus sanguinis* (i.e. biological descent rather than territorial residence). The law, which remains in force today, was designed to enable people of German origin living outside Germany, particularly in Eastern Europe and what is now the former Soviet Union, to retain German citizenship rights. While the initial driving force behind this system was German self-inclusion, it has at the same time carried important exclusionary implications. Because of their different biological and territorial origins, most immigrants of non-German descent who settle in Germany remain permanently outside the national community, and the same applies to their children and grandchildren.

It would be over-simplistic to see this system as an expression of crude biological racism. Brubaker (1992) has argued that it is ethno-cultural rather than ethno-racial in intent, if not in effect. As parents generally attempt to rear their children in the cultural traditions which they themselves have inherited, the transmission of nationality through filiation is the juridical corollary of this cultural transaction. Significantly, when the rights of ethnic Germans in the Soviet Bloc were strengthened by additional laws adopted in Germany after the Second World War, evidence of German culture was officially recognized as an acceptable alternative to proof of biological descent for those wishing to exercise these rights.

Rather than focusing on biological or territorial origins, a directly cultural view of ethnicity takes as its starting-point participation in a shared system of meaning and values. Thus defined, ethnic minorities are characterized by linguistic, religious or moral codes different from those of the dominant population. The Spanish-speaking population in the US, Hindus in Britain, and Muslims in France are examples of groups liable to be categorized in this way. The cultural view of ethnicity involves no biological component. In common with the other approaches already considered, however, it includes a politico-territorial dimension. Minority and majority groups appear as such only when they are positioned within politic-ally structured spaces. Hispanics are not a minority group in Mexico; nor are Hindus in India, nor Muslims in Algeria. They appear so only within the confines of a territory which is under the sovereignty of a state dominated by cultural norms of a different order.

Whether the emphasis falls on biological, territorial or cultural criteria, the cardinal feature of ethnic minorities is that they are in some way marked as originating outside the national society within which they now live. The central question to which this gives rise is how far minorities of this kind genuinely stand apart from the majority population. Do the members of minority ethnic groups belong wholly or primarily to their countries of origin, to the national societies in which they live, to separate collectivities in the margins of both, or to wider trans-national entities? While the terminology of 'ethnic minorities' is seldom used in France, fundamentally similar questions lie at the heart of the French debate over 'integra-tion'. When academics and politicians talk of a crisis of integration (Wieviorka 1990), they mean that there is a danger that people of immigrant origin are being inadequately incorporated into French society.

Unlike their German neighbours, the French have a long tradition of mixing *jus sanguinis*, giving citizenship through filiation, and *jus soli*, through which birth within the national territory brings entitlement to citizenship. An important underlying assumption has always been that both methods of bestowing citizenship were built on a strong foundation of cultural cohesion. While immigrants from other countries could be naturalized only if they furnished proof of cultural assimilation, it was assumed that their children, socialized from birth in France, would be sufficiently French in outlook to justify the automatic acquisition of citizenship on reaching adulthood. These and many other related assumptions have been called into question in recent years.

Until quite recently, the overwhelming majority of immigrants came from countries which share with France a tradition of Catholicism. Today, almost half come from countries where the dominant faith is Islam, a religion which until their arrival had virtually no significant history within France.[7] Most Muslim immigrants come from North and West Africa and are visually recognizable as originating outside the country. Because their children display similar somatic features, it is widely (though not always correctly) assumed that they, too, are Muslims. Incidents such as the Islamic headscarf affair of 1989 – when a nationwide furore was sparked by the refusal of three Muslim girls to remove their headscarves during school classes – were symptomatic of widespread anxieties over the compatibility of Islamic culture with French norms. Doubts over the commitment of young people of immigrant origin to the dominant values of French society found their most powerful symbolic expression in the reform of French nationality laws enacted in 1993. As revised, those laws now require most immigrant-born children to request French nationality instead of receiving it automatically.

If there is a crisis of integration, it is not only cultural and political but also socio-economic in nature. The immigrant communities which have recently been settling in France have been doing so in a context of rising unemployment, fitful growth, and major economic restructuring. The opportunities for effective socio-economic incorporation have therefore been far less plentiful than during earlier periods. It is, indeed, arguable that the roots of present fears concerning ineffective integration lie far more in socio-economic circumstances than in cultural differences between recent Third

World immigrants and their European predecessors. As Noiriel (1988: 247–94) has pointed out, bouts of xenophobia similar to that currently directed against immigrants of Third World origin marked the economic downturns of the 1880s and the 1930s, when Italians and Poles were castigated as 'unassimilable', which in the language of the day was equivalent to saying they were impossible to integrate.

Charges of this kind were less a reflection of the cultural differences characterizing immigrants than of an unwillingness among the French themselves to incorporate relative newcomers at a time of economic difficulty. In this respect, the current problematic of integration runs closer than it might sometimes appear to that of race relations, for both are concerned (albeit from different perspectives) with patterns of social differentiation marked by discriminatory behaviour against people of foreign origin. In France, as in Britain, the somatic features of people of Third World origin frequently arouse exclusionary attitudes. Immigrants of African and Asian descent originating in the DOM-TOM often suffer from discrimination of this kind, despite the fact that they are French by nationality and to a large extent by cultural affiliation. Paradoxically, exclusionary reflexes among the French themselves are tending to create in all but name racially constructed ethnic minorities of precisely the kind that cut across the much-vaunted project of integration.

It is doubtful, however, whether it makes sense to import wholesale into France the discourse of race relations. While discriminatory behaviour triggered by somatic features may be described in broad terms as racist, there are no 'races' in France (any more than there are in Britain) among whom 'relations' can be said to exist. Even if they are triggered by skin colour, many acts of discrimination rest on cultural prejudices against people of foreign origin rather than on theories of biological racism. More fundamentally, the rhetoric of 'racial' or cultural discrimination may be little more than a cloak for the more hard-nosed objective of imposing unfair handicaps on easily targeted groups in the competition for scarce resources such as jobs and housing. To categorize all this as 'race relations' is unhelpful from an analytical point of view, for it carries the risk of reifying epiphenomena instead of looking beyond these to the root causes of social differentiation.

The discourse of integration has its own drawbacks. The most important of these is a tendency among those who speak of integration to assume that the effacement of differentiation through ever fuller incorporation into the national community is not simply a useful model for analytical purposes but also a self-evidently desirable goal. Often, as Beaud and Noiriel (1991) have pointed out, integration is implicitly and uncritically equated with assimilation, i.e. the wholesale elimination of differences through the generalization of pre-existing national norms. A classic exposition of the analytical model of assimilation with particular reference to the US is that of Gordon (1964). In France, the normative equation of integration with assimilation is championed explicitly by Barreau (1992). In a milder form, similar presuppositions structure many governmental and academic analyses in France. In this respect, the discourse of integration functions as part of the project of nationalization (Miles 1993: 175–6, 207–11; Lorcerie 1994a).

By contrast with normative approaches of this kind, functionalist views of integration focus on the the social, economic or political participation of people of minority origin without assuming that the end product of this process is, or should necessarily be, their assimilation into pre-existing French norms. Stretched between these normative and functionalist poles, 'integration' has now become such a catch-all term that its meaning is often ill-defined (Bonnafous 1992; Bastenier and Dassetto 1993). When schematic definitions are attempted, they vary from one analyst to another. Lapeyronnie (1993) distinguishes between integration (defined as identification with national cultural norms) and participation (defined as involvement in the processes of socio-economic production and exchange). Dubet (1989) prefers a threefold distinction between socio-economic integration, cultural assimilation, and national identification, the last being associated with political participation. The state-appointed Haut Conseil à l'Intégration (HCI) appears to propose a functionalist definition of integration based on the notion of participation in French society (HCI 1991: 18–19), but its reports implicitly favour a normative approach by claiming to measure the 'progress' of integration by reference to indicators such as crime rates, educational qualifications and mixed marriages (ibid.: 38–48).

In view of these difficulties, I shall refrain in the present study as far as possible from using the word 'integration'. However, because of its ubiquity in popular, academic and political discourse in France, the term cannot be avoided altogether. It will be used only when citing statements or arguments advanced by those who use the term in France. When its meaning is clear in the original source, I will explicate it accordingly. As many users leave the word undefined, explication is not always possible, and in such cases the reader is left to infer from the context what may be meant.

The word 'assimilation' will also be avoided, except when referring to the use made of this term by others. In general, I find it more useful to speak of 'acculturation', meaning the acquisition of pre-existing cultural norms dominant in a particular society. Assimilation tends to imply not only acculturation but also the complete abandonment of minority cultural norms. As will be shown in Chapter 3, this is a rather simplistic way of conceiving of the cultural intercourse generated by international migration. Acculturation does not necessarily imply the obliteration of cultural differences, for it is perfectly possible for people to be simultaneously competent in more than one culture.

One of the most important and least scrutinized aspects of the paradigm of integration lies in the assumption that the framework of social incorporation is, or should be, coterminous with the boundaries of the nation-state. Such an assumption was never wholly valid, and the increasingly global scale on which labour, capital, goods and services circulate is rendering it ever more obsolescent. International migration is itself one of the most tangible expressions of this process. Yet there is an important sense in which immigrants (or, rather, certain groups of immigrants), more than others, remain constrained by the power of the nation-state. Since the 1950s, obstacles to intra-European migration have been steadily removed by a growing number of states, at any rate where their own nationals are concerned. To facilitate freedom of movement within the European Union, member states are being driven to harmonize their entry policies vis-à-vis third country (i.e. non-EU) nationals by creating a common policy on external frontiers. Once inside the EU, however, immigrants from non-member states remain almost entirely subject to the regulatory framework of the particular country to which they have been admitted. Their residence and work permits do not extend beyond the boundaries of that country, and even within it their rights are restricted in ways that do not apply to EU nationals. The horizon of opportunities open to non-EU nationals is in this respect bounded by the state on whose territory they reside. For this reason, it makes sense to analyse their experiences within such a framework.

The fundamental issue with which the present study is concerned is the extent to which recent immigrants and their descendants, when compared with the rest of the population, are characterized by a process of 'differential incorporation' (Rex 1986b: xii) within

French society. Incorporation is both a subjective and an objective process. Individuals are incorporated objectively within a society to the extent that they are *de facto* participants in the full range of activities and relationships that characterize the national collectivity. Subjective incorporation depends both on self-perceptions and on the perceptions of others. While immigrants and their descendants may feel a personal identification with the national community or at least characteristic parts of it, members of the majority population may adopt exclusionary attitudes. There is a constant cross-over between subjective and objective processes. How people interact depends in part on their perceptions and aspirations; the manner in which an individual is treated by others affects in turn the way he or she feels and thinks.

For analytical purposes, three main axes of social experience may be distinguished: the economic (concerned with the production and consumption of material resources), the cultural (centred on the construction and communication of meaning and value); and the political (focusing on the acquisition and use of power). Few, if any, experiences are ever mono-dimensional. In practical terms, power cannot be wielded without using cultural instruments, most obviously language. Control over economic resources gives a very real kind of power, even if it is not expressed through the channels of formal politics and public policy-making (elections, state intervention, etc.). Cultural production is impossible without access to certain economic resources, and cultural products may in turn take the form of commodities bought and sold in the marketplace. It is clear that if we wish to measure the breadth and depth of social incorporation, all three axes must be considered, including the ways in which they reinforce or cross-cut each other.

The main emphasis of Chapters 2 and 3 is on the experiences and attitudes of minority groups. Chapters 4 and 5 focus on the majority population. In Chapter 2, we shall consider the extent to which people of immigrant origin occupy a distinctive position in France's socio-economic structure. Chapter 3 asks how far minority and majority groups are separated by different systems of meaning and value. Chapter 4 considers how and why the citizenship rights of immigrants and their descendants have been redefined in recent years. As the key to incorporation into formal politics, citizenship is of major symbolic importance. French politics and public policy have also had enormous practical consequences for the population of immigrant origin. These are examined in Chapter 5.

Should we describe people of immigrant origin as ethnic minorities? To the extent that they originate in territories outside France, there is an objective sense in which they could be classified in this way. The nub of the issue, however, is how far they now belong to the society in which they live. Within the race-relations paradigm, their stigmatization by members of the majority population would suffice to label them as ethnic minorities. It would, however, be a mistake for social scientists to model their own concepts on the prejudices of particular social actors. At least as important as the attitude of the majority population is the extent to which immigrants and their descendants feel committed to French society, as well as their *de facto* participation in its structures. To avoid ambiguity, I think it wise to make these important conceptual differences explicit in the present analysis. Accordingly, a tripartite distinction will be made between what I propose to call *ethnic groups*, *ethnicized groups* and *ethno-cultural groups*.

In the present context, membership of a minority ethnic group is defined by the objective fact of common origins in a territory outside the state in which the group now resides, and within which (an)other group(s) occupies/occupy a dominant position. Those foreign origins may be direct (in the case of immigrants) or indirect (in the case of their descendants). Whether this territorial and biological legacy is of real social significance depends to a large extent on how it is perceived by different social actors. A minority ethnicized group is one whose members are considered by members of the majority population to be in a significant sense separate from the national community;[8] racialized minority groups (categorized by somatic features such as skin colour) are a sub-type of ethnicized minorities. An ethno-cultural group is one whose members feel united by a shared system of meaning and value associated with common origins.

None of these three types of group is necessarily united by formal organizational structures, though ethno-cultural groups are generally more inclined than the others to organize themselves in such a way. Some sociologists active in the field of ethnic relations, notably Rex (1986a), prefer to speak of unorganized groups as quasi-groups, but this seems unnecessary provided the use of the word 'group' is carefully defined, as above. The formal organization of minority ethno-cultural groups, through associational and community structures, is discussed in Chapter 3.

The boundary lines between ethnic, ethnicized and ethno-cultural groups are seldom if ever neatly isomorphic (cf. Mason 1990, 1991). The French are inclined to talk about anyone with the physical appearance of a Maghrebi as an 'Arab', though many Maghrebis in fact come from Berber- (rather than Arab-) speaking areas. In this respect, 'Arabs' as an ethnicized group are very different from 'Arabs' as defined by shared territorial or cultural origins. Many of the children of Arab immigrants identify only weakly or inter- mittently with the cultural heritage of their parents; as such, while they are generally perceived by the public at large as part of the ethnicized Arab population, they belong only marginally to the ethno- cultural Arab community.

As will be shown in Chapters 3 and 4, if the French are often anxious over what is seen as the threat of ethno-cultural minorities, it is in part because they mistake the phantoms created by their own ethnicization of minority ethnic groups for the much more diffuse modes of ethnicity which characterize many people of immigrant origin. Before examining these attitudinal indicators, however, we shall begin by considering in the next chapter some basic data on the position of recent immigrants and their descendants within the socio- economic structure of France.

Chapter 2

Socio-economic structures

INTRODUCTION

Economic production sets the material framework within which social structures and individual life opportunities are shaped. Together with child-rearing, which continues to impact differentially on men and women, the business of earning a living takes up more of the average adult's waking life than any other activity. At the same time, it provides the resources which are indispensable to virtually every other part of life. The single most important resource to which it gives access is housing, the location and quality of which provide the context for numerous other social experiences. If people of immigrant origin are atypical in their employment and residential patterns, compared with the rest of the population, they are by the same token marked as significantly different in some of the most basic aspects of social incorporation.

People suffering from acute disadvantage in the labour market are referred to by certain commentators as an 'underclass', and localities containing dense concentrations of those affected in this way are sometimes labelled as 'ghettos'. Both terms are customarily linked with notions of ethnic alterity: ghettos and the underclass associated with them are equated primarily with concentrations of disadvantaged minority ethnicized groups.[1] In the US, where both terms are more widely used than in Britain or continental Europe, they have been forged into an explicit collocation by Wilson (1987, 1989), whose work has focused on mainly black inner-city areas of acute disadvantage in major American conurbations. Earlier American usage of these terms was adapted to the context of British 'race relations' by such sociologists as Rex and Tomlinson (Rex and Tomlinson 1979; cf. Rex 1988), and in recent years they have begun to feature in discussions of continental Europe, including France (see, e.g., Lapeyronnie 1993).

However, European social scientists generally prefer not to use these terms, for two main reasons. First, everyday usage has become heavily politicized, with strong connotations of moral opprobrium: in political debate, membership of the ghetto and its underclass is frequently attributed to dysfunctional behaviour such as high crime rates and low standards of personal morality. Wilson and others have done their best to dispel such myths, grounding their analysis in empirical investigations of social disadvantage. Even at this second level, however, the applicability of such an approach to Europe is generally doubted, mainly because few if any European cities contain ethnicized concentrations of the density found in the US (Wacquant 1992). In France, traces of both approaches are fused in censorious references to the ghetto as an Anglo-Saxon (i.e. British and American) model which must not be allowed to develop in French cities.[2] Viewed from this perspective, the ghetto is the antithesis of successful integration: a spatially distinct enclave inhabited by people who deviate from the moral and material norms of the majority population.

Because they are so ideologically tainted, terms such as the ghetto and the underclass are probably best avoided in scholarly analyses. The questions which they raise are nevertheless highly pertinent to an understanding of the social incorporation of immigrants and their descendants. How far do minority ethnic groups in France occupy distinct positions in the labour and housing markets? This is the guiding theme of the present chapter. While it is important and relatively simple to formulate this question, it is far more difficult to produce an empirically reliable answer. The most important reason for this lies in the absence of official data on a large part of the population of immigrant origin. Census, labour-force and other surveys in France usually distinguish only between French nationals and foreigners; because most people born to immigrant parents become French on or before reaching adulthood, it is generally impossible to identify them and their children in surveys of this kind. If minority ethnic groups can be said to occupy particular positions in the class structure, this implies a considerable degree of stability. Longitudinal data (i.e. information documenting trends over time) are therefore potentially very significant, and the most convincing evidence of this kind would be inter-generational. Unfortunately, the blindspots in most official statistics make it impossible to establish

a reliable picture of the employment patterns and spatial distribution
of second- and third-generation members of minority ethnic groups.

An important survey designed to remedy some of these gaps was
initiated by the Institut National d'Etudes Démographiques (INED)
in conjunction with the Institut National de la Statistique et des
Etudes Economiques (INSEE) in the early 1990s, but no results
relating to employment and housing have yet been published.
Fragmentary data of a longitudinal nature do exist and will be drawn
on where appropriate, but throughout the following analysis we need
to keep in mind the limitations of the available evidence.

EMPLOYMENT

Before the recruitment freeze imposed in the mid-1970s, immigrants
throughout Western Europe were characterized by high rates of
economic activity and low rates of unemployment. Unlike the
indigenous populations, a large proportion of which consisted of
young and retired people outside the labour market, foreigners were
far more likely to be in paid employment, and they were heavily
concentrated in badly paid, low-skilled jobs. It was therefore
possible to argue with some justification that, together with indigenous workers at the lower end of the socio-economic hierarchy, they
were objectively part of the working class, even if this was not
acknowledged subjectively by many of the individuals concerned
(Castles and Kosack 1973). Since then, there have been major
demographic and economic changes. At the time of the 1946 census,
some 60 per cent of all foreigners in France were part of the formal
labour force (i.e. were economically active in the sense of holding a
job or seeking one), compared with 51 per cent of French nationals.
By the end of the 1960s, family settlement was already sufficiently
advanced to have reduced the share of the foreign population that
was economically active to 48 per cent, compared with 41 per cent
among French nationals. By 1990, only 45 per cent of France's
foreign population was economically active, a figure almost identical
to that of the national population as a whole (INSEE 1992a: 19). At
the same time, unemployment has risen sharply, particularly among
non-nationals. Among French nationals, the unemployment rate
(defined in the census as the share of the economically active
population out of work, whether receiving unemployment benefit or
not) stood at 10 per cent in 1990, compared to 20 per cent among
the foreign population (ibid.: Tables 13 and 19).

Table 2.1 Labour-force participation rates among 15–64 age group, by nationality and sex, 1990

	% All	% Male	% Female
French	67.7	75.8	59.8
Foreign	63.4	77.6	44.6
EC	68.8	80.2	55.2
Spanish	64.6	76.1	51.3
Italians	61.7	74.7	40.2
Portuguese	74.1	84.8	61.7
Algerians	59.3	76.2	34.1
Moroccans	56.1	74.5	29.6
Tunisians	61.7	79.9	30.9
Other Africans*	58.2	69.5	39.8
S.-E. Asians**	67.1	75.7	56.6
Turks	57.6	80.5	25.9

Source: Derived from INSEE 1992a: Tables R9, 4, 15.
* Ex-French sub-Saharan Africa   ** Ex-French Indo-China

Table 2.2 Unemployment rates, by nationality and sex, 1990

	% All	% Male	% Female
French	10.4	7.5	14.1
Foreign	19.5	16.3	26.8
EC	11.3	8.6	16.0
Spanish	12.5	10.3	16.3
Italians	12.2	9.3	20.9
Portuguese	10.2	7.4	14.5
Algerians	27.5	23.1	42.3
Moroccans	25.4	20.7	42.5
Tunisians	25.7	22.0	41.7
Other Africans*	27.6	21.5	45.2
S.-E. Asians**	26.8	19.5	38.6
Turks	28.9	23.0	47.9

Source: Derived from INSEE 1992a: Tables 13, 19.
* Ex-French sub-Saharan Africa   ** Ex-French Indo-China

Women have been disproportionately affected by the rise in unemployment. The female participation rate in the formal labour market has always been lower than that of men, but since the late 1960s it has risen steadily – from 28 to 38 per cent among French nationals between 1968 and 1990, and from 20 to 31 per cent among non-nationals during the same period. Unemployment rates are, however, almost twice as high among French women as among their male counterparts (14 per cent as against 7 per cent in 1990), and the same is true of foreign women, who in 1990 had an unemployment rate of 27 per cent compared with 16 per cent among foreign men. Tables 2.1 and 2.2 show that female groups with low rates of participation in the formal labour force also suffer the highest jobless rates. Women from the Maghreb and Turkey have the lowest rates of formal economic activity, a pattern which appears in part to reflect the cultural norms prevailing in Islamic countries, where female employment outside the home is often discouraged.[3] Those seeking work experience extremely high unemployment levels, making these women doubly disadvantaged where socio-economic incorporation is concerned.

It is a mark of how economic conditions have changed in the industrialized world that today, when some analysts of social stratification attempt to locate minority ethnic groups within the parameters of an underclass, they appeal to very different criteria from those invoked by Castles and Godack in their 1973 study of immigrant workers. Instead of hyper-concentration in low status jobs, wholesale disconnection from the labour market is advanced by Wilson, Lapeyronnie and others as a cardinal feature of the 'underclass'. Yet if permanent, or at least long-term, unemployment is fundamental to membership of such a class, a glance at the unemployment rate among documented foreigners in France suffices to show that most of them do not fall within it. While, as we shall see, some ethnic groups have unemployment rates well in excess of the average for the foreign labour force, none can be said to be wholly disconnected from the job market. Moreover, the inclusion of documented migrants and their dependants within the framework of the welfare state – which in France and other European countries provides more extensive social protection than is available in the US (Heisler and Schmitter Heisler 1986: 19–20) – locks even those who are unemployed into a close relationship with the institutional authorities of the receiving society. While undocumented migrants cannot, by definition, be quantified with precision, it is beyond doubt that they account for only a fraction of minority ethnic groups. It is also likely that, lacking the social protection afforded by the welfare state, they have relatively high levels of labour-market participation – albeit in poorly paid, insecure jobs.

Despite these important structural developments, it is arguable that the functional role of the foreign labour force has changed less than might at first appear. During the years of post-war economic expansion, immigrant workers served as what, in Marxist terminology, is known as a reserve labour army. The international division of labour had created in ex-colonial and other territories large pools of unemployed or under-employed people. By drawing on this reserve workforce, capital was able to remedy labour shortages in industrialized countries without increasing wage costs unduly, for the status of most of those recruited in this way was too insecure to permit them seriously to challenge employers over pay or working conditions. The high unemployment rates now suffered by foreign workers, and their concentration in insecure, low-grade jobs, suggest that they have become a reserve labour army which is based within France rather than outside its borders (Talha 1989: 165–237; Marie 1992: 27–8). Moreover, while the evidence concerning second-generation members of recently established minority groups is patchy, there are strong indicators that they tend to occupy a structural position which is similar to that of their parents.

Cross (1995), who rejects the 'underclass' as a useful analytical concept, has instead proposed a three-pronged approach for assessing the extent to which minority groups are differentially incorporated into society as a consequence of their position within the labour market. Using Cross's grid in a slightly modified form (his own definitions are somewhat narrower than those employed here), we may speak of *segmentation* as the concentration of certain groups of workers within particular sectors of the economy and at certain levels of the occupational hierarchy. *Marginalization* is the condition of workers who hold particularly insecure jobs. Those who are unemployed, particularly over long periods, may be described as the victims of *exclusion*. On all three counts, people of immigrant origin are generally less well placed than the rest of France's population, and certain minority groups – essentially non-Europeans – are more adversely affected than others.

Segmentation

We may usefully begin by considering the overall distribution of foreign workers within the French economy; concentrations of particular ethnic groups will be highlighted later in this chapter. The foreign labour force has traditionally been over-represented in the industrial sector. In 1975, two-thirds of foreign workers held industrial jobs, including more than a quarter in the construction industry (Table 2.3). By contrast, well over half of French nationals were employed in the service sector. Many of these had left industrial jobs during the post-war boom, taking more attractive opportunities in the tertiary (i.e. service) sector. Less desirable jobs vacated in the industrial sector were filled by immigrant workers. Since the mid-1970s, wide-scale restructuring has brought an overall decline in manufacturing industry, and an ever stronger tertiarization of the economy as whole. By 1990, almost two-thirds of French nationals were employed in the service sector, as was half of the foreign labour force.

There are marked differences in the employment patterns of men and women (Tables 2.4 and 2.5). Men, particularly non-nationals, have traditionally been to the fore in industrial jobs, whereas women are heavily concentrated in the service sector. Most foreign men are still in industry, but the majority of their French counterparts now hold tertiary-sector jobs. In 1975, almost one-third of the foreign male labour force was in the construction industry, and this share has declined relatively little since then. The steepest decline has been in the share of those holding other industrial jobs, down from almost 40 per cent of foreign male workers in 1975 to only 28 per cent in 1990. At the same time, the proportion employed in services has more than doubled, rising from 19 to 40 per cent. Very few women, French or foreign, are found in the construction industry. More than one-third of female non-nationals were employed in other parts of industry in 1975, a significantly larger share than among French women. By 1990, the proportion had dropped to one-fifth, and the gap between nationals and non-nationals was also much smaller. Almost identical proportions of French and foreign women – more than three-quarters of the total – held jobs in the service sector.

Despite similarities in overall sectoral trends among French and foreign members of the labour force, there are major differences in the types of jobs held (Tables 2.6–2.8). At 22 per cent, the proportion of foreign women employed in 1990 within the census category of 'personal service' staff – usually implying low-status domestic work – was almost three times greater than among French women. Some 40 per cent of French women held non-managerial white-collar jobs in offices or shops, compared with only 23 per cent of non-nationals. Among the male labour force, 70 per cent of foreigners were manual workers, compared with 40 per cent of French nationals. Only 12 per cent of French men were in unskilled manual jobs, against 32 per

Table 2.3 Sectoral distribution of French and foreign labour force, male and female combined, by percentage, 1975–90

	1975		1982		1990	
	French	Foreign	French	Foreign	French	Foreign
Agriculture	10.3	5.7	8.2	4.4	5.8	3.4
Industry*	28.8	38.7	26.0	33.7	22.5	26.2
Construction	7.8	26.9	8.2	22.3	6.6	20.6
Services	53.1	28.7	57.6	39.6	65.1	49.8
Total	100	100	100	100	100	100

Source: INSEE 1992a: Table R10.
* Excluding construction

Table 2.4 Sectoral distribution of French and foreign male labour force, by percentage, 1975–90

	1975		1982		1990	
	French	Foreign	French	Foreign	French	Foreign
Agriculture	11.6	6.3	8.9	4.9	6.7	3.8
Industry*	31.8	39.5	30.3	35.3	27.6	28.4
Construction	11.6	32.5	12.6	28.5	10.5	28.0
Services	45.0	21.7	48.2	31.3	55.2	39.8
Total	100	100	100	100	100	100

Source: INSEE 1992a: Table R10.
* Excluding construction

Table 2.5 Sectoral distribution of French and foreign female labour force, by percentage, 1975–90

	1975		1982		1990	
	French	Foreign	French	Foreign	French	Foreign
Agriculture	8.4	3.0	7.1	2.6	4.7	2.0
Industry*	23.6	35.2	19.4	27.5	15.9	20.6
Construction	1.4	1.6	1.5	1.2	1.4	1.3
Services	66.6	60.2	72.0	68.7	78.0	76.1
Total	100	100	100	100	100	100

Source: INSEE 1992a: Table R10.
* Excluding construction

Table 2.6 Socio-economic groups as percentage of labour force, males and females combined, by nationality, 1990

	Fr	Fo	EC	Sp	It	Po	Al	Mo	Tu	Af	As	Tk	Ot
Farmers	4.3	0.5	0.9	1.1	1.3	0.2	0.1	0.3	0.1	0.1	0.2	0.7	1.5
Artisans, tradespeople, company heads	7.4	6.1	6.9	6.5	12.9	4.7	5.8	3.7	6.8	3.8	6.7	6.3	7.6
Senior managers and professionals	11.1	5.8	5.9	4.0	6.1	0.9	2.4	2.6	3.4	6.8	2.9	1.0	21.6
Junior managers and professionals	19.6	7.8	8.9	9.2	12.6	4.8	5.9	4.6	6.4	9.5	6.6	2.8	15.9
Non-manual workers	28.2	18.8	21.1	24.9	15.0	22.3	16.7	14.5	15.8	22.4	19.9	7.1	20.9
personal service staff	4.5	8.8	11.6	14.8	6.0	13.6	5.9	6.5	6.7	8.3	8.6	2.2	8.0
Manual workers	28.4	57.9	55.4	53.4	51.2	66.1	64.8	69.9	63.8	50.8	57.9	75.2	29.5
skilled	16.3	26.1	27.9	27.9	31.9	31.1	30.0	25.2	29.4	16.6	24.6	26.0	14.4
unskilled	11.1	29.2	25.2	20.5	18.4	32.6	34.2	35.4	31.4	33.9	32.2	45.8	14.4
agricultural	1.0	2.6	2.3	5.0	0.9	2.3	0.6	9.3	3.0	0.3	1.1	3.4	0.7
Unemployed with no previous job	1.0	3.1	0.9	0.9	0.9	1.0	4.3	4.4	3.7	6.6	5.8	6.9	3.0
Total	100	100	100	100	100	100	100	100	100	100	100	100	100

Source: Derived from INSEE 1992a: Table 17.
Key: Fr=French; Fo=Foreign; EC=European Community; Sp=Spanish; It=Italian; Po=Portuguese; Al=Algerians; Mo=Moroccans; Tu=Tunisians; Af=Other Africans; As=South-east Asians; Tk=Turks; Ot=Others

Table 2.7 Socio-economic groups as percentage of male labour force, by nationality, 1990

	Fr	Fo	EC	Sp	It	Po	Al	Mo	Tu	Af	As	Tk	Ot
Farmers	4.9	0.6	1.1	1.3	1.3	0.3	0.0	0.3	0.1	0.1	0.2	0.8	1.7
Artisans, tradespeople, company heads	9.0	7.5	9.4	8.8	15.4	6.9	6.6	4.1	7.6	4.6	7.5	7.1	9.5
Senior managers and professionals	14.0	6.2	6.9	4.8	6.5	1.0	2.3	2.7	3.5	7.2	3.9	1.0	25.9
Junior managers and professionals	19.6	7.6	9.5	10.8	13.7	6.1	5.4	4.3	6.2	9.5	8.0	2.5	13.4
Non-manual workers	11.3	7.0	5.0	6.4	5.2	4.1	7.2	5.7	9.0	14.1	14.6	2.6	10.2
personal service staff	1.2	2.9	2.0	2.5	2.0	1.8	3.0	2.4	3.9	5.0	7.4	1.0	4.0
Manual workers	40.6	69.6	67.7	67.5	57.7	81.2	76.8	81.1	72.4	61.5	63.1	82.2	37.5
skilled	26.9	35.0	40.8	41.2	39.9	47.2	37.6	30.8	35.0	21.2	29.6	29.9	20.7
unskilled	12.3	31.4	24.3	19.9	16.8	31.6	38.5	39.2	35.0	39.9	32.4	48.9	15.9
agricultural	1.4	3.2	2.6	6.4	1.0	2.5	0.7	11.1	3.4	0.4	1.1	3.4	0.9
Unemployed with no previous job	0.6	1.5	0.4	0.4	0.2	0.4	1.7	1.8	1.2	3.0	2.7	3.8	1.8
Total	100	100	100	100	100	100	100	100	100	100	100	100	100

Source: Derived from INSEE 1992a: Table 17.
Key: Fr=French; Fo=Foreign; EC=European Community; Sp=Spanish; It=Italian; Po=Portuguese; Al=Algerians; Mo=Moroccans; Tu=Tunisians; Af=Other Africans; As=South-east Asians; Tk=Turks; Ot=Others

Table 2.8 Socio-economic groups as percentage of female labour force, by nationality, 1990

	Fr	Fo	EC	Sp	It	Po	Al	Mo	Tu	Af	As	Tk	Ot
Farmers	3.5	0.4	0.7	0.7	1.0	0.1	0.1	0.2	0.0	0.0	0.2	0.1	1.3
Artisans, tradespeople, company heads	5.4	2.9	2.7	2.5	5.5	1.3	3.0	2.0	3.4	1.7	5.2	2.5	4.6
Senior managers and professionals	7.7	4.8	4.1	2.6	5.0	0.7	2.7	2.4	2.8	5.5	1.3	1.3	15.0
Junior managers and professionals	19.5	8.4	7.9	6.5	9.1	2.7	7.8	5.9	7.1	9.3	4.4	4.1	19.7
Non-manual workers	48.8	45.7	48.9	56.2	44.8	51.4	48.3	46.1	45.6	46.2	28.5	26.7	37.6
personal service staff	8.4	22.4	27.8	35.5	18.1	32.5	15.7	21.6	19.4	17.5	10.5	7.1	14.4
Manual workers	13.7	30.9	33.8	29.7	31.8	41.8	25.2	29.5	26.4	20.6	49.5	45.0	16.9
skilled	3.6	5.8	5.3	5.6	7.7	5.6	4.9	5.1	5.1	3.7	16.7	19.2	4.5
unskilled	9.6	23.7	26.8	21.6	23.5	34.2	19.8	21.6	20.4	16.8	31.7	32.4	12.1
agricultural	0.5	1.4	1.7	2.5	0.6	2.0	0.5	2.8	0.9	0.1	1.1	3.4	0.3
Unemployed with no previous job	1.4	6.9	1.9	1.8	2.8	2.0	12.9	13.9	14.7	16.7	10.9	20.3	4.9
Total	100	100	100	100	100	100	100	100	100	100	100	100	100

Source: Derived from INSEE 1992a: Table 17.
Key: Fr=French; Fo=Foreign; EC=European Community; Sp=Spanish; It=Italian; Po=Portuguese; Al=Algerians; Mo=Moroccans; Tu=Tunisians; Af=Other Africans; As=South-east Asians; Tk=Turks; Ot=Others

cent of non-nationals. At the opposite end of the scale, 14 per cent of French males were senior managers or professionals, compared with just 6 per cent of foreigners; among women, the figures were 8 and 5 per cent respectively.

After halting labour migration in 1974, the administration presided over by Giscard d'Estaing had hoped to curb unemployment among French nationals by encouraging foreign workers to return home; forcible repatriations were also planned, though it proved impossible to effect them. An important assumption underlying this strategy was that French nationals would be willing to fill the jobs vacated by departing foreigners. Government ministers were irritated when a report which they had commissioned called this assumption into question. Taking the construction and automobile industries as examples, Le Pors (1977) reported that as the posts occupied by foreigners were mainly of the kind that the French themselves had been keen to quit, it was unlikely they would now return to such jobs, even at a time of rising unemployment. In both absolute and proportional terms, these industries were the two largest employers of foreign labour in France. In different ways, they exemplified the fact that immigrant workers, concentrated in certain segments of the labour market, were a structural rather than a temporary feature of the national economy.

The building trade, which remains by far the biggest single employer of foreign workers, was characterized during the post-war period by increasingly poor rates of pay, compared with those offered in other sectors, and carried particularly unattractive working conditions – high accident rates, poor hygiene, low job security, etc. Small wonder, then, that French nationals were increasingly inclined to leave the industry, leaving immigrants to fill the gaps. A similar trend was visible in the car industry, where automation had lowered the general level of skills required of the workforce, for whom repetitive assembly-line tasks were the norm; shiftwork and the anti-social hours which this implied were a further disincentive. While robotization led to wide-scale redundancies among immigrant car workers from the late 1970s onwards, this brought few job opportunities for French nationals. According to labour-force surveys, between 1973 and 1982 the number of foreigners employed in the car industry dropped by 151,000; because many of these jobs disappeared altogether, it is estimated that no more than 10,000 French nationals found employment as a result (Hessel 1988: II, 43).

There has been heavy labour-shedding in the building industry, too, and foreign workers have borne the brunt of this. Non-nationals accounted for three-quarters of all the construction jobs lost between 1975 and 1982 (Marie 1992: 27). While this helped to protect French workers from the worst of the recession, as overall employment levels in this sector have declined the laying-off of large numbers of foreign workers has created relatively few new jobs for French nationals.

Public cleaning services in large cities such as Paris offer a rare example of the systematic substitution of French for foreign workers. In 1976, the Paris City Council stopped recruiting foreigners to sweep the streets. Because permanent employment by central and local arms of the state is reserved by law for French nationals, the council was able to effect this shift without breaking other statutes forbidding racial discrimination. Until 1976, most street-sweepers had had the formal status of temporary auxiliaries, which had enabled the council to hire foreigners. By 1985, 1,500 of them had left their jobs, while 2,000 French nationals had been taken on. This reduced the proportion of foreigners among the city's street-sweepers to 32 per cent in 1985, compared with 72 per cent in 1975. Even here, however, major improvements in pay and working conditions made the process a less than direct substitution of nationals for non-nationals, for the jobs taken up by the former were substantially upgraded in comparison with those vacated by the latter (Merckling 1987: 81).

Marginalization

The concentration of foreign workers in unattractive segments and at low levels of the economic hierarchy is compounded by their vulnerability to job insecurity. This insecurity, which in one sense marginalizes them, is nevertheless structurally important. Capitalist economies are increasingly characterized by what are known as split or dual labour markets (Berger and Piore 1980). The primary market offers relatively stable, skilled and well-paid jobs, whereas in the secondary market employment is more likely to be insecure, poorly paid and unskilled. It is no accident that France's heaviest concentrations of foreign workers are in the construction industry, for this, more than any other, is characterized by high levels of job insecurity (Beaugé 1990). Textile manufacture, which also relies heavily on immigrant workers, is another industry vulnerable to sharp fluctuations in the demand for labour (Berrier 1985). The fact that permanent employment by the state is reserved for French nationals excludes foreigners from the most secure part of the tertiary sector; non-nationals are concentrated in services such as domestic work and catering (i.e. hotels, cafés and restaurants), where employment is often poorly paid and subject to seasonal and other fluctuations (Verhaeren 1990: 128–30; Maurin 1991: 48–9).

Since the late 1970s, economic restructuring forced by the quickening pace of globalization has been marked in France, as in many Western countries, by the decline of manufacturing industry, the growth of the service sector, higher levels of female economic activity, and increased casualization, i.e. the introduction of weaker employment contracts than those previously enjoyed by employees. The effect of these closely intertwined trends has been to favour the development of the secondary labour market. Some of this has been achieved by substituting part-time and/or temporary contracts for full-time, permanent jobs; increased sub-contracting by large firms has pushed in the same direction (Abou Sada 1990). Legally sanctioned forms of casualization have been accompanied by the development of the informal or underground economy, which circumvents legislation designed to protect the labour force. By not declaring part or all of their activities to the authorities, employers escape tax and social security payments as well as regulations on health and safety, minimum wage levels, maximum working-hours, and security of employment. By the same token, those employed in this way work in extremely insecure conditions. Undocumented immigrants are only a small part of the total underground economy, but their fear of expulsion if reported to the authorities makes them one of the most vulnerable groups within it (HCI 1993b: 100).

The jobs initially taken by immigrant workers have generally been in the secondary labour market (Piore 1979; Courault 1990). The fixed-term contracts prescribed in the official procedures laid down in 1945 by the Office National d'Immigration (ONI) for the recruitment of foreign workers were designed to ensure flexibility. Seasonal workers – tens of thousands of whom are still granted temporary work permits each year, mainly in the agricultural sector – represent a continuing and acute form of institutionalized impermanence. The ONI has never succeeded in fully controlling the recruitment process. Algerians were always exempt from it, and during the 1960s most other foreign workers obtained residence and work permits only after they had taken up jobs, reversing the order of the formally prescribed procedures. The dividing line between the formal and informal parts of the secondary market was thus relatively weak: undocumented foreign workers who, in breach of the law, obtained temporary contracts of employment found it easy to regularize their situation.

As their period of settlement lengthened, immigrants generally acquired longer-term residence and work permits, together with more stable employment, while nevertheless remaining subject to more frequent changes of jobs than French nationals (Maurin 1991: 42). After the recruitment freeze imposed in 1974, the more difficult economic climate which was then developing probably slowed the pace at which settled labour migrants were able to move from the secondary to the primary labour market (Tribalat 1991: 196). Following the second oil crisis of 1979, economic restructuring brought huge job losses in sectors with heavy concentrations of foreign workers, among whom unemployment rates rose steeply, forcing a renewed willingness to accept insecure work rather than none at all (Courault 1990). At the same time, the state's refusal to accept new foreign entrants sharpened the divide between the formal and informal parts of the secondary market. Despite rising un-employment, many employers welcomed illegal immigrants, whose weak bargaining position they were keen to exploit. A similar pattern persists today (HCI 1993c).

An analysis by Marie (1988) of those who benefited from the amnesty declared by the incoming Socialist administration in 1981–2 provides a telling picture of the role of undocumented foreign workers within the French economy. Most were of Third World origin, reflecting the dominance of Africans and Asians in recent migratory flows. The great majority held jobs in sectors dominated by small firms. Two-thirds worked for businesses employing fewer than ten people. Construction, catering, domestic service and the clothing industry together accounted for more than half of all those regularized. As Marie (1992: 31) later observed, this sectoral profile matches up very closely with the most dynamic features of the role currently played by foreign workers in the formal labour market. A follow-up survey conducted two years after the amnesty found that more than 80 per cent of the total now held regular jobs, usually in the same sector where they had previously been working illegally. This was clear evidence that, as undocumented workers, they had been meeting a structural need within the French economy. Their working conditions after regularization changed very little. Low pay, long and anti-social working hours and insecure contracts of employ-ment were the hallmarks of this system, enabling employers to respond to shifts in demand with maximum flexibility (Marie 1988: 554–74). An analysis of police reports concerning employers accused of circumventing the laws regulating hired labour in 1989–90 found that the pattern had changed very little: two-thirds of the reported cases concerned the building, catering and retail-distribution sectors (Marie 1992: 32).

While most of those regularized in 1980–1 were young men, one-fifth were women. Again, this replicated almost exactly the gender balance among salaried foreign workers in the formal labour market (ibid.: 30). Three-quarters of the regularized women were unmarried. The largest single group among them – almost one-third of the total – was composed of Portuguese nationals. They accounted for the bulk of undocumented domestic staff, who together represented half of the female contingent in the regularization operation. About one-fifth of undocumented women were employed as cleaners or clothing workers. Even after regularization, two-thirds of women were being paid less than the official minimum wage, as were one-quarter of regularized men.

Among undocumented workers as a whole, a tendency towards ethnic segmentation was clearly visible, with Turks, Moroccans and Tunisians together accounting for almost two-thirds of those regularized in the building industry; sub-Saharan Africans represented 41 per cent of other industrial workers, and the Portuguese alone accounted for an identical share of regularized domestic staff. In many, though not all, respects this, too, parallels the sectoral distribution of national groups within the formal economy (Tables 2.9–2.11). Ethnic concentrations were still more marked among the 20 per cent of regularized workers employed by foreign nationals. Some 75 per cent of those working for Algerians were themselves of Algerian nationality; among Turks the equivalent figure was 80 per cent, and among Tunisians and Moroccans it exceeded 90 per cent (Marie 1988).

It should be noted that the 1981 amnesty was targeted at foreign workers who held neither residence nor labour permits. The informal economy employs not only illegal immigrants but also many French nationals, as well as foreigners who, despite holding both residence and labour permits, cannot find suitable work in the formal economy. In particular, it is likely that the official figures on female labour-participation rates significantly under-represent the true contribution of women, particularly Maghrebis, to economic activity (Tapinos 1992: 37, 42).

Table 2.9 Sectoral percentage distribution of labour force, male and female combined, by nationality, 1990

	Agriculture	Industry excluding construction	Construction industry	Services	Total
French	5.8	22.5	6.6	65.1	100
Foreign	3.3	26.3	20.6	49.8	100
EC	3.3	24.3	24.7	47.7	100
Spanish	6.1	24.4	19.4	50.1	100
Italians	2.2	28.4	27.1	42.3	100
Portuguese	2.6	24.0	29.9	43.5	100
Algerians	0.6	26.9	21.9	50.6	100
Moroccans	10.6	29.6	18.9	40.9	100
Tunisians	3.3	21.8	24.6	50.3	100
Other Africans*	0.3	23.6	6.9	69.2	100
S.-E. Asians**	1.1	42.7	3.4	52.8	100
Turks	4.3	43.7	28.5	23.5	100
Others	2.5	21.6	6.9	69.0	100

Source: INSEE 1992a: Table 18.
* Ex-French sub-Saharan Africa ** Ex-French Indo-China

Table 2.10 Sectoral percentage distribution of male labour force, by nationality, 1990

	Agriculture	Industry excluding construction	Construction industry	Services	Total
French	6.7	27.6	10.5	55.2	100
Foreign	3.9	28.4	28.0	39.7	100
EC	3.7	26.3	37.1	32.9	100
Spanish	7.6	29.6	29.4	33.4	100
Italians	2.3	29.7	34.1	33.9	100
Portuguese	2.8	24.8	46.4	26.0	100
Algerians	0.6	29.3	26.5	43.6	100
Moroccans	12.0	32.5	22.4	33.1	100
Tunisians	3.8	22.5	28.6	45.1	100
Other Africans*	0.3	26.9	8.3	64.5	100
S.-E. Asians**	1.0	42.3	4.9	51.8	100
Turks	4.3	43.2	32.6	19.9	100
Others	2.9	23.8	10.4	62.9	100

Source: INSEE 1992a: Table 18.
* Ex-French sub-Saharan Africa ** Ex-French Indo-China

Table 2.11 Sectoral percentage distribution of female labour force, by nationality, 1990

	Agriculture	Industry excluding construction	Construction industry	Services	Total
French	4.7	15.9	1.4	78.0	100
Foreign	2.0	20.6	1.3	76.1	100
EC	2.5	20.7	1.5	75.3	100
Spanish	3.4	14.9	1.4	80.3	100
Italians	1.8	23.8	2.5	71.9	100
Portuguese	2.2	22.8	1.5	73.5	100
Algerians	0.4	16.4	1.3	81.9	100
Moroccans	3.6	15.4	1.3	79.7	100
Tunisians	0.9	17.3	1.2	80.6	100
Other Africans*	0.2	10.6	1.1	88.1	100
S.-E. Asians**	1.2	43.4	0.4	55.0	100
Turks	4.5	46.7	2.6	46.2	100
Others	1.9	17.8	0.9	79.4	100

Source: INSEE 1992a: Table 18.
* Ex-French sub-Saharan Africa ** Ex-French Indo-China

Exclusion

It is a cruel irony that immigrants, who in popular discourse used to be synonymous with immigrant workers, now suffer from exceptionally high levels of unemployment. Until the late 1970s, while marginalized and segmented, they were nevertheless more fully integrated into the world of work – in the simple sense of holding jobs of one kind or another – than French nationals themselves. Today, while far more settled in France than was the case twenty years ago, many foreigners face a much higher risk of social exclusion as a consequence of unemployment.

There is a sharp distinction here between Europeans and others. As can be seen from Table 2.2, documented unemployment levels among EU nationals are very similar to those of the French. Africans and Asians, by contrast, are almost three times as likely to be out of work. The gap between French workers and Third World nationals is higher still when the male labour force is considered separately. More than two in five African and Asian women are unemployed, compared with one in seven French women.

Tribalat (1991: 195–237) has suggested that differential unemployment rates reflect the relatively recent nature of migratory flows from certain countries. The available data provide only limited evidence in support of this. While unemployment is even higher among Africans and Asians who have arrived in France since 1982, mainly within the framework of family reunification procedures, Europeans entering since then suffer only marginally worse unemployment than their longer-established compatriots, who in turn are in a very similar position to French nationals (HCI 1993b: 37). Recent entrants may be handicapped by poor language skills, but there is no reason to believe that Third World nationals are worse affected by this than Europeans. As most of those from Africa and Asia come from former colonies where French is still widely used, they should if anything have an advantage in this respect. Lack of qualifications and discrimination on the part of employers are more likely explanations.

As the educational systems of many Third World countries are far less developed than those in European states, African immigrants in particular appear to be disadvantaged in this regard. Labour-force surveys indicate that 75 per cent of Maghrebis have no formal qualifications at all, compared with only 35 per cent of French workers. Yet even when controlled comparisons are made with French nationals of identical age and skills, Maghrebis are almost twice as likely to be out of work, which strongly suggests that they are the victims of discriminatory practices. Similarly, as only 45 per cent of South-East Asians lack qualifications, compared with 82 per cent of Portuguese workers, it is likely that the much higher levels of unemployment suffered by the former are due in part to discrimination against them (Maurin 1991: 39–41).

Similar differences in unemployment rates have been visible since the wave of economic restructuring which began in the late 1970s. On average, the jobless rate among foreigners has been about twice as high as among French nationals, but the real division has been between Third World nationals (whose unemployment rate has been roughly three times that of French nationals) and Europeans (who have remained close to the French figure). The steep rise in unemployment among foreign workers has been partly a consequence of their concentration in unskilled jobs within sectors which have shed particularly large numbers of workers. The shake-out was particularly vigorous in the late 1970s and early 1980s. In the industrial sector as a whole (including construction), foreigners represented two-fifths of the jobs lost between 1979 and 1982, though they accounted for only about one-tenth of the total industrial labour force (Anstett 1992: 113).

In 1982, foreigners constituted about one-sixth of the building industry's labour force, but they had suffered seven out of every ten job losses over the previous ten years (ibid.: 114). At the time of the 1975 census, vehicle production was the second largest industrial employer of foreign labour. With robotization, the industry suffered heavy job losses in the early 1980s, and most of the manual workers replaced in this way were non-nationals. By 1990, the foreign workforce had been reduced by more than half, while French nationals in this sector were down by only one-sixth.

Contrasts of this kind cannot always be accounted for by differences in the level of skills offered by French and by foreign workers. In the electrical industry, for example, unskilled non-nationals suffered job losses during the 1980s at a rate five times higher than French workers in the same category (Maurin 1991: 44). While its effects are difficult to quantify with precision, discrimination by employers does appear to have disadvantaged certain groups of foreign workers, particularly non-Europeans, within the formal labour market. At the same time, the generally poor level of qualifications found among Africans in particular is in itself a serious handicap when competing for jobs in expanding sectors demanding higher levels of skills than were required in some declining industries.

The cumulative effect of all this has been to push a growing proportion of certain groups into long-term unemployment. A labour-force survey conducted in 1992 found that 40 per cent of unemployed foreigners had been out of work for over a year, compared with 32 per cent of French nationals. While long-term joblessness affected 25 per cent of unemployed Portuguese nationals, among out-of-work Maghrebis the rate was 44 per cent, and among other Africans it stood at 48 per cent (INSEE 1994: 85).

Ethnic business

The term 'ethnic business' is widely used to denote economic activities by people of minority ethnic groups who are self-employed, and who in many cases also employ others.[4] In France and other countries, the last twenty years have brought a marked rise in small businesses of this kind. In the present context, these businesses raise two questions which are particularly pertinent: how far have they served to alleviate the difficulties experienced in the labour market by minority ethnic groups, and how far have they strengthened or diluted the segmentation of these groups?

The statistical data available in France usually distinguish three main categories among the self-employed: artisans (i.e. skilled manual workers), people in the retail, wholesale or catering trades (generically referred to hereafter as tradespeople), and the owners of businesses employing ten or more people. All but 7 per cent of self-employed foreigners fit into the first two categories (Echardour and Maurin 1993: 510). As foreign entrepreneurs employing more than a handful of people are few in number, there is relatively little scope for the development of full-blown 'enclave economies', i.e. concentrations of particular minority groups within businesses owned, managed and staffed entirely on a mono-ethnic basis (Portes 1981).

By comparison with their share of the general population, foreigners have traditionally been under-represented among the self-employed, partly because of restrictive regulations which were not lifted until 1984. Not surprisingly, those wishing to set up in business have been characterized by above-average naturalization rates, as a consequence of which statistics based on nationality significantly underestimate the number of self-employed immigrants. Since the mid-1970s, however, there has been a steady rise in the number of self-employed foreigners. This began even before the restrictions on them were lifted.

From only 2 per cent of all artisans in 1975, foreign nationals rose to 4 per cent in 1982 and 6 per cent in 1990, a figure only fractionally less than their share of the total labour force (Auvolat and Benattig 1988: 39; INSEE 1992a: Table 17). It is no accident that this rise has taken place at a time of radical economic restructuring and weaker job security. Many large companies have increased the share of their activities sub-contracted out to small businesses sometimes consisting of one 'self-employed' individual who, because of that status, is formally exempt from the security of employment traditionally enjoyed by salaried employees. In the mid-1980s, a survey by Auvolat and Benattig (1988) found that half of all recently registered artisans, both French and foreign, had previously been out of work. Among foreign artisans, southern European (particularly Portuguese) and Maghrebi nationals were dominant. Most set up in sectors where they had previously worked as employees. More than two-thirds of foreign artisans, compared with only two-fifths of French artisans, were in the building industry, where there have been heavy job losses, particularly among immigrant workers, since the late

1970s. Significantly, two-thirds of the self-employed foreigners in the construction sector surveyed by Auvolat and Benattig were sub-contractors, compared with less than one-third of French nationals. Thus many self-employed foreigners appear to owe their status to a combination of labour-shedding and sub-contracting practices devised by larger French firms to gain flexibility in the hiring and firing of their workforce (Garson and Mouhoud 1989). In these circumstances, it is only in a relatively weak sense that the majority of foreign artisans might be included under the umbrella of 'ethnic business'. While certainly over-represented in certain segments of the labour market, they remain to a very large extent dependent upon, and dominated by, contracts in the mainstream economy.

A clear pattern of ethnic segmentation is also visible among tradespeople of immigrant origin. In 1990, foreigners represented 5 per cent of all tradespeople in France, compared with 3 per cent in 1982 (Echardour and Maurin 1993: 510). In the mid-1980s, Ma Mung and Guillon (1986: 108) found that in the Paris conurbation more than 60 per cent of foreign-owned small businesses were accounted for by grocery stores and catering establishments, i.e. hotels, cafés and restaurants. French tradespeople were far more widely spread. The businesses in which foreigners were most strongly represented were either in decline among French tradespeople (this was true of both grocery stores and catering in general) or offered 'exotic' produce unavailable in French establishments (the cuisine proposed by foreign-owned restaurants being the best example). Certain nationalities were also heavily over-represented, with Maghrebis accounting for 61 per cent of all foreign tradespeople, against only 39 per cent of the foreign population at large. This was partly because, under the terms of the Evian agreement granting independence to Algeria in 1962, Algerians had been exempted from the controls on self-employment by foreigners. It should also be said that because of exceptionally high naturalization rates among South-East Asians, their business activities – which are particularly strong in the catering sector – are always grossly underestimated in analyses based on nationality.

A more recent survey by Ma Mung (1992), based on ethnic origins (as judged by family names) rather than nationality, confirms the current dynamism of tradespeople of immigrant origin, and the predominance among them of Maghrebis and Asians, with a marked segmentation in particular niches. More than one in five of all the shops and catering establishments in the Paris conurbation which changed hands in the first half of 1989 were bought by Maghrebis (15 per cent of the total) or Asians (5.6 per cent); as measured by nationality, these groups account respectively for just 2.5 and less than 1 per cent of the general population. While gradually extending into a wider range of businesses, both groups remain heavily concentrated in food shops and catering, with Maghrebis to the fore in general grocery stores, and Asians strongly represented in the restaurant trade.

The extent to which a particular pattern of economic activity may be described as 'ethnic business' depends on the ethnic complexion of four main variables: the capital with which businesses are acquired, the staff who run them, the services or products sold, and the customers for whom they cater. The more these variables correspond to the same ethnic group, the more the businesses in question function as a distinct economic circuit outside the dominant patterns of the national economy. While businesses run by people of immigrant origin in France are frequently dependent for their capital on minority ethnic networks, and some target clienteles which are primarily of a similar ethnic complexion, most depend for the lion's share of their custom on the majority population. According to Ma Mung and Guillon (1986: 128), the two most typical types of foreign-run small businesses are Maghrebi-owned grocery stores selling a 'normal' (i.e. unexotic) range of products in mainly French districts, and Asian restaurants serving oriental dishes to French customers.

It should be remembered that both the retail-food and catering sectors have been in decline among French tradespeople, who have proved increasingly unwilling to work the long and anti-social hours which are necessary to make a success of such businesses. Businesses of this kind certainly attest to the dynamism found among groups of immigrant origin, and it is also true that small, user-friendly grocery stores in mainly French districts play a valuable public-relations role on behalf of minority ethnic groups; but they also tend to reinforce the pattern of ethnic segmentation noted earlier in connection with salaried workers, without necessarily bringing real independence or even higher living standards to the self-employed.

Longitudinal data

Granted the low level at which most immigrants enter the labour market, evidence of upward social mobility is one of the key indicators of the extent to which they are being incorporated into the full spread of French society, rather than confined to its margins. A labour-force survey of workers aged between 30 and 60 in 1989 found that among those who had been unskilled labourers in 1981, 13 per cent of Portuguese nationals had been promoted to skilled jobs, compared with 6 per cent of French nationals and 3.5 per cent of Maghrebis. Among those who were already in skilled manual employment in 1981, 8 per cent of the Portuguese, 6.5 per cent of the French and 3.5 per cent of Maghrebis had been promoted to office jobs (Maurin 1991: 44). As labour-force surveys are based on less comprehensive soundings than censuses, it would be unwise to treat these findings as an exact description of the national situation, but it is likely that they provide a reasonably accurate indication of underlying trends.

There have to date been very few attempts to collect similar data on foreign workers over a longer period. The only significant study of this kind which has so far been published is that of Borkowski (1990). Again, the findings must be treated with caution, partly because some of the criteria by which Borkowski measures social mobility are less than wholly objective. It is also regrettable that the size of the sample is not indicated. The survey is based on interviews conducted in the mid-1980s with immigrants who had arrived in France before 1968. Respondents were asked to indicate their occupation, that of their father, and that of their children. In addition, the interviewer assessed the financial circumstances of each respondent, though the criteria by which this was done are not specified, and Borkowski acknowledges that it was a largely subjective process. A tripartite categorization was used: respondents were described as well off, badly off, or of average means. Some 27 per cent of respondents were placed in the higher category, 22 per cent in the lower, and 51 per cent in the middle category. Combining these assessments with information on inter-generational occupational trends, Borkowski described respondents as having experienced a social trajectory that was either upward, middling or poor. On this basis, 29 per cent of respondents were said to have moved upwards, 23 per cent ranked as middling, and 48 per cent were found to be poor. Among particular ethnic groups, the least successful were Maghrebis, with 57 per cent ranked as poor, and 22 per cent placed on an upward trajectory. The most successful were West Europeans, with 46 per cent moving upward and 29 per cent classed as poor.

The imprecision and subjectivity involved in these rankings make it necessary to treat them with great caution. A more reliable picture may be obtained by confining the analysis to the data on occupational status, within which Borkowski distinguished three main categories: white-collar, manual, and others. While the fathers of 50 per cent of respondents were classed as manual workers, 54 per cent of interviewees were placed in this category. Some 17 per cent of fathers had held white-collar jobs, while 36 per cent of interviewees fell in this category. Among the remaining 33 per cent of fathers, 20 per cent had worked on the land, while 13 per cent had been artisans or tradespeople; only 2 per cent of interviewees were in agriculture, while 8 per cent were artisans or tradespeople. Overall, the evidence for significant upward mobility among immigrants as a whole is not particularly strong.

Borkowski's data suggest that a greater degree of upward mobility may have been achieved by the children of immigrants. All those covered by the survey were born before 1968. While the fathers of 67 per cent were manual workers, only 35 per cent of the younger generation fell into this category. Some 54 per cent of immigrant-born children were placed in the white-collar category, compared with 13 per cent of their fathers. Of the remaining 11 per cent among the younger generation, 9 per cent were artisans or tradespeople; their fathers accounted for 20 per cent of immigrants, among whom 11 per cent had been artisans or tradespeople. Despite the clear trend away from manual occupations, it should not be assumed that white-collar work necessarily signifies a higher social status. As noted earlier, many jobs in the service sector are unskilled and poorly paid. Unfortunately, Borkowski's data are not sufficiently refined to permit a satisfactory analysis of this factor.

As with the inter-generational data on immigrants and their parents, when Borkowksi's assessments of financial circumstances are added and combined with a breakdown by ethnic origins, the resulting league table of social mobility among immigrant-born children, compared with their fathers, includes too many subjective elements to count as in any way an authoritative guide. The children of West Europeans come out best, with 55 per cent moving upward, and only 19 per cent classed as poor. A similar proportion of young Maghrebis, 53 per cent, was also said to have moved upward, but as 29 per cent were classed as poor, Borkowski described them as more divided than other ethnic groups.

The main lesson of Borkowski's study is the inadequacy of the data currently available for the assessment of inter-generational change among immigrants and their descendants. Traditional census data based on nationality are of little help, since the majority of immigrant-born children have automatically acquired French citizenship on or before reaching adulthood. Studies such as that of Palidda and Muñoz (1988) on the labour-market position of young foreigners throw at best only limited light on the descendants of immigrants, for non-nationals over the age of 18 are likely to have been born abroad and have in many cases spent part or all of their childhood there, making them atypical of immigrant-born children socialized in France. Census forms do record the birthplace of all residents (though not that of their parents), which in principle can help to fill some of the gaps in our knowledge of the socio-economic condition of minority ethnic groups, but INSEE has so far released very little information of this kind. The first significant, though still limited, study to draw on such data is that of Tribalat (1993).

Tribalat's methodology is similar to that used with data derived from the 1981 census in Britain, when the ethnic minority population was officially calculated on the basis of the number of people living in households headed by a person born in the New Commonwealth, i.e. former British colonies where Europeans had never formed more than a very small part of the population. At the time of the 1990 census in France, 1,726,000 children aged below 17 were living in immigrant-headed households. (For the purposes of Tribalat's analysis, *rapatriés* and French nationals from the DOM-TOM are not classed as immigrants.) More than half of these children were already French; only 864,000 were foreign nationals, and all but 274,000 were born in France. In these same households, there were 1,030,000 people in the 15–24 age bracket (which, it should be noted, overlaps slightly with the 0–16 age group), two-thirds of whom were born in France. By focusing on this age group it is possible to estimate the unemployment rates experienced by young people of different ethnic origins.

The contrasts which emerge are similar but not identical to those characterizing first-generation members of different immigrant groups. Calculated on this basis, the nationwide unemployment rate among 22-year-old men, including those in non-immigrant households, is 19 per cent. Among men of that age in immigrant-headed households, the rates are 12 per cent in homes headed by an immigrant from Portugal, 23 per cent where the head is from Spain, 39 per cent where the head is from Morocco, and 51 per cent where the head is from Algeria (Tribalat 1993: 1940–1). Tribalat does not give any comparable 1990 data for women, but in a more limited household survey in 1982 she found a substantially similar pattern among both sexes. The unemployment rate among 21-year-olds still living with French mothers was 12 per cent for men and 18 per cent for women; among the sons and daughters of Portuguese women the figures were 7 and 18 per cent respectively, compared with 39 and 49 per cent among those born to Algerian mothers (Tribalat 1991: 165). Even allowing for the fact that these calculations do not include adults born to immigrant parents who now have their own homes – many, if not most, of whom must be supporting themselves by gainful employment – the unemployment rates among young people of Maghrebi origin make shocking reading.

Exact comparisons with young people from households headed by South-East Asians and sub-Saharan Africans are difficult because a larger proportion of them are still in full-time education, but their unemployment rates are certainly lower than those of young Maghrebis. The stronger rates of participation in higher education among the children of South-East Asians serve to reproduce the superior qualifications found among this group, compared with other immigrants, and this is clearly beneficial in the employment market. Research on the educational attainment of the children of immigrants has consistently shown that the socio-professional status and educational qualifications of parents (which tend to be interlinked) are by far the most important variables, as they are for youngsters among the French population at large. Foreign children generally fare less well at school than French nationals. Certain groups, such as Maghrebis, do particularly badly. These same groups are characterized by far higher levels of socio-economic disadvantage, with poorly educated manual workers accounting for a large proportion of immigrant parents. When children from similar socio-economic backgrounds are compared, the differences between national groups are almost insignificant; if anything, foreign children tend to do slightly better than their French peers (Aissou 1987; Boulot and Boyzon-Fradet 1988; Conseil Economique et Social 1994: 58–79).

Compared with the school population as a whole, young Maghrebis leave full-time education much earlier, and with much poorer qualifications. Yet this alone does not suffice to explain their chronic rates of unemployment. The children of Portuguese immigrants also tend to finish their education early, but their unemployment rate is well below the national average. While young people of Portuguese origin benefit from family and other networks in finding jobs, particularly in the building industry, it is clear that they also suffer far less discrimination than young Maghrebis.

The rise in unemployment seen in most West European countries since the beginning of the 1980s has hit young people particularly hard, forcing governments to devise a variety of schemes designed to alleviate the problem. In France, the first such initiative was the creation in 1982 of *Missions locales pour l'insertion professionnelle et sociale des jeunes*, local advice centres targeting young people (essentially in the 16–25 age group) experiencing serious difficulties in finding work. Since then, state-aided youth-employment, work-experience and training schemes have also been introduced. In 1992, the labour inspectorate produced a report on the experiences of young people of immigrant origin within the employment market based on information collected through these local advice centres (IGAS 1992). The official ban on ethnic monitoring made it impossible to produce exact figures (for reasons already explained, nationality is an inadequate indicator), but local officials estimated that youngsters from immigrant families, who probably make up less than 15 per cent of the 16–25 age group as a whole (Tribalat 1993: 1930) accounted between 30 and 60 per cent of their clients (IGAS 1992: 17). As the *Missions locales* are designed to assist young people facing particularly acute employment problems, there is strong evidence here that the descendants of immigrants are encountering exceptionally severe difficulties.

It is true that immigrant-born youngsters are over-represented in relatively poor households with unskilled family heads, and that this pattern tends to reproduce itself in an inter-generational way regardless of ethnic origins. The inspectorate found, however, that in addition to the handicap of poor qualifications, which they shared with many unemployed youths from non-immigrant families, youngsters of immigrant origin were subject to widespread discrimination. Every local advice centre reported that this was the case. Bearing in mind that discrimination has been prohibited by law since 1972, the frequency with which employers engage in such practices even when dealing with official agencies of the state is very striking. The full force of these practices can best be conveyed by quoting from the report:

All the *Missions locales* and local employment offices included in the survey emphasized the growing importance of discrimination in job offers, based on the origins, the name or simply the address of candidates, particularly if this is an area where disturbances have occurred.

The unwillingness to take on certain people is not always spelt out explicitly. The employer may indicate reservations or refusals of certain candidates by saying nothing at all or simply rejecting them without explanation; in some cases, employers explain their refusals by saying they already have too many foreigners on the payroll or blame refusals on the reaction of other members of staff or customers, when the job involves dealing with the public. Often, though, particularly when contacting local employment offices, employers are straight to the point, signalling their refusal with remarks such as 'no coloured people', 'no Arabs', 'no Maghrebis'.

The *Missions locales* included in the survey estimated that one in three and in some cases one in two job offers were discriminatory.

(IGAS 1992: 49–50)

As one of the co-authors of the report has noted, those worst hit by practices of this kind are young people from Maghrebi and sub-Saharan African families, as well as those originating in the DOM-TOM, despite the fact that many of the former and all of the latter are French nationals (Lemoine 1992: 175). There is an important cross-over here between the attitudinal factors examined in Chapter 4 and the material circumstances of people of immigrant origin. Employment opportunities are fundamental to life chances, and it is clear that certain ethnicized groups suffer severe handicaps in this respect.

HOUSING

Housing and employment are linked in two main ways. At a regional level, the practicalities of daily travel are such that most people live fairly close to their place of work. More locally, housing opportunities are heavily conditioned by income levels, which in turn depend primarily on employment. France's foreign population is heavily concentrated in urban areas (Figure 2.1), reflecting the predominance of industrial employment among non-nationals. Only 8 per cent of foreigners live in rural areas, compared with 27 per cent of French nationals. Foreign residents are more concentrated than the general population in large cities, with Greater Paris, France's largest conurbation, accounting for well over one-third of the foreign population, compared with only 15 per cent of French nationals.

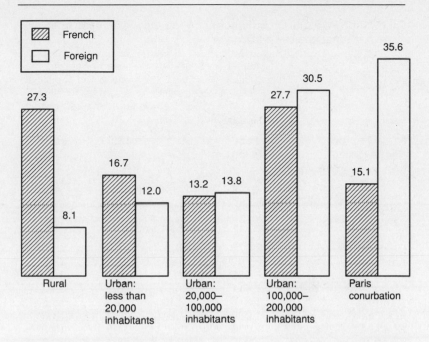

Figure 2.1 Population percentage distribution, by nationality and type of locality, 1990
Source: INSEE 1994: 103.

The Paris conurbation makes up the bulk of the population in Ile-de-France, one of the twenty-two administrative regions into which metropolitan France is divided. Each region contains on average four or five *départements*, which are roughly equivalent to British or American counties. As can be seen from Table 2.12, 59 per cent of the foreign population, compared with 36 per cent of the population as a whole, is concentrated in just three of these regions: Ile-de-France (centred on the city of Paris, which, uniquely, also has the status of a *département*), Rhône-Alpes (where the largest city is Lyon) and Provence-Alpes-Côte d'Azur (of which Marseille is the administrative centre). Ile-de-France is by far the most important region in both absolute and proportional terms. It contains almost two-fifths of France's total foreign population, and the foreign share of the regional population is greater here than in any other part of France. Other important concentrations include those in the old northern and eastern industrial regions of Nord–Pas-de-Calais, Alsace and Lorraine. The least industrialized parts of France lie in

Table 2.12 Population distribution, by region, type of district and nationality, 1990

	Total population	Share of foreign population	Foreign share of regional population	Foreign share of population in jointly aided districts
	(thousands)	(%)	(%)	(%)
Ile-de-France	10,660	38.3	12.9	24.8
Rhône–Alpes	5,355	12.0	8.0	22.3
Provence–Alpes–Côte d'Azur	4,259	8.4	7.1	16.2
Nord–Pas-de-Calais	3,968	4.6	4.2	11.7
Lorraine	2,308	4.3	6.7	21.4
Languedoc–Roussillon	2,116	3.7	6.3	15.3
Alsace	1,624	3.6	7.9	23.6
Centre	2,373	3.2	4.9	25.5
Aquitaine	2,798	3.2	4.1	18.1
Midi–Pyrénées	2,433	2.9	4.3	21.3
Bourgogne	1,611	2.3	5.2	25.6
Picardie	1,814	2.1	4.2	14.6
Franche-Comté	1,099	1.9	6.2	33.2
Champagne–Ardenne	1,350	1.8	4.8	14.5
Haute-Normandie	1,739	1.6	3.2	11.8
Auvergne	1,323	1.5	4.1	12.1
Pays de la Loire	3,060	1.3	1.5	10.1
Bretagne	2,797	0.8	1.0	9.4
Poitou–Charentes	1,597	0.7	1.6	7.4
Corse	250	0.7	9.9	8.1
Basse-Normandie	1,394	0.6	1.6	9.0
Limousin	723	0.6	2.8	13.0
Total	56,651	100	6.3	18.3

Source: INSEE 1994: 103, 105.

the west of the country, where foreigners are in general far less numerous (Georges 1986: 72–129).

As they are concentrated in relatively low-level jobs and exposed to high levels of unemployment, most foreign workers have below-average incomes (INSEE 1994: 91). Africans and Asians generally have larger families than French and EU nationals, which further depresses their per capita income levels. Their purchasing power in the housing market is therefore tightly constrained. Discrimination by gatekeepers such as landlords and estate agents has imposed additional limits. People of immigrant origin have consequently tended to become concentrated in certain localities and types of housing. The informal mutual-support networks associated with 'chain' migration have also contributed to this process. When first seeking work or accommodation, many immigrants head for localities where family members or people originating in the same village or region have already settled, thus creating a recruitment chain by word-of-mouth (Sayad 1975). In some cases, these informal recruitment chains are strengthened by a desire for mutual support and protection in the face of racist behaviour. There have also been cases of what the Americans call 'white flight', i.e. large-scale departures to other localities by members of the majority population who, fearing an influx of visible minorities, precipitate a self-fulfilling prophecy (Battegay 1992).

During the early post-war period, when France faced an acute housing shortage, some immigrant workers were provided with hostel-style accommodation by their employers, but most had to fend for themselves. Many lived in cheap lodging houses in dilapidated inner-city districts, which in some cases were run by *marchands de sommeil* (sleep merchants), racketeers who rented out beds on a shift basis. Others – particularly those who were joined by their families – moved into *bidonvilles* (shantytowns) set up on spare ground, often in outlying districts. Most of the makeshift buildings in these shanty-towns lacked the basic facilities, such as mains electricity, running water and sewers, that the majority of the population took for granted. By the mid-1960s, 75,000 people were officially classed as living in *bidonvilles*, though the true figure was probably at least three times as high (Lallaoui 1993: 44–5). As four-fifths of the officially acknowledged total were foreigners – among whom half were Maghrebis and a quarter Portuguese – the *bidonvilles* exemplified the way in which unbridled market forces tended to create dense, ghetto-like concentrations of economically weak ethnic groups.

Some of the public-policy initiatives designed to remedy excesses of this kind have also proved segregationist in their effects. The first such initiative came in 1956, with the creation of the Société Nationale de Construction de Logements pour les Travailleurs Algériens (SONACOTRAL), a state agency set up to provide hostel accommodation for Algerian immigrant workers. In 1963, the organization was renamed the Société Nationale de Construction de Logements pours les Travailleurs (SONACOTRA), when its remit was extended to include foreign workers of all nationalities. The hostels built by SONACOTRA certainly offered better basic facilities than many tenants had been able to find in the private sector, but as the accommodation was intended solely for foreign workers, it effectively separated them from the mass of the population (Ginesy-Galano 1984). Since the mid-1970s, this type of housing has been called increasingly into question, partly as a consequence of growing disquiet over the regimented living conditions characterizing many hostels, and because of their unsuitability for family occupation at a time when family settlement has largely displaced the rotation of 'lone' immigrant workers. Even so, almost 100,000 foreigners – virtually all men, and 85 per cent Africans – still lived in hostel acccommodation at the time of the 1990 census (INSEE 1992a: 81).

Recognizing the shift towards family settlement, and committed since the early 1970s to the eradication of *bidonvilles*, the state ceased investing in the construction of new hostels in 1975 and at the same time began directing substantial sums of money into public housing for immigrant families. A key mechanism for this lay in the adaptation of a payroll tax initially created in 1953 to help ease the overall housing shortage in France. All companies with more than ten employees were required to invest 1 per cent of their total payroll in housing programmes. Beginning in 1975, companies were instructed to earmark one-fifth of their contributions to the housing of immigrant workers, and most of the funds created in this way were invested in family-style accommodation in *Habitations à Loyer Modéré* (HLMs), the French equivalent of British council housing and American housing projects. Although these funds were sometimes misused and the overall level of the payroll tax was later reduced, as was the share earmarked for immigrants, the net effect was substantially to increase the presence of immigrant families within the public-housing sector. Many of these families had previously lived in *bidonvilles*; others had been forced out of run-down inner-city areas when these were transformed by property developers into up-market units beyond the purchasing power of low-income families.

In 1975, only 15 per cent of households headed by a foreign national lived in HLMs. By 1982, the figure had climbed to 24 per cent, and in 1990 it stood at 28 per cent, compared with only 14 per cent of households headed by a French national. As can be seen from Table 2.13, well over half of all French heads of household are now owner-occupiers, compared with only a quarter of foreigners. The owner-occupation rate is very much lower among Africans and Asians than among Europeans. These differentials reflect the lower income levels generally found among non-Europeans, who find it

Table 2.13 Housing-tenure patterns, by percentage, and nationality of head of household, 1990

	Owner-occupier	Private un-furnished tenant	Private furnished tenant	HLM un-furnished tenant	Free housing	Total
French	56.2	23.0	1.2	13.7	5.9	100
Foreign	26.4	34.8	4.2	28.0	6.7	100
EC	39.9	31.6	2.1	18.4	8.0	100
Spanish	38.1	31.1	1.7	20.5	8.6	100
Italians	55.9	22.0	1.2	14.2	6.8	100
Portuguese	28.7	36.1	1.8	24.8	8.6	100
Algerians	14.9	30.9	7.4	43.4	3.5	100
Moroccans	8.7	35.8	4.6	44.3	6.6	100
Tunisians	11.8	45.3	4.2	34.4	4.3	100
Other Africans*	9.6	41.4	8.3	36.6	4.2	100
S.-E. Asians**	19.7	31.4	2.5	43.4	3.0	100
Turks	8.4	41.7	3.2	45.1	1.7	100
Others	25.6	43.0	6.3	15.3	9.7	100

Source: INSEE 1992a: Table 33.
* Ex-French sub-Saharan Africa ** Ex-French Indo-China

much harder to raise the level of funds required to become home-purchasers. A similar contrast is visible in the rented sector, where private accommodation is usually more costly than social housing. French and European tenants are more numerous in the private than in the public rented sector, whereas Africans and Asians are heavily concentrated in HLMs. In all, 42 per cent of Maghrebi-headed households, 43 per cent of South-East Asians and 45 per cent of Turks live in HLMs, compared with 18 per cent of European- and 14 per cent of French-headed households.

The majority of HLMs constructed after the war took the form of large-scale high-rise developments in suburban districts, many of which were designated as *Zones à Urbaniser en Priorité* (ZUPs). Although ZUPs were officially superseded in 1967 by *Zones d'Aménagement Concerté* (ZACs), the term has remained in common usage as a label for large estates consisting mainly of social housing. While HLMs were built primarily to accommodate tenants of limited means, significant numbers of lower middle-class French families lived there during the early post-war period. By the late 1970s many of these had moved out, becoming owner-occupiers in the private sector. French tenants who remained in HLMs often felt trapped in an urban environment where social facilities had seldom been good and were often visibly deterioriating. The growing presence of immigrant families was sometimes regarded by French tenants as a mark – if not indeed the cause – of the deteriorating conditions in HLM estates. Instead of being spread evenly across those estates, foreign tenants have generally been allocated to less popular, more run-down properties, rather than to new units financed by the payroll tax (Boumaza, Rudder and Maria 1989; Weil 1991: 254–6; Blanc 1992; Rudder 1992).

Since the late 1970s, a variety of government policies has been devised to assist urban areas experiencing acute social difficulties. At the time of the 1990 census, more than 500 districts containing a total of almost 3 million inhabitants were receiving special assist-ance in programmes jointly run by city councils, regional authorities and the central state. As recorded by the census, unemployment across France as a whole was 11 per cent. Within jointly aided districts the figure was 20 per cent, and almost one-third of the jobless in these neighbourhoods had been out of work for at least two years. A study by Castellan, Marpsat and Goldberger (1992) shows that foreigners – and non-Europeans in particular – are over-represented in these localities. While non-nationals make up only 6 per cent of the general population, they account for 18 per cent of the inhabitants of jointly aided districts (Table 2.12). Non-EU nationals represent 63 per cent of the foreign population as a whole, but their share of the foreign population within jointly aided districts is 81 per cent.

Most of these districts are in the suburbs of large cities. Neighbour-hoods of this kind are commonly referred to as *banlieues*, a term which until recently denoted suburban districts in general, but which has now become synonymous with areas of acute social disadvantage (Hargreaves forthcoming). In the English-speaking world, suburbs generally connote relatively pleasant living conditions, in contrast with those obtaining in inner-city areas, where the densest concentra-tions both of poverty and of minority ethnic groups are to be found. There are relatively few districts of this kind close to the centre of French cities. In Paris, the best-known examples are La Goutte d'Or, just to the north of the Gare du Nord (Toubon and Kessamah 1990; Vuddamalay, White and Sporton 1991) and Belleville, to the east of the Place de la République (Simon 1992). Even here, redevelopment programmes are now pushing many low-income families out into suburban areas offering cheaper public-sector accommodation.

Though differently located, the French *banlieues*, as currently connoted, are the sociological equivalent of British and American inner-city areas. Typically, these districts are dominated by high-rise HLM estates catering for the poorest sections of society. Across France as a whole, 15 per cent of households live in HLMs; in jointly aided districts, the figure is 55 per cent. The northern and western suburbs of Paris contain many such estates in districts such as La Courneuve, Nanterre and Sartrouville. Similar districts in the eastern suburbs of Lyon include Vaulx-en-Velin and Vénissieux. In Marseille, the main concentrations of this kind are known as *les quartiers du Nord* (the northern districts). Often, these neighbourhoods are hemmed in by communications arteries which, paradoxically, separate them from other parts of the city. Seven out of ten are close to railway lines, but only four out of ten are served by a station. One-third are bounded on at least one side by an *autoroute* (i.e. motorway or freeway); more than four-fifths are boxed in by other major roads (Castellan, Marpsat and Goldberger 1992).

The peripheral location of most jointly aided districts, their poor facilities and physical separation from other parts of the city, combined with high unemployment levels and dense concentrations of mediocre or poor-quality housing, have turned these areas into a byword for social exclusion (Dubet and Lapeyronnie 1992). Widespread media coverage of violent confrontations between police and disillusioned youths has helped to give these neighbourhoods a reputation for lawlessness (Body-Gendrot 1993). As noted earlier, youths of immigrant origin suffer exceptionally high unemployment rates. They have often been to the fore in street disorders provoked by what they see as aggressive policing. Little-reported incidents of this kind occurred in districts such as Nanterre and Vaulx-en-Velin during the 1970s. Greater publicity was given to similar incidents on the Minguettes housing estate in Vénissieux in the early 1980s, and a veritable torrent of media coverage was unleashed during the early 1990s when serious disorders occurred in localities such as Vaulx-en-Velin, Sartrouville and the Val-Fourré estate in Mantes-la-Jolie, fifty miles to the west of Paris (Begag and Delorme 1994: 107–21). Most of these recent disturbances have been characterized by a very similar pattern: an unarmed youth of immigrant origin involved or suspected of involvement in petty crime (most commonly, the theft of a motor vehicle) has been shot dead by a police officer, and this has been followed by an outbreak of street violence by other youths.

In media coverage of these events, frequent comparisons have been made with American inner-city areas marked by heavy concentrations of poverty, crime and minority ethnicized groups, mainly blacks. In drawing this connection, French journalists and politicians have been increasingly inclined to refer to the most disadvantaged of French *banlieues* as 'ghettos'. As Wacquant (1992) has shown, however, the parallel is far from exact. The sheer scale of racialized ghettos in major American cities has no direct equivalent in France. The black ghetto of Chicago's South Side contains between 400,000 and 700,000 inhabitants; there are similar concentrations in the South Central and Compton districts of Los Angeles, and almost 1 million people live in the black ghettos of New York City's Harlem, Brownsville and South Bronx districts. In French cities, the largest comparable concentrations come nowhere near this. Val-Fourré, France's biggest single ZUP, has 28,000 inhabitants. Even at its height (several tower blocks have now been demolished), the population of the Minguettes estate in Vénissieux was 35,000. America's black ghettos are sufficiently large to contain a complex division of labour, which in the past enabled some of these districts to function almost as closed micro-societies (with the departure of many middle-class blacks this is less true today). Despite deficiencies in public transport, most inhabitants of French ZUPs who have jobs work outside the estates where they live; although people from other districts tend not to enter disadvantaged areas, there are regular flows in the other direction.

In the US, it is not uncommon for large neighbourhoods to be almost entirely mono-ethnic, i.e. inhabited almost exclusively by members of a single ethnicized group, particularly blacks. There are very few sizeable estates in France where French nationals are in a minority. In most districts where minority ethnic groups are highly visible, they remain minorities, except for occasional micro-concentrations within particular blocks or buildings. Areas containing relatively large concentrations of foreign residents are almost always multi-ethnic, i.e. it is common to find people of many different national origins within the same neighbourhood; while a few groups often dominate, it is extremely rare for a single group to make up virtually the whole of the minority population. In Val-Fourré, for example, where non-nationals account for almost half of the total population, the largest single group is composed of Moroccans, who represent two-fifths of the foreign contingent and just under one-fifth of all residents (Poiret and Guégan 1992: 172). La Goutte d'Or is often regarded as a Maghrebi 'ghetto'; in fact, foreigners account for only one-third of its residents, and when Algerians, Moroccans and Tunisians are combined they make up little more than half of the foreign population, i.e. only about one-sixth of the total population (Vuddamalay, White and Sporton 1991: 249). The area's reputation owes much to its dense concentrations of minority ethnic shops and businesses, which dominate the street façades and act as a magnet to shoppers of immigrant origin who, while highly visible during trading-hours, actually live in other districts scattered across the the Paris conurbation.

Although living-conditions in many HLM estates compare unfavourably with other parts of France, Wacquant (1992) has shown that unemployment and poverty are less severe than in American ghettos. Better welfare-provision and other public-policy initiatives help to explain these differences. Violent crime is also far less prevalent in the French *banlieues*. While firearms are sometimes turned against young people of immigrant origin by police officers and other French nationals, there are relatively few recorded cases of guns being used or even possessed by law-breakers of foreign origin. Homicide rates are well below those found in American ghettos, and the street disturbances seen in districts such as Vaulx-en-Velin and Sartrouville have been tiny in scale compared with the massive eruptions seen in many American cities during the late 1960s and in the South Central district of Los Angeles in 1992.

It is true that the statistical data available on minority ethnic groups in France are woefully inadequate compared with those produced in the US. The almost exclusive reliance on nationality significantly underestimates the true size of France's minority ethnic groups. Across the country as a whole, the *département* in which foreigners account for the largest share of the population is Seine-Saint-Denis, in the northern suburbs of Paris. It includes La Courneuve and many other districts containing high-rise HLM estates. The foreign share of the total population in Seine-Saint-Denis is 19 per cent. Foreign children account for an identical share of the 0–14 age group, but Tribalat's study shows that when nationality is discounted, children living in immigrant-headed households make up 38 per cent of the 0–16 age group in Seine-Saint-Denis (Tribalat 1993: 1935). No systematic information is available on adult French nationals descended from immigrants who have left the parental home and set up households of their own, but it would be surprising if all had left the localities in which they were raised. It is therefore reasonable to suppose that a significant number of such households are to be found in Seine-Saint-Denis. In addition, this *département* houses large numbers of French nationals originating in the DOM-TOM. If they and French nationals who are second- and third-generation members of other minority groups were to be added to the foreign populations on which most analyses are based, minority ethnic concentrations in socially disadvantaged districts would undoubtedly be seen to be more dense than they appear on the basis of nationality alone. The inclusion of undocumented migrants would swell the figures further.

Even so, it is clear that mono-ethnic districts are far less developed than in the US, and as disadvantaged areas are generally smaller in French cities, they are less prone to function as self-contained entities divorced from the wider social fabric surrounding them. Minority groups are over-represented ·in disadvantaged parts of French cities, but it is empirically misleading and ideologically dangerous to speak of these areas as 'ghettos'.

GROUP PROFILES

Residential concentrations of particular ethnic groups are conditioned not only by employment patterns and other factors already mentioned, but also by social networks and culturally specific opportunities or constraints. Taken together, these factors have produced considerable diversity in the pattern of settlement characterizing different groups, and it is worth examining these in more detail.

Europeans

Though now much smaller in number than in the past, Italians dominated migratory inflows into France during a large part of the twentieth century. There is still a strong Italian presence in old industrial regions such as Nord-Pas-de-Calais and Lorraine, together with south-eastern regions, which are geographically close to Italy, and the Greater Paris area. The Spanish are mainly concentrated in southern France, as well in the central part of the Paris conurbation. The southern concentrations reflect the proximity of the border with Spain, across which there is a long tradition of agricultural labourers coming to work on French farms. The Spanish population of southern cities such as Bordeaux and Toulouse was also swollen by the arrival of political exiles after the Fascist victory in the Spanish Civil War. In the Paris area, Spaniards are found particularly in well-to-do central *arrondissements* (districts) such as the seventh, eighth and sixteenth, and up-market suburbs such as Neuilly-sur-Seine and Saint-Mandé. This is seldom because they are themselves well-off, but because many Spaniards – particularly women – are employed as domestic staff by wealthy families, who require them to live in (Taboada-Leonetti 1987).

The Portuguese are now the largest national contingent among the foreign population as a whole (Cunha 1988). Female labour-participation rates are particularly high, with strong concentrations in the domestic-service sector. Non-European women are far less frequently employed in French homes. The Portuguese are more scattered than many other groups, partly because Portuguese men are over-represented in the building industry, where employment tends to be quite widely spread and often requires considerable mobility. Almost half of Portuguese men in employment hold construction-industry jobs, a far higher share than is found among any other national group. This is one of the reasons why, despite their large absolute numbers, they are less immediately visible than other, particularly non-European, groups. Similarly, the subordinate position of Spanish and Portuguese domestic staff in households providing free accommodation prevents them from displaying visible markers of their presence within wealthy areas. Foreign tenants in poorer districts may feel less inhibited, and for tradespeople serving minority groups or hoping to attract French customers in search of exotic cuisine a prominent display of ethnic markers is often judged to be good for business (Rudder and Guillon 1987). Compared with Maghrebis and Asians, Europeans are under-represented in the retail and catering sectors. For these and other reasons, including most obviously skin colour, even relatively dense concentrations of Europeans tend to be less visible than those of other groups (Taboada-Leonetti 1989; White 1989).

Maghrebis

Algerians constitute France's oldest and largest immigrant group of Third World origin (Gillette and Sayad 1984). They remain heavily concentrated in regions where significant numbers of them were first hired as manual labourers: in the suburbs of major conurbations, notably Paris (particularly northern disricts), Lyon and Marseille, and in the old industrial regions of the north and east. Desplanques and Tabard (1991: 56, 61) have shown that in Île-de-France,

Algerians are over-represented in districts which have experienced severe economic decline and loss of population. As they have tended to remain in these districts and are under-represented in areas of strong technology-led job creation, they are particularly vulnerable to unemployment and urban decay. Two-thirds of the Portuguese, as of the Algerian, labour force consists of manual workers, but the Portuguese are far less concentrated in densely working-class districts (Desplanques and Tabard 1991: 59). In common with other Maghrebis, Algerians are over-represented in suburban HLM estates. While Maghrebis make up 39 per cent of the nationwide foreign population, they account for 56 per cent of foreigners residing in jointly aided districts. EU nationals represent 36 per cent of all foreign residents, but their share of the foreign population in jointly aided districts is only 19 per cent (Champion, Goldberger and Marpsat 1993: 27).

The 1990 census puts the Algerian population at 614,000. As with other national groups, this leaves out of account naturalized immigrants and people of immigrant descent who automatically acquire French nationality. Where Algerians are concerned, there is a further complication arising from the process of decolonization. During the war of independence, Algerian auxiliary troops known as *harkis* were used by the French in their struggle against the nationalist guerrillas. With the advent of independence in 1962, many *harkis* were killed by nationalist forces, but tens of thousands escaped to France, together with other Algerian Muslims who had sided with the French. Today, they and their descendants are about 500,000 strong. All are and always have been French nationals, yet they are regarded as outsiders by many members of the native population and have experienced extreme marginalization in both housing and employment markets. When they first arrived in France, many *harkis* were housed in old army camps and similar forms of makeshift accommodation in isolated locations. Gradually, most were rehoused in less remote areas near the Mediterranean littoral, together with northern towns such as Roubaix and Amiens. They often remain in dense micro-concentrations, however, and suffer acute unemployment levels (Roux 1991; Hamoumou 1993). In the summer of 1991, when unemployment among the 18–25 age group in *harki* families was reported to be running at 80 per cent (*Le Monde*, 30 June 1991), youngsters in southern towns such as Narbonne staged violent street demonstrations similar to those which had recently occurred in more northerly cities characterized by acute social disadvantage.

Alhough Moroccans are now almost equal in number to Algerian nationals, their migratory history is more recent. Many found manual jobs in the car industry during the 1960s, and this helps to explain their concentration in the western part of Ile-de-France, stretching from the western suburbs of Paris along the Seine valley to Mantes-la-Jolie. Others worked in the now defunct coal mines and other declining industries of the north, where significant numbers of Moroccans still live. Moroccans are more widely distributed across rural parts of the south-west, and account for more than half the foreign population in Corsica; in both cases, agricultural employment – which occupies a larger share of the total Moroccan labour force than of any other national group – is to the fore.

The Tunisian population in France is only about one-third of the size of each of the other Maghrebi groups. The settlement of Tunisians is also more recent than that of Algerians and Moroccans. There are few Tunisians in the old industrial regions of the north and east. They are more concentrated than other Maghrebis in the central parts of major conurbations such as Paris and Lyon (Rimani 1988). There is also a large concentration of manual workers, especially in the building industry, along the south-east littoral between Marseilles and Menton (Chauviré 1993: 539–40).

Sub-Saharan Africans

Sub-Saharan Africans provide a classic example of how, among certain groups, immigration has rapidly accelerated since the formal 'end' of non-EC migration to France. A year after the freeze on migration was announced, the 1975 census recorded only 82,000 nationals of African countries, excluding those of the Maghreb. By 1982, the total had almost doubled to 158,000, and by 1990 it had climbed to 240,000. The vast majority come from former French colonies in sub-Saharan Africa, together with the ex-Belgian colony of Zaïre and the former British Indian Ocean colony of Mauritius, in both of which French is widely spoken. Within the formal economy, non-Maghrebi Africans are more highly concentrated in the service sector than any other group, including French nationals: almost nine out of ten women and two out of three men hold service-sector jobs. These are generally low-grade jobs, particularly in sectors such as cleaning and street-vending. Like most other groups of recent immigrant origin, sub-Saharan Africans are heavily over-represented in the Ile-de-France region. Two-thirds of them live there, and half of the documented total are found in just two *départements*: the city of Paris and Seine-Saint-Denis (Barou 1992b; INSEE 1992a: Table 35).

The true size of these groups is generally acknowledged to be considerably larger than the official figures suggest, partly because polygamous families – of which there are significant numbers among the population of West African origin – experience major difficulties in securing appropriate documentation. The precise number of polygamous African families in France is not known. The most reliable estimates are those of Poiret and Guégan (1992), who put the number of polygamous households in the Ile-de-France region at between 3,000 and 15,000. As each household involves a minimum of two wives, each of whom is likely to have several children, the total number of people concerned is by no means insignificant, even on the lower estimate. For polygamous families, the quest for suitable housing is often extremely arduous. These difficulties have been highlighted by the prominence of African families in recent demonstrations by homeless people. The most widely publicized of these involved dozens of Malian families evicted from their run-down Paris homes in 1992 to make way for property developers. They were offered makeshift accommodation by the local authorities only after camping for six months in parkland near the château de Vincennes (Sindonino 1993).

The shortage of affordable accommodation large enough to house polygamous families decently, combined with the reluctance of both public- and private-sector gatekeepers to respond to their needs, has forced those concerned to rely heavily on their own social networks. When polygamous families succeed in finding suitable accommodation, they not uncommonly pass the word to others, who may well seek to move into the same area. In this way, dense micro-concentrations sometimes develop. During the 1980s, for example, special promotional deals on properties built in new towns on the edge of the Paris conurbation unexpectedly enabled a small number of African families to move into localities such as Evry and Marne-la-Vallée. In a period of four years, several blocks in the district of Emerainville, in Marne-la-Vallée, were sold almost entirely to foreign purchasers, most of whom were polygamous Africans. With low incomes, these families were at one and the same time massively indebted and seriously overcrowded. Each African household contained on average eight people (compared with three among their French neighbours), and their per capita income was estimated to be

40 francs per day, against 200 francs per person in French households and an official poverty line of 50 francs per day (Poiret and Guégan 1992: 234–58).

Asians

Small numbers of Asians have been present in France throughout the twentieth century, but large-scale settlement on their part, like that of sub-Saharan Africans, dates essentially from the mid-1970s. In the space of fifteen years, the number of Asian nationals more than quadrupled, rising from 104,000 in 1975 to 425,000 in 1990 (INSEE 1992a: Table R6). About one-third are from South-East Asia and another third originate in Turkey, with the remainder made up of many different nationalities (*Asiatiques en France* 1994).

Turks have exceptionally low levels of employment in the service sector. They are the only sizeable national group where women in industrial employment outnumber those with service-sector jobs. Only 20 per cent of Turkish men work in the service sector, compared with 40 per cent of foreigners among the male labour force as a whole. Turks of both sexes have a strong presence in the textile and clothing industries, which often rely on labour-intensive small businesses characterized by low rates of pay and a significant element of undocumented employment (Morokvasic, Phizacklea and Rudolph 1986; Morokvasic 1990). While one-fifth of France's Turks live in Ile-de-France, two-fifths are concentrated in three eastern regions: Rhône-Alpes, Alsace and Lorraine, the last two of which are close to the border with Germany, where by far the largest part of the Turkish diaspora is found (*Migrations société* 1992).

South-East Asians, both men and women, are also very active in the textile and clothing industries. In addition, they represent a vigorous force in the service sector, particularly catering, running restaurants and cafés as well as retail shops. Like the garment industry, these businesses make extensive use of a low-wage and sometimes undocumented labour force; not uncommonly, they also rely on unpaid work by family members. Because so much of the work is done within family businesses or, in the case of the garment industry, as outwork (Brunel 1992: 205), the higher rates of female economic activity found among South-East Asians, compared with those of Turkish and Maghrebi women, do not necessarily imply a wider network of social contacts. Nearly half of the South-East Asians without French nationality live in Ile-de-France. The rest are fairly widely scattered across other urban areas, no doubt reflecting the fact that Asian restaurants have now become a standard part of the dining facilities patronized in many towns.

Because South-East Asians have been marked by exceptionally high naturalization rates – there are now more naturalized Vietnamese in France than Vietnamese nationals (INSEE 1992a: Tables 10 and 10b) – it is particularly difficult to construct an accurate statistical profile of them. As naturalization rates tend to be above average among the self-employed and well qualified professionals, the available census data (Tables 2.6–2.8) almost certainly underestimate the proportion of South-East Asians who run their own businesses. The statistical picture is further complicated by the fact that most of those who fled Indo-China in the mid-1970s were of Chinese origin, though they were of Vietnamese, Cambodian or Laotian nationality (Yok-Soon 1991: 121). Mainly tradespeople, particularly restaurateurs and shopkeepers, they were joined by Chinese traders from Taiwan and Hong Kong who entered France as self-employed entrepreneurs; often, the capital necessary for this was raised through a global network of family and social contacts which has made Chinese traders a uniquely mobile group (Ma Mung and Guillon 1986).

An older-established and little-noticed concentration of Chinese settlers, mainly from what since 1949 has been the People's Republic, was already present in the Arts et Métiers neighbourhood of Paris's third *arrondissement*. Ethnic Chinese entering after the end of the Vietnam War regrouped near the Porte de Choisy, on the southern edge of the thirteenth *arrondissement* of Paris, and to a lesser extent in Belleville. Today the Porte de Choisy offers a rare example of an almost mono-ethnic micro-district. The majority of businesses in a small area known as the Choisy Triangle are now ethnic Chinese, and in a few apartment blocks there are similar residential concentrations (Guillon and Taboada-Leonetti 1986). Compared with France's total immigrant population, the number of Chinese living in the Choisy Triangle is of course very small, and the area remains untypical of the districts inhabited by the majority of the foreign population.

DOM-TOMiens

Far more typical are immigrants originating in the DOM-TOM. Although they are all French nationals, those living in metropolitan

France have a socio-economic profile which is very similar to that of many foreign immigrants. The DOM-TOM are characterized by lower living standards and higher levels of unemployment than those prevailing in metropolitan France, where many of their inhabitants have therefore sought work. All but about one-tenth of the 339,600 DOM-TOMiens now resident in France come from three of the overseas *départements*: the Caribbean islands of Guadeloupe and Martinique, and the Indian Ocean island of Réunion. A quarter of the entire population born in Martinique and Guadeloupe now lives in metropolitan France. The labour-force participation rates of DOM-TOMiens exceed those of foreign immigrants, and are particularly high among women, a significant proportion of whom came as economic migrants in their own right rather than as dependants of male breadwinners. In total, women slightly outnumber men among immigrants originating in the DOM-TOM. Within the labour force of metropolitan France, DOM-TOMiens are exceeded in absolute numbers only by two foreign groups: those of Portuguese and of Algerian nationality (Marie 1993a, 1993b; Condon and Ogden 1991).

Most DOM-TOMiens live in the Paris conurbation, often in areas containing dense concentrations of foreign immigrants from Third World countries, whom they also resemble by their low levels of owner-occupation and high rates of HLM tenancy. Almost a quarter are found in just two of metropolitan France's ninety-five *départements*: the city of Paris, particularly the working-class northern and eastern *arrondissements*, which include La Goutte d'Or and Belleville, and the contiguous *département* of Seine-Saint-Denis. This predilection for the Paris region, where the central administrative organs of the state are located, is partly explained by the exceptionally high concentrations of DOM-TOMiens in public-sector employment. Eight out of ten immigrant workers from the DOM-TOM are in the service sector, and half are employed by the state, compared with only one-third of the labour force as a whole (Marie 1993b: 9). Foreign immigrants are largely excluded from state employment. Despite this important difference, there is an underlying similarity in the low level of the jobs acceded to by most foreigners and DOM-TOMiens. Less well qualified than women native to metropolitan France, those originating in the DOM-TOM are over-represented in low-grade hospital and other health-service jobs, while men are concentrated in the lower ranks of the postal service, school ancillary work and other parts of the public sector. Unemployment among immigrants from the DOM-TOM is only a little higher than the national average, but among their children, as among those born to foreign immigrants, it is almost twice the national average. While poor qualifications offer a partial explanation, labour-inspectorate reports indicate that discrimination by employers also weighs heavily in the high jobless rates among young people descended from DOM-TOMiens (Marie 1993b: 10–11; IGAS 1992).

CONCLUSION

The experiences of people originating in the DOM-TOM suggest that, despite its centrality in official thinking, formal nationality status is of less significance than other factors in shaping the incorporation of immigrants and their descendants into French society. The social capital that immigrants bring with them, particularly in the form of certified skills, together with discriminatory treatment by members of the native population, are of much greater importance in the employment and housing markets. The discrimination suffered by certain groups shows that despite their *de facto* presence within French society, at an attitudinal level people of immigrant origin may still be regarded as outsiders. In practical terms, their occupational segmentation and uneven spatial distribution may also make it difficult for some groups – particularly Africans and Asians – to establish more than superficial social contacts with the indigenous population. Because of their lower rates of participation in the formal labour force, women tend to be particularly constrained in this respect. Yet in their cultural practices and aspirations, people of immigrant origin are increasingly inclined to embrace French values, seeking inclusion rather than exclusion. It is to a consideration of the cultural dimension of their experience that we now turn.

Chapter 3

Ethnic identification and mobilization

INTRODUCTION

Most labour migrants initially expected to be only temporary residents in France. Under the 'rotation' system of labour recruitment which initially prevailed in many parts of the Third World, dependants generally remained in the country of origin, where they were supported by remittances sent home by workers in France. Even when they were joined by their families in France, many immigrant workers saw this as a temporary arrangement, at the end of which they would return to their country of origin, having saved enough to buy a more comfortable home than they could previously afford, or perhaps to set up a small business. Like the native population in France, they saw the migratory process as an essentially, if not indeed exclusively, economic phenomenon. In reality, it carried important cultural implications from the outset, and these have become steadily more apparent with the passage of time, especially with the development of permanent family settlement. Participation in the labour market demands at least a minimal level of acculturation, i.e. the acquisition of cultural codes prevalent in the receiving country. At the same time, immigrants have carried into France a large and very different store of cultural baggage accumulated in their countries of origin. With the increasing visibility of differences of this kind, a significant part of French public opinion is now persuaded that immigration – particularly from Islamic countries – represents a fundamental threat to the cultural cohesion of the nation.

The main purpose of this chapter is to assess the extent to which recent immigrants and their descendants are culturally distinct from the majority population in France. All minority groups have in some degree acculturated, but this is not necessarily incompatible with the retention of pre-migratory cultural practices and/or the development of new syntheses drawing on a variety of sources. Some analysts regard acculturation as part of a process of 'modernization', but this term is in my view best avoided, partly because it often implies, even if only at an unconscious level, a positive value judgement in favour of acculturation, and a negative view of its presumed opposite, 'traditionalism'.[1] No less importantly, it misleadingly implies that extremely complex processes can be understood in terms of a simple polarization between binary opposites, with a one-way street connecting the two. Immigrants and their descendants are not confined to tramlines carrying them ineluctably through acculturation to complete assimilation, with the only significant variable being the pace at which they adopt the norms of the receiving society while simultaneously abandoning those of the sending society. As we shall see, the cultural options open to minority groups are far wider than this.

Cultures, nations and states

The word 'culture' is used in many different ways, so it is important to spell out its meaning in the present context. In its most basic sense, culture may be understood as the human production of meaning and value. Beyond this generic sense we may speak of particular cultures as group codes of meaning and value. Ethno-cultural groups, as defined in Chapter 1, are characterized by shared codes associated with common origins. Individual members of ethno-cultural groups do not always agree in every particular, but can at least disagree in mutually intelligible ways, for they share and communicate with each in the same cultural codes. The most fundamental of cultural codes is language. The ability or inability to speak French, Portuguese, Arabic or Turkish gives access to or excludes a person from a wealth of communicative acts. Other fundamental cultural codes govern cosmological beliefs, personal morality and a sense of territorial belonging.

Just as it is impossible wholly to disentangle culture and economics, so there are significant overlaps between culture and politics. While some cultural practices are a purely private matter or, if publicly visible, are not subject to state regulation, others are formally codified in law. Some of these touch on extremely intimate parts of personal life, such as sexuality and family relationships.

Others concern potent symbols of national identity, such as language and, in certain cases, religion. Yet only very rarely do the boundaries of cultural practices match up exactly with those of political geography. Although English, French and other tongues are often referred to as 'national' languages, and are indeed enshrined in law as the official languages of certain states, the spatial distribution of English- and French-speakers is by no means isomorphic with the boundaries of those countries. Nor do the boundaries of linguistic groups necessarily coincide with those of religious or other cultural groups.

The myth of a culturally distinct and homogenous nation-state has been central to the political history of modern Europe. During the twentieth century it has been taken up by many Third World states. The many wars which punctuated European history up to 1945, and which have recently been renewed in Eastern Europe, like those in post-independence Africa and Asia, have often been marked by a disjunction between political and cultural boundaries. Basques in Spain and France, Berbers in the Maghreb, and Kurds in Turkey and neighbouring countries are examples of the many linguistic minorities scattered within or across state boundaries. Conversely, some important cultural traditions, including religions such as Christianity, Buddhism and Islam, are supra-national in scale.

Wholly distinct and autonomous national cultures have never existed. In at least two major respects, however, modern states have pushed towards the nationalization of cultures. Often at the cost of hugely destructive wars, they have pursued this project externally by attempting to establish international boundaries consonant with the spatial distribution of certain cultural groups. Within its own frontiers, the state has exercised enormous – though never exclusive – power over the means of cultural reproduction.

Today, three main forces predominate in the transmission of cultural systems. The earliest influence in the life of every individual is the family. Next comes the formal system of education through which the child passes in preparation for adulthood. Concurrently with this, and throughout the rest of his or her life, the mass media disseminate images and information which have a powerful influence on the individual's view of the world. While it is difficult for the state to exercise direct control over day-to-day family life,[2] it exerts a strong and sometimes decisive influence over education and the media.

In the modern world, the state controls most, and in some cases all, of the formal educational process. Not surprisingly, the knowledge dispensed by state educational systems tends to takes the nation as its 'natural' frame of reference. The national language occupies pride of place, while history and geography lessons familiarize the child with landmarks and events of national significance.

State control over the media has generally been less complete, though in authoritarian countries it is often very extensive. Before the rise of electronic media such as radio and television, communication processes were dominated by print media and to a lesser extent by the cinema. Economies of scale and the central role of formal education in creating a readership literate in a common language favoured the rise of a national press even when this remained in private, rather than state, ownership; at the same time, technological limitations made it difficult to distribute newspapers much beyond the national territory within an acceptable time frame. The electronic media have in many ways cut through these constraints. Radio dispensed with the need for a literate audience, though language barriers still imposed significant limits on the medium. Moving pictures, first developed via the pre-electronic technology of the cinema, traverse linguistic and other boundaries far more easily. While the cinema is relatively cumbersome and limited in its audience penetration, television has brought instantaneous audio-visual communication into the home, and with the rise of satellite technology audiences are increasingly global in scale. When television broadcasting was limited to a handful of terrestrially based frequencies in each country, it was in principle relatively easy for the state to regulate the system. In practice, the high production costs associated with television have often made it necessary to purchase programmes abroad. The advent of domestic video recorders, together with cable and satellite broadcasting, has further weakened state control over the medium.

Immigration and culture

The children of immigrants, like those born to the native population, are initially exposed primarily to family influences. Linguistic, moral and other codes inherited from the country of origin naturally dominate during these early years. The mutual support systems associated with chain migration provide a wider network of social contacts drawing on cultural practices shared by immigrants originating in the same village or region. These are often supplemented by formally constituted associations pursuing welfare, cultural and sometimes political objectives.

Until 1981, these efforts were hampered in France by legal restrictions on foreigners' rights of association. After these restrictions were removed by the incoming Socialist-led administration, the number of associations mushroomed (*La Tribune Fonda* 1991). Even now, however, the sending and receiving states continue to exert a significant influence over voluntary associations. The limited resources available on a self-help basis oblige many associations to seek public subsidies from either the sending or the receiving state (cf. Schmitter Heisler 1986: 82–6). Some sending states attempt to control practically all the organizational activities of their nationals and harass emigrants who set up independent associations (Miller 1981: 38–40), but they are seldom successful in this.

In a study of Marseille, Cesari (1993) found that subsidies awarded by the French state, either centrally or through the city council, were of crucial importance in shaping the activities of local associations run by people of immigrant origin. Public funding of this kind is channelled mainly through the Fonds d'Action Sociale pour les travailleurs immigrés et leurs familles (FAS), which is controlled by the Ministry for Social Affairs. The prime purpose assigned to the FAS is to support the state project of integrating immigrants and their descendants into French society. It assists voluntary associations run by members of minority ethnic groups whose activities are conducive to integration, but not if they are driven by separatist ambitions.

Within the formal educational system, the cultural codes of migrants are overwhelmingly marginalized in favour of those prevalent among the majority population.[3] In France all children, regardless of their nationality, are required by law to attend school from the age of 6 to 16. Generous state provision of nursery schools means that the majority of children enter the educational system three or even four years before the age of 6; most remain in it well beyond the minimum school-leaving age. Immigrants are not entirely powerless in the face of the state educational system. Under French law, they are free to set up schools of their own. In practice, most immigrants have neither the economic resources nor the organizational skills necessary for such an undertaking. Among foreign children of primary-school age, only 3 per cent are educated outside the state sector; at the secondary-school level the figure is 7 per cent (Conseil Economique et Social 1994: 45).

Private schools providing educational programmes based on those of foreign countries generally charge high fees and are frequented only by the children of relatively affluent, professionally qualified foreign residents. For most immigrant-born children, the schooling provided free of charge by France's state educational system is the only practical option. Small elites within minority ethno-cultural groups often try to counterbalance this pattern by organizing extra-curricular classes, and sending states sometimes provide trained personnel and other assistance, but the resources at their disposal are no match for those poured into the mainstream educational system.

Low levels of literacy among many immigrants, particularly those from Third World countries, have placed severe limitations on their use of print media, though there is a long history of newspaper and magazine production by cultural elites of foreign origin in France (*Presse et mémoire* 1990). The electronic media are more easily accessible to large audiences. Radio broadcasts from home countries can often be picked up quite easily on receivers in France. During the 1970s, a brisk trade in imported audio cassettes developed, enabling immigrants to hand-pick programmes to suit their own listening tastes (Lehembre 1984). Since 1981, when the newly elected Socialist-led administration liberalized the air-waves, dozens of local radio stations run by and for minority ethno-cultural groups have been licensed (Barbulesco 1985). While these have often helped to build a sense of community among such groups, the state has nevertheless exercised considerable control over them. Rather than risk fostering cultural separatism, the state-appointed agencies responsible for granting licences have generally favoured multi-ethnic rather than single-ethnic stations (HCI 1992b: 131). Many of them depend on public subsidies, channelled mainly through the FAS, which insists that those benefiting from its support subscribe to the objective of integration (Moreau-Desportes 1990).

Television, by far the most powerful mass medium, has in its dominant forms been the least responsive to minority interests (UNESCO 1986). Until the mid-1980s, France had only three terrestrial channels, all of them state-owned. Although there are now three private channels as well, commercial pressures have dictated programming aimed at maximizing mass audiences, rather than catering for minority groups (Hargreaves 1992b). A small amount of specialist programming on terrestrially based state channels has been funded by the FAS (Humblot 1989; Hargreaves 1993b), but for a fuller diet minority ethno-cultural groups are obliged to turn to other forms of television.

Domestic video recorders became widely available in France during the 1980s. Significantly, they are one of the few consumer durables in which foreign-headed households are now better equipped than those headed by French nationals (*Le Monde*, 11 June 1991). With substantial video-cassette production centres in both Asia and the Arab world and easily accessible retail outlets in French cities, many people of immigrant origin are now able to construct home-viewing schedules reflecting their ethno-cultural roots. It should not be assumed, however, that facilities of this kind are used in a mono-ethnic fashion. While the children of Asian immigrants, for example, enjoy imported martial-arts films (a genre which is also popular among a significant number of French youngsters), they are avid viewers of American movies, and also enjoy both French and American rock-music videos. The viewing habits of their French peers often involve a similar trans-national amalgam (Raulin 1990). While Maghrebian immigrants sometimes watch Islamic cassettes, their children generally have more secular tastes (Chaabaoui 1989). Kastoryano (1986: 99) reports a similar split between the viewing habits of first- and second-generation members of the Turkish population in France.

Cable and satellite television are now further widening the choices available in suitably equipped homes. Cable television is still relatively underdeveloped in France. At the beginning of 1994 there were only 1.3 million subscribers across the country as a whole (*Le Monde*, 30 January 1994), but as the system is designed primarily to serve urban areas, where minority ethnic groups are over-represented, the potential for specialist programming aimed at these groups is considerable. However, the broadcasting licensing authority, the Conseil Supérieur de l'Audiovisuel (CSA), has proved extremely reluctant to allow television stations based in the home states of immigrants access to the French cable network – which would effectively remove editorial control from French hands – despite the technical feasibility of this. The Moroccan channel 2MI was first made available to cable subscribers in the northern town of Roubaix in 1989. The service was later extended to Mantes-la-Jolie and other towns with substantial concentrations of Maghrebis, but it was discontinued in 1993. It is far less easy for the French authorities to control satellite broadcasting by foreign states. During the early 1990s, television channels based in countries ranging from Morocco and Tunisia to Turkey and Poland became available to viewers in France equipped with suitable satellite dishes. While the number of satellite receivers across the country as a whole totalled little more than half a million in 1993, sales among minority ethnic groups were reported to be accelerating the following year (*Le Monde*, 11 September 1994).

French anxieties over cultural imports, particularly in the audio-visual sector, were a major factor in the 1993 GATT negotiations on world trade. Only when her negotiating partners agreed to exempt cultural goods from free-trade measures did France finally clear the way for the conclusion of a world-wide deal. Under this agreement, France continues to imposed tight quotas on foreign programmes broadcast on prime time terrestrially-based television. The main target of these protectionist measures lies not, of course, in any of the Third World countries in which most immigrants originate, but in the US, which has long occupied a globally dominant position in the field of popular culture. A long series of similar protectionist measures has failed to prevent the partial Americanization of many aspects of French culture during the post-war period. To speak of 'French culture' as if it were a wholly autonomous national entity is, indeed, and always has been, seriously misleading. Like the culture of every other nationally defined space, it is composed in part of elements which extend, and in some cases originate, beyond the country's frontiers. Before the current influx of Americana, France and her European neighbours exchanged many cultural influences. For example, her Judaeo-Christian heritage has its origins in the Middle East. While it is permissible to speak of French culture as a set of norms which are dominant in France, it is important to remember that not all of them are exclusive to France; nor are they shared to an identical extent by every French national. While the French language is now common to practically the whole of the indigenous population, there is still considerable diversity over matters such as religious belief and personal morality.

This is not always fully appreciated by the French themselves. Like the natives of other states, they have been encouraged to think of themselves as a more coherent and self-contained cultural community than they really are. Research conducted among members of minority ethno-cultural groups has often found a similar appearance of national consciousness dominating over cultural diversity. Le Huu Khoa, for example, reports that, when given *carte blanche* to define their identity, Vietnamese respondents in France always spoke first and foremost of themselves as Vietnamese and in some cases as French, or as a mixture of the two; though many were Buddhists or Catholics, none spontaneously defined themselves by their religious affiliation (Le Huu Khoa 1985: 173–82). Kastoryano found a more ambiguous over-writing of religious by national identity among Turkish immigrants and their descendants. When she asked the children of immigrants to state their religion, most replied: 'I'm a Turk' (Kastoryano 1986: 89), perpetuating an equation between religious affiliation and national belonging commonly found among their parents. In Turkey, the state has formally distanced itself from the religious sphere more than is the case in virtually any other predominantly Islamic country. While the state tells its citizens that they are first and foremost Turks, Islamic beliefs remain strong, particularly in the rural areas where many immigrants originate. The potential gap between the two strands is elided by using 'Turkish' as a synonym for 'Muslim'.

Culture and identity

The limits of state propaganda machines are vividly illustrated by Kastoryano's findings. Despite (or perhaps because of) their relatively limited education, the Turks interviewed by Kastoryano inflect the official view of national identity with a more religious slant than the state might wish. Their replies also illustrate some of the enormous complexities which often lie behind the seemingly simple concept of 'identity'. Following Hall (1992), we may usefully distinguish between three main approaches to this concept. The first, inherited from the Enlightenment, views identity as a relatively fixed and autonomous form of selfhood, an inner personality largely immune to outside influences. A second approach, symbolic interactionism, developed during the early decades of the twentieth century, puts the emphasis on social influences in the construction of more malleable personal identities. Most recently, theorists of postmodernism have argued for an unanchored, constantly open and self-generating form of identity. As these contrasting approaches suggest, one of the main difficulties attaching to the term 'identity' is the fact that in everyday usage it is often understood to denote something fixed, whereas social psychologists and other researchers have produced abundant evidence to show that few if any human beings may be said to have an entirely stable, unchanging identity.

If we define identity as the pattern of meaning and value by which a person structures his or her life, it is clear that this involves a dynamic process rather than an immutable condition. Individuals construct meaning and value with the aid of cultural codes shared by particular groups. Personal identity is in this sense inseparable from – though not necessarily reducible to – socio-cultural identity. It is not uncommon for a person to switch between codes. By the same token, he or she moves between a variety of socio-cultural identities.

Socio-cultural ties based on collective origins distinct from those of other groups are the foundation of ethnic identities. The cultural codes associated with ethnic identities have been described by Geertz as 'primordial attachments' (Geertz 1963: 109). There are at least three senses in which this description might appear apt. First, the cultural codes on which ethnic identities are built tend to be of a fundamental nature, setting a general framework of meaning within which particular acts are constructed. This applies to language, for example, as well as to religious beliefs. Second, cultural codes of this kind are usually, though not always, learnt at an early age, and in this sense enjoy ontological primacy. Third, they are by the same token associated with deep-seated affective ties which may make them difficult to dislodge or replace. New codes may be learnt in later life, however, and in certain circumstances may supersede those acquired at an early age. Moreover, code-switching is not necessarily an essentially affective affair. Individuals or groups may invoke ethnic identities in a calculated fashion, sometimes with the aim of achieving objectives which owe relatively little to the original codes inherited by ethno-cultural groups. This is sometimes referred to as an instrumentalist (as against a primordial) form of ethnicity. Drawing on rational choice theory, Banton (1983) and Hechter *et al*. (1982) have argued that ethnic allegiances owe more to this kind of calculation than to primordial sentiments.

The behaviour of all human beings is marked by a mixture of rational and affective features. The rational dimension is most easily visible in the economic sphere, where employers and employees make calculated judgements about the most effective ways of maximizing their material gains. When they first migrate, foreign workers often expect to pursue an economic project without this affecting their cultural identity. In reality, it is impossible to keep the two wholly separate, just as it is impossible to separate politics from culture. As already noted, the state plays a major role in cultural reproduction. At the same time, certain kinds of cultural competence are indispensable to effective economic participation. Most immigrant workers are obliged to acquire at least minimal competence in the language of the receiving country if they are to function effectively in the employment and housing markets. They may take a purely instrumental view of foreign-language acquisition, thereby retaining a primordial attachment to their native tongue, but in this and other respects their cultural repertoire widens significantly as the length of their stay extends.

However, the most important challenge to minority ethno-cultural groups concerns the second and third generations (Liebkind 1989). The majority of immigrants arrive in the receiving country as adults, with their primordial cultural attachments already formed in the country of origin. By contrast, the formative years of their children are spent in the land to which the older generation has moved. These youngsters are often encouraged by their parents to work hard at school, for education is seen as a passport to better jobs than those held by most immigrant workers. At the same time, many parents are initially anxious to ensure that the cultural codes inherited from the country of origin are sustained by the younger generation. Their children are therefore expected to profit instrumentally from school while remaining affectively distanced from the cultural norms dominant in the receiving country. In most cases, it proves impossible wholly to reconcile these contradictory demands. As they pass through the educational system and mix with children from the majority population, immigrant-born youngsters tend to internalize the cultural codes of the dominant population not simply as means to an end but as desirable objects in their own right.

During the colonial period, European minorities were able to sustain their ethno-cultural identity by virtue of their privileged position in overseas territories. Today's post-colonial immigrants occupy a diametrically opposite position: they are disempowered minorities, without citizenship in most cases, and with very little leverage over the formal education system. As Banton (1983: 154) has observed, in the industrialized world only a handful of cases can be cited of minority ethno-cultural groups which have succeeded in remaining almost wholly separate from the majority populations over more than three generations. The best-known examples are the Amish communities in the US, which have managed to exist as almost entirely self-contained entities, controlling entry and exit, information flows, employment for adults and the education of children. This has been possible only because of their spatial isolation in rural communities. There are very few examples of a comparable degree of ethno-cultural separation being sustained in cities, where the physical proximity of densely packed and diverse population groups make inter-group contacts almost inevitable.

As noted in Chapter 2, immigrants and their families are heavily concentrated in urban areas, and they are particularly over-represented in France's largest conurbations, notably Paris. Mono-ethnic districts are virtually non-existent, except for a few micro-localities. Some groups, such as the *harkis*, were initially housed in isolated areas, but their children have all been educated in state schools, and their parents are in any case fiercely pro-French, having fought against Algerian independence. Kastoryano's fieldwork on Turkish immigrants reveals an interesting contrast between those who have settled in the Paris conurbation and those she interviewed in Terrasson, a small provincial town in south-west France. Though smaller in absolute numbers than their compatriots in Paris, the Turks in Terrasson are more densely concentrated, and this has made it easier to establish social networks beneficial for the reinforcement of their distinct cultural codes. Yet even here, separation from the indigenous population is by no means absolute. Almost all the men work in nearby French factories, while their children all attend local state schools. The erosion of their ethno-cultural identity is less marked than among Turks dispersed across the Paris conurbation, but it is nonetheless underway (Kastoryano 1986; cf. Tripier 1990: 211–66).

Measuring ethnicity

Measuring the strength of ethno-cultural groups is no easy task. It should be remembered that these are not the same as ethnic groups, whose members are defined for the purposes of the present study simply on the basis of shared territorial origins. Despite the in-adequacies of official statistics, we saw in Chapter 2 that data on nationality do enable us to conduct at least partial socio-economic analyses of minority ethnic groups in France. No directly comparable data are available on ethno-cultural groups. There are no census questions, for example, on language usage or religious beliefs. We therefore have to rely on much smaller surveys conducted by a variety of researchers. The representativeness of sampling pro-cedures is often open to question, and there are huge variations in the methodologies used by different researchers, making accurate comparsions based on their data difficult if not impossible.

The central role of subjective processes in the constitution of cultural groups raises even more fundamental difficulties. Unlike employment and housing patterns, which are in principle open to direct empirical observation, ethno-cultural belonging revolves around intellectual and attitudinal processes which cannot be directly apprehended by an outside observer. Traces of those processes are visible in behavioural patterns, but their interpretation is by no means a simple or mechanical task. It is, of course, possible to ask people about their values and beliefs (many of the surveys drawn on later in this chapter do so), but this always involves complex methodological problems, and there is no guarantee that potential interviewees will be willing to respond to questions in such personally sensitive areas or, if they do, that their replies will be wholly truthful.

In assessing the strength of ethno-cultural groups, it is useful to distinguish between cultural *competence*, cultural *performance*, ethnic *identification* and ethnic *mobilization*. Cultural competence, the capacity to use a particular cultural code, is intertwined but not identical with cultural performance, i.e. the actual use of such codes. Ethnic identification, the affective association of an individual with an ethno-cultural group, may lead to involvement in ethnic mobilization (i.e. the collective organization of such a group), but this is not automatic.

In many cases, cultural competence is acquired unreflectingly through cultural performance. Perhaps the best example of this is the acquisition of a person's native language. That language is often known as the mother tongue because it is learnt by deciphering and copying utterances heard during the child's earliest years, when parental influences are at their strongest. While parents often correct errors in particular utterances made by their children, they seldom if ever give formal grammar lessons. Yet at an unconscious level the child masters an enormously complex set of rules governing the formulation of intelligible utterances in the language concerned. In this way, linguistic competence is derived from linguistic performance. When second or third languages are learnt later in life, often at school, the pattern is usually very different. Although there are considerable variations in language-instruction methods, it is not uncommon for teachers to begin by explaining general rules, which are then illustrated and practised through particular utterances. In this way, linguistic performance is preconditioned by linguistic competence.

It is important to note that neither linguistic competence in particular nor cultural competence in general is a zero-sum game. Just as individuals may acquire new languages without this in any way reducing their competence in their native tongue, so they may grasp other types of cultural code without losing those already mastered. Elements drawn from diverse cultures frequently co-exist within a person. While conflicts may sometimes arise, this is by no means always the case. Frequently, cultural diversity provides a stimulus for the creation of new syntheses.

At the same time, an individual may be competent in a particular code and make active use of it without identifying with the ethno-cultural group with which it is most closely associated. For instance, immigrants often learn to use the dominant language of the society in which they live while nevertheless regarding it as a code which remains fundamentally foreign to them. Even if the native tongue falls into disuse, at an affective level it is likely to retain a strong hold on the mind of the immigrant, for whom it remains a more natural vehicle of expression or communication. Similar observations apply to non-linguistic codes. Spiritual values, for example, may be understood, and in some cases religious practices may be performed, without the person concerned necessarily believing in the doctrines on which they are based. Children are often encouraged to join in the religious practices of their parents and may feel pressurized to conform outwardly with them as long as they remain in the family home even if their inner thoughts are at variance with these traditions. Cultural performance cannot therefore be equated with ethnic identification.

As a general rule, ethnic mobilization[4] is a more reliable sign of ethnic identification. While individuals may sometimes feel pressurized into joining or supporting 'voluntary' organizations, on the whole these are run by activists who are strongly committed to particular goals. It is nevertheless important to distinguish between mobilization *for* ethnicity and mobilization *through* ethnicity. Some associations – those promoting language teaching or religious observance, for example – draw on the bonds of ethnic affiliation to further cultural objectives. Others may be organized by and for members of ethnicized or ethno-cultural groups, but not necessarily with the aim of strengthening ethnic identity. Membership of certain anti-racist organizations, for example, may be ethnically based, but the objective may be equality of treatment alongside the indigenous population rather than the promotion of distinctive cultural codes.

LANGUAGE

Competence in French

Although most immigrants were poorly educated and have learnt little if any French at school, they generally acquire at least a minimal level of competence in the language, particularly if their working environment requires this. Few employers offer linguistic training. Adult literacy classes are organized by a number of voluntary agencies, but the availability of courses is patchy; women, particularly from Islamic countries, have often found it difficult to attend, partly because their menfolk are reluctant to endorse female activity outside the domestic sphere (*Le Monde*, 28 May 1994).

Table 3.1 French-language competence among immigrants, by nationality, sex and date of arrival in France, 1992

	Average date of arrival in France	Schooling included some French %	Difficulty in understanding French TV news %	Speak little or no French %
Portuguese – male	1970	17	14	38
Portuguese – female	1972	20	20	35
Algerian – male	1964	35	10	16
Algerian – female	1972	25	46	57
Moroccans + Tunisians – male	1972	35	26	40
Moroccans + Tunisians – female	1979	29	51	65
Turks – male	1977	10	65	83
Turks – female	1979	0	85	100

Source: INSEE 1994: 61.

A household survey conducted jointly by INSEE and INED in 1992 found a close correlation between the length of settlement of immigrants and the degree of proficiency which they had acquired in the French language (Table 3.1). Only a minority had had any formal education in French, with those from former colonies in a slightly stronger position in this regard. The proportion of Algerian men who said they had had some schooling in French was twice as large as that reported by Portuguese men, and with a longer average period of settlement Algerian men still speaking little or no French were far less numerous than their Portuguese counterparts.

The lower rates of linguistic competence generally reported by women migrants are primarily a reflection of their later arrival in France, but there are some significant differences between different national groups. In spite of having the same average length of settlement as Portuguese women and slightly greater exposure to French while at school, Algerian women were much weaker in the language. Some 57 per cent said they could speak little or no French, compared with only 35 per cent of Portuguese women, who, uniquely, reported higher levels of proficiency than men of the same nationality. It is likely that this reflects employment patterns. As many Portuguese women are employed as domestic staff by French nationals, they work in a basically French-speaking environment, whereas men employed in the construction industry – as are many Portuguese – are more liable to work in ethnically segmented teams. Participation rates in the formal labour market are much lower among Algerian women than among those of Portuguese nationality, and very few work within a French residential environment. Their greater isolation at home is reflected in lower levels of competence in French. Still greater linguistic difficulties are reported by Turkish women, who suffer from all three handicaps: a comparatively short period of residence in France, no schooling whatever in French, and very low levels of employment outside the home.

Few of their children experience comparable difficulties. Those who arrive in France after reaching school age are often handicapped initially, but special support classes are provided to help reduce the linguistic gap as quickly as possible. Among those born in France, the initial trauma of stepping from a home dominated by the mother tongue into the French-speaking environment of school is soon overcome. So complete is the mastery of French acquired by most immigrant-born children that it generally supplants the mother tongue as their primary language. Frequently, their command of the mother tongue becomes stunted, failing to progress beyond the level reached at the beginning of their schooling. Very commonly, the younger generation uses French within the family home. At first, parents may continue speaking to their children in their native language, while receiving replies in French. Later, many parents find themselves forced to switch to French. In some cases, parents deliberately use French because they believe that proficiency in this language will give their children better opportunities in the French labour market. Le Huu Khoa (1985: 210), for example, reports that this is common among Vietnamese families.

Mother-tongue teaching

In the mid-1970s, the French government agreed to allow sending states to provide, at their own expense, tuition in *Langues et Cultures d'Origine* (Homeland Languages and Cultures – LCO) for the children of immigrants within French primary schools. By the early 1980s, agreements had been signed with eight states, but despite considerable investment in specialist teaching only a minority of immigrant-born children has been covered by these programmes (*Revue de linguistique et de didactique des langues* 1990). In school year 1988–9, the proportion of foreign children receiving language instruction paid for by the sending state was as follows: Algerians 14 per cent, Moroccans 15 per cent, Tunisians 15 per cent, Spaniards 23 per cent, Italians 137 (*sic*) per cent, Portuguese 31 per cent, Turks 35 per cent, Yugoslavians 20 per cent (Ministère de l'Education Nationale 1989: Table 4). Other sending states, such as those in sub-Saharan Africa and South-East Asia, fund no classes of this kind. The fact that the number of primary-school children learning Italian is larger than all those of Italian nationality combined reflects the fact that some French parents have used the system as a way of obtaining early foreign-language tuition for their own children. Other languages spoken by minority ethnic groups exert no comparable attraction. Even among nationals of the countries concerned, there are often misgivings about attending these classes, for in many cases this means missing other parts of the curriculum. Affective ties with the country of origin are not uncommonly outweighed by the low status attached to 'immigrant' languages in the eyes of the majority population, and a concern to maximize skills directly applicable within France.

LCO classes last no more than three hours a week, and the language taught is in any case often quite different from the child's mother tongue. Maghrebis, for example, are taught a standardized version of Arabic, which at best bears only a distant resemblance to the dialects spoken by their parents (Jerab 1988). For a sizeable proportion of Maghrebi children it is a completely foreign language, for their parents are not Arabic-speakers at all but Berbers. About half of the Moroccans in France today are Berbers, and until quite recently Berber-speakers were in a majority among Algerian immigrants (Chaker 1988). Yet there are no state-funded classes in their language. The Algerian government has done everything in its power to stifle the Berber language, insisting that all Algerian citizens should speak Arabic, the sole 'national' language. Similarly, the Kurdish language has only recently been granted limited recognition in Turkey. Many children effectively find themselves in the position of trying to learn a foreign tongue from scratch on the basis of only a few hours' tuition a week; the lack of linguistic reinforcement at home reduces still further the chances of making significant progress at school.

Mother-tongue teaching is even more marginalized at the secondary-school level. Although major languages spoken in a number of sending countries are in principle available on demand, very few immigrant-born youngsters opt to study them. Like their French peers, the overwhelming majority choose English as their first foreign language. This is partly because of the negative images associated with languages spoken by immigrants of low socio-economic status, in sharp contrast with the images of glamour and commercial utility associated with English. In 1984–5, Portuguese was being studied by no more than 15 per cent of Portuguese secondary-school children; only 7 per cent of Maghrebis were learning Arabic (Boulot and Boyzon-Fradet 1987: 179), and the proportion has since declined. Only fragmentary information is available on language classes organized by voluntary associations, but their efforts are unlikely to alter significantly the overall picture of very limited formal education in the mother tongue of most immigrant-born children (Bazin and Vermes 1990).

A recent language survey conducted jointly by INSEE and INED indicates that all the main immigrant groups are also fighting a losing battle on the home front (Héran 1993). The survey, conducted in 1992, asked approximately 2,000 parents living in France who were brought up speaking a language other than French which language they usually spoke when addressing their children. As dozens of different native languages – including some spoken by regional, rather than immigrant, minorities – were included in this aggregate total, sample sizes for individual languages were often small. The results should therefore be treated as indicative rather than as definitive measures of language performance. Certain overall trends nevertheless emerge very clearly.

Though it is not their native tongue, the overwhelming majority of interviewees say they usually speak in French to their children (Table 3.2). The main variations between different groups of immigrants are accounted for by differences in the length of settlement. Berber parents, for example, who use French with their children

Table 3.2 Language usage by parents resident in France brought up speaking a language other than French, 1992

Language of parents	Proportion usually speaking French to their children %
Creole (DOMs and Mauritius)	90
Italian	90
Spanish	80
Portuguese	55
Arabic	50
Berber	70
Turkish	5
Vietnamese	55
Miscellaneous sub-Saharan	75

Source: INSEE–INED 1992 Education Survey in Héran 1993:2.

more frequently than Arabic-speakers, have on average lived in France for a longer period. A similar point applies to Italian- and Spanish-speaking parents as compared with Portuguese-speakers. The very small use of French reported by Turkish interviewees reflects their recent arrival in France. Sub-Saharan Africans are also relatively recent arrivals, but it is likely that they were more exposed to the French language than Turks before emigrating, hence their greater propensity to use French with their children. Right across the board, the practice of conversing within the family in French increases steadily with the length of settlement, irrespective of the parents' native tongue or indeed of their sex. Given an equal period of residence in France, women, who are sometimes portrayed as more conservative guardians of tradition than men, in fact have a slightly higher propensity to use French when talking to their children.

It would be wrong to jump to the conclusion that the habit of speaking mainly in French can be directly equated, as Héran (1993: 2) rather misleadingly puts it, with the 'rate of loss' of the parental language. In a survey conducted by the Education Ministry almost simultaneously with the INED–INSEE survey, the proportion of foreign parents who said they regularly spoke to their children in a language other than French was as follows: 99 per cent of Turks, 91 per cent of both Spaniards and Portuguese, 88 per cent of Moroccans, 87 per cent of South-East Asians, 83 per cent of Algerians, and 82 per cent of Tunisians (Conseil Economique et Social 1994: 77).

These findings are not necessarily at odds with those of the survey previously quoted. It is perfectly possible for parents to speak 'usually' in French while nevertheless also speaking 'regularly' in their native tongue, though their children may well reply in French. Even if, at the level of day-to-day performance, French clearly dominates, linguistic competence is not a zero-sum game: while acquiring competence in French and perhaps other languages, the children of immigrants are likely to retain at least a passive understanding of their mother tongue even if their active command of it is largely lost. Precisely because it is the language of their parents, many young people continue to identify affectively with their mother tongue even when they lack competence in it altogether, a posture summed up in a remark made by a young interviewee of Algerian origin questioned in a survey by Dabène and Billiez (1987: 66): 'Arabic is my language but I can't speak it.'

This affective relationship is clearly different and less intense, however, from that felt by immigrants who are wholly at one with their native tongue. In purely practical terms, moreover, few second-generation members of minority groups are in a position to pass on their mother tongue to their own children, though many express an idealistic desire to do so. In most cases they have so internalized the French language that it comes as naturally to them as their native tongue to their parents. Functionally, it has in fact replaced their native language, for it serves not only instrumental purposes at school or at work but also as the principal vehicle of self-expression, whether in personal relationships (such as within the family) or for creative purposes such as literary production.

Variants and inflexions

For many immigrants from former colonies, French is still perceived, even if only at an unconscious level, as a language of external domination. Traces of such anxieties are sometimes found among their children, despite their formal mastery of French, and this perhaps helps to explain a frequent tendency to inflect the language in directions which de-centre it. By injecting liberal doses of slang, and expressions imported from other tongues, they re-appropriate the language so as to make it perceptibly their own. A form of slang much favoured by young people of immigrant origin is *verlan* (backslang), which re-invents words by reversing the order of their syllables (Bachmann and Basier 1984; Mela 1988). A now famous example of this is the neologism *Beur*, which was initially adopted as a self-designation by young Parisians of Maghrebi origin during the 1970s. *Beur* is a partial contraction and reversal of *Arabe*, a word which in French usage often carries pejorative connotations inherited from the colonial period. Anyone of Maghrebi appearance is liable to be referred to by a French observer as an Arab, despite the fact that many of those concerned are from Berber families. Aware that when they were called Arabs this frequently connoted an inferior status, young Maghrebis began calling themselves Beurs. As the term was completely new, its meaning was moulded by its creators instead of being tainted by negative accretions from the past.

The word entered public usage in 1981, when Radio Beur became one of the first local radio stations to be licensed in Paris. Within a few years, heavy usage of the term by the mass media made it part of the vocabulary of the general public throughout France. Precisely because of this, those to whom the term is applied are now increasingly reluctant to accept it, for they no longer control its meaning and fear that, as used by others, *Beur* is acquiring connotations similar to those of *Arabe*. This has not dampened the enthusiasm of young Maghrebis for the principle of backslang. Provided terms reappropriated by outsiders are renewed by the in-group (*Rebeu*, for example, is sometimes used as a reversal of *Beur*), a sense of community can be sustained by linguistic inflexions of this kind.

One of the great attractions of *verlan* is that it enables language-users to position themselves outside the standard categories of social identification. Those who called themselves Beurs circumvented the simplistic choice with which outsiders tended to confront them, insisting that they be labelled as *either* French *or* Arab (Barbara 1986: 135). Open identification with France is a particularly sensitive matter for the descendants of Algerians, since their parents generally supported the nationalist movement during the struggle for independence. Although the younger generation owes more of its cultural repertoire to France than to Algeria, there is a tendency to emphasize sub- or supra-national elements within the French cultural space, thereby avoiding directly national forms of identification (Hargreaves 1992a, 1993a). For example, forms of slang unique to a particular region or town are often cultivated, while at the other end of the scale there is a strong interest in international youth culture, especially when marked by American and/or black influences.

Mixtures of this kind frequently mark the literary production of

young Maghrebis, dozens of whom have published mainly autobiographical novels since the early 1980s (Hargreaves 1991a). The
emphasis on local roots is exemplified in the title of Azouz Begag's
Le Gone du Chaâba (The Kid from the Chaâba 1986). While the
author's Arab ancestry is signalled in *Chaâba*, the Arabic name of
the shanty town where Begag was brought up in the city of Lyon,
gone (kid) is part of the local slang indigenous to the town. Only
those who really belong to a locality can fully master its slang. Begag
was born in Lyon, and by calling himself a *gone* he signals the depth
of his roots in France's second city. While this implicitly cuts across
those who argue that people of immigrant origin can never be part
of the French national community, the emphasis on local slang
enables the author to establish his French credentials without directly
identifying himself with a specifically national representation of
French culture.

The title of Soraya Nini's autobiographical novel, *Ils disent que
je suis une Beurette* . . . (They Call Me a Beurette . . . , 1993), reflects
the wariness now felt by many young Maghrebis in relation to the
term *Beur* and its feminine variant, *Beurette*, which is sometimes
used by French journalists. There is also a deep reluctance among
many young women to accept the gender roles traditionally assumed
in Maghrebi families (an issue explored in greater detail later in this
chapter). When talking with her Maghrebi girlfriends, Nini's fic-
tional *alter ego*, Samia, mixes linguistic codes so as to escape the
repressive surveillance of her family. The girls' secret language
blends together *verlan*, southern French slang and English, produ-
cing cocktails of the following kind: 'La mother a técontra au
KGB que tu treren tous sel srios présa eighteen o'clock! (La mother
a raconté au KGB que tu rentres tous les soirs après dix-huit heures)'
(Nini 1993: 112) ('Mother told the KGB [a nickname for Samia's
elder brother] that you don't get home until after six o'clock each
evening').

While the English expressions which pepper this and other pieces
of writing by young Maghrebi authors may sometimes draw on
school lessons, they are more commonly inspired by the mass media,
which are deeply impregnated with material originating in the US
despite the efforts of the French state to hold back the tide. The title
of another autobiographical narrative, Ferrudja's Kessas's *Beur's
Story* (1990), is directly inspired by two American movies, *West Side
Story* and *Love Story*, both of which feature romances between an
American boy and an immigrant-born girl. When the Maghrebi-born

Smaïn, now one of the most popular humorists in France, staged his first major show he called it *A Star is Beur*, a playful allusion to the Judy Garland movie *A Star is Born*. In his autobiography (written at the youthful age of 32), Smaïn recalls that his childhood was saturated with American influences transmitted nightly on French television. His first role-model was the American humorist Jerry Lewis, the first record he bought was a George Gershwin album (which he could not resist because of its photograph of New York at night), and he dreamed constantly of waking up to find himself in Hollywood-sur-Seine (Smaïn 1990).

American popular culture is no more monolothic than the cultural practices of the many countries into which it has penetrated. While Smaïn fell under the spell of white entertainment establishment figures, many other young Maghrebis in France, particularly those who have become political activists, have been more influenced by black Americans. Some of the most important tensions which lie just below the surface of American popular culture are exemplified in the field of rock music. Although rock and roll first came to international prominence through white American performers, the musical forms on which they drew were largely the creation of black Americans. Today, many variants of rock music – including some of its most politicized forms – are dominated by black rather than white performers. It is significant that in France the earliest stirrings of political mobilization among young people of Third World, mainly Maghrebi, origin were organized at the beginning of the 1980s under the title Rock Against Police. The name was directly inspired by the Rock Against Racism concerts organized a few years earlier in Britain by young Afro-Caribbeans, who in turn looked for their own role-models to black Americans. Thus in France the English label 'Rock Against Police' was a way of attracting young supporters through the excitement associated with rock music, while at the same time pointing to the political example provided by minority groups in Britain and North America, where mobilization against racism was more advanced (*Questions clefs* 1982: 52–63).

The use of English by people of minority ethnic origin is a complex and politically ambivalent phenomenon. Some, such as Smaïn, equate it with an ethic of personal socio-economic advancement, while for others it is an emblem of collective mobilization by oppressed minorities. No less important is the cultural ambivalence of English usage, which allows young people of immigrant origin to position themselves both within and beyond the cultural norms dominant in France. English is now such a standard part of international youth culture that its adoption places the descendants of immigrants on a par with their French peers without their ostensibly submitting to a specifically French norm, which would be deeply troubling to many of their parents.

GENDER ROLES AND FAMILY RELATIONSHIPS

Personal values

Family relationships are of importance not only in the transmission of cultural values from one generation to the next but also as a key locus in which individuals establish their personal status within the framework of collectively structured signifying practices. The cultural structuring of gender roles is a crucial part of this process. Historically, men have tended to ascribe to themselves a dominant role in most, though not all, socio-cultural systems. In recent decades, legislation has been adopted in many industrialized countries aimed at establishing at least formal equality between men and women, though in practice many inequalities persist. Most immigrants of Third World origin come from countries where even formal equality does not exist: power is vested primarily in the father, whose authority extends over most decision-making areas and who generally serves as the breadwinner while the mother attends primarily to domestic tasks.

There are exceptions to this general pattern. In parts of West Africa, for example, matrilineal kinship systems place mothers at the centre of family units (Barou 1992a: 48). When the ancestors of Afro-Caribbeans – some of whom are descended from families of this type – were forcibly transported across the Atlantic as slaves, they suffered major socio-cultural dislocation and were often prevented from forming stable family units. Today, a relatively high proportion of Afro-Caribbean households consists of single-parent families, which are almost always headed by women. In the US, a similar pattern applies to black Americans. It is replicated in turn by immigrants from the Caribbean who have settled in European countries such as Britain, France and the Netherlands. The 1990 census found that a quarter of the families in metropolitan France originating in the French West Indies were headed by a single parent, almost invariably female; this proportion is roughly twice the national average (Marie 1993b: 12). The high profile of Afro-

Caribbean women as breadwinners is reflected in the exceptional levels of female emigration and labour-force participation found among the population originating in the DOM-TOM, as noted in Chapter 2.

In many regions outside the industrialized world, fertility is a highly prized female attribute. Women achieve status and respect by bearing children, and this favours fertility rates which are high when compared with those prevalent among the indigenous population in industrialized countries such as France. These fertility rates are initially replicated by women migrants, but the gap almost always closes as the length of settlement increases. Among Algerians in France, for example, the fertility rate fell from 8.5 children per woman of child-bearing age in the early 1960s to 4.2 in the early 1980s. At the same time, a narrower gap between French nationals and women migrants from southern Europe virtually disappeared. In the early 1960s, it was not uncommon for women of southern European origin to have three or four children each. By the early 1980s, their fertility rates were very similar to the French average of about 1.8 children per woman of child-bearing age (Desplanques 1985: 39).

The rising living standards and improved health care associated with industrialization are generally accompanied by what is known as the demographic transition: a fall in mortality rates accompanied (sometimes a little later) by a reduction in birth rates. The net effect has been smaller families, with each member enjoying greater life-expectancy than in pre-industrial societies. Many parts of the Third World have yet to make this demographic transition, but among women migrants originating in these countries there is a steady decline in fertility rates as their length of settlement increases. Between 1981 and 1990, when the average number of children per French woman of child-bearing age remained more or less stagnant (slipping from 1.8 to 1.7), there were sharp falls among women of African and Asian origin. The average number of children fell from 4.2 to 3.2 among Algerian women, from 5.2 to 3.5 among Moroccans, and from 5.3 to 3.7 among those of Turkish nationality. Although the fall – from 5.1 to 4.8 – was less marked among nationals of sub-Saharan African states, whose arrival in France is particularly recent, there is nevertheless already a widening gap between them and women remaining in the countries of origin, where on average each woman has more than six children (INSEE 1992b).

The long-term trend towards families similar in size to the French norm is undoubtedly sustained among the descendants of immigrants, though as most are French nationals by the time they reach child-bearing age it is difficult to document this with precision. A significant indicator is a rise in the average age at which immigrant-born women marry, compared with their mothers. An analysis by Tribalat of INSEE survey data collected in 1982 found that while 70 per cent of Algerian migrant women had been married before the age of 20, this was true of only 15 per cent of their daughters. A similar trend was apparent among Moroccans and Tunisians. The relatively low age at which the daughters of Turkish women were marrying was attributed to the fact that, compared with Maghrebis, Turks had tended to migrate at a later age. Because of this, many had daughters of marriageable age who had been socialized in rural parts of Turkey, where early marriages were still the norm. Young women of Maghrebi origin, who had spent longer in France, were thought to be delaying marriage partly because they were in some cases unwilling to accept Muslim spouses proposed by their parents (Tribalat 1991: 151–8).

The desire to exercise personal control in the fields of sexuality and matrimony is indicative of important attitudinal changes among young people of immigrant origin compared with their parents. Second- and third-generation members of minority ethnic groups tend to model themselves on their French peers, most of whom regard sexual relations and marriage as matters in which personal decision-making should be paramount. By contrast, in many parts of Africa and Asia extra-marital sexual relations are strictly taboo, and matrimony is seen as a matter to be arranged between families. When families migrate, the choice of marriage partners becomes of crucial importance for the inter-generational reproduction of ethno-cultural differentiation. The higher the rate of endogamy, i.e. marriage within an ethno-cultural group, the better are the chances of sustaining its distinctive cultural values. Exogamy (i.e. marriage outside the group) often reflects a desire for personal independence and signals the erosion of the group's traditions.

In most Third World countries it has been customary for parents to arrange marriages for their children. Those who migrate often expect to retain this prerogative and to use it in such a way as to ensure that succeeding generations remain faithful to the cultural heritage of their ancestors. Immigrants seeking to arrange marriages in this way, usually through extended family and social networks, are engaged in a very important form of ethnic mobilization. As children brought up in France are inclined to expect the same personal freedoms as their French peers, they sometimes find themselves on collision course with their parents. In a survey by the Centre de Formation et de Recherche de l'Education Surveillée (CFRES) conducted among five hundred teenagers in the late 1970s, 68 per cent of Maghrebi interviewees, compared with only 29 per cent of the Iberian (i.e. Portuguese and Spanish) sample and 27 per cent of their French peers, said their parents were opposed in principle to marriages between people of different nationalities. Asked to give their own opinion, only 9 per cent of Maghrebi boys and 15 per cent of Maghrebi girls took the same view. The figures among Iberian youths were 4 and 13 per cent; among French interviewees they were 8 and 7 per cent (Zaleska 1982: 186–8). Whatever their origins, most interviewees said that neither nationality nor religion mattered where their own preferences for a marriage partner were concerned; the important thing would be personal attraction (Taboada-Leonetti 1982: 224). A survey by Muxel of three similarly defined groups of teenagers in the mid-1980s found almost universal agreement for the proposition that cohabitation outside marriage was acceptable (Muxel 1988: 932) – a view with which very few Muslim parents would be likely to agree.

There are also deep inter-generational differences over gender roles. Some 85 per cent of the young Maghrebis questioned in the CFRES survey said their fathers felt women should stay at home and look after the family while men went out to work; 68 per cent said their mothers agreed. The equivalent figures were 67 and 60 per cent among Iberian interviewees, compared with 33 and 24 per cent among the French. When asked to state their own views, the younger generation favoured a more equal distribution of roles among men and women, though boys were less committed to this than girls. Only 10 per cent of Maghrebi girls, compared with 38 per cent of boys, agreed with the traditional distribution of gender roles. The figures were almost identical among young Iberians, while among French girls and boys they were 3 and 20 per cent respectively. Muxel's survey found a very similar inter-ethnic convergence on the question of gender roles among young people from native French, immigrant Catholic and immigrant Muslim backgrounds (Muxel 1988: 932).

Parental expectations tend to constrain daughters more than sons, for the dominant role traditionally enjoyed by men makes endogamous marriages contracted by male descendants appear less threatening than those of females. In Islamic countries, non-Muslim women who marry Muslim men are expected and sometimes legally required to accept that their children will be brought up as Muslims; because of the dominant role traditionally attributed to men, marriages between Muslim women and non-Muslim men are strongly discouraged and may not be legally recognized at all. In France, daughters of Muslim immigrants marrying non-Muslims run a much higher risk of being shunned by their families than do sons who take non-Muslim spouses (Streiff-Fenart 1993).

It is difficult to know how many marriages are contracted between partners from different ethno-cultural groups. The nationality of spouses is often a relevant indicator, but the data compiled in France do not include marriages contracted in the home countries of immigrants. Moreover, as the descendants of immigrants are generally French nationals by the time they reach adulthood, it is impossible to make even approximate estimates of inter-generational trends based on the nationality of spouses. The most thorough study so far conducted on the basis of nationality shows that marriages between foreigners and French nationals generally increase with the length of settlement and that foreign men enter more frequently than women into unions of this kind (Muñoz-Perez and Tribalat 1984). While this gender balance no doubt corresponds in part to the statistical dominance of men in adult migratory inflows, it may also reflect the heavier pressures brought to bear on women by members of groups anxious to sustain a separate ethno-cultural identity through endogamous unions (Abelkrim-Chikh 1991).

Studies of mixed marriages (i.e. those between spouses of different ethnic origins) show that it is difficult, if not impossible, to insulate the family home from the wider political struggle between the different cultural traditions in which the partners have their roots. As a general rule, these marriages are marked by a cultural imbalance against the minority group. Thus immigrants in mixed unions are less likely than those married to a partner of the same ethnic origin to use their mother tongue when speaking to their children (Héran 1993: 3). The names given to the children of mixed unions are highly symbolic indicators of identity. When parents choose names, they implicitly indicate how they want their children to be perceived in relation to their diverse ethno-cultural origins. Those perceptions depend in part on popular preconceptions attaching to different ethnicized groups. Varro and Lesbet (1986) report that as Franco-American couples generally consider their two countries of origin to enjoy roughly equal public esteem, they tend to favour names which are common to both. More commonly, immigrants fear that the nominalization of foreign origins may expose their children to discriminatory treatment. For this reason, French names are often preferred.

The historical legacy of colonization invests the deliberations of some couples with particular sensitivity. Algerian immigrants who experienced the war of independence are generally reluctant to accept French names for their children or grandchildren, though they know that Arab names render social acceptance more difficult in France. In most mixed unions, the desire not to handicap children with stigmatized names eventually wins out over the wish to display a sense of historical pride. In a study of the names given to six hundred children of mixed Franco-Maghrebi (mainly Franco-Algerian) parentage, Streiff-Fenart found that 58 per cent had identifiably French names, compared with only 18 per cent that could be classified as Arab. This overall imbalance was compounded by gendered inequalities. Among couples where the Maghrebi partner was male French names still predominated, with 44 per cent of the total, but the proportion of Arab names rose to 29 per cent. By contrast, where the female partner was Maghrebi 73 per cent of names were French and only 6 per cent Arab (Streiff-Fenart 1993: 235).

Almost a quarter of the names given to the children of Franco-Maghrebi couples were found to be 'neutral', i.e. they could be identified with both cultural traditions or neither. Popular examples straddling the cultural divide included Nadia for girls and Hedi/ Eddie (the Americanized diminutive for Edouard) for boys. Names such as Joris, Tahnee, Vadim and Nolwen were drawn from cultural spaces such as Scandinavia, which were free from the rivalry and/or stigmatization marking Franco-Maghrebi relations. These names are important symbols of the capacity for renewal and invention often seen in the cultural practices of ordinary individuals faced with the contrasting traditions of majority and minority groups. As Streiff-Fenart (1989) and others (Muller 1987; Déjeux 1989; Barbara 1993) have shown, similar compromises and creative syntheses in matters ranging from language and dress to schoolwork and leisure permeate the daily lives of families based on mixed unions.

Legal clashes

Syntheses of this kind are possible because both partners in mixed unions share a personal bond which enables them to look beyond the cultural boundariès of the groups in which they originate. In other circumstances, cultural differences sometimes lead to serious conflicts. Some of the most basic aspects of personal relationships are codified in laws governing kinship systems, which vary from one state to another. Practices which are perfectly lawful in an immigrant's home country may render him or her liable to prosecution in France (HCI 1992b). Family law in France is based on the premise of monogamy. In recent years, immigration from countries where polygamy is widely practised has opened up a legal minefield.

Although polygamous practices existed before Islam, they were formally codified in the Koran, which permitted husbands to take up to four wives provided they were all treated equally. In many parts of the Islamic world, including the Maghreb, polygamy has now fallen into disuse, and some predominantly Islamic countries, such as Tunisia, have made it unlawful. Most of the polygamous families in France are Muslims originating in the Soninké, Bambara and Toucouleur peoples of Mali and Senegal, in former French West Africa, where the practice is both widespread and lawful. While French nationals are not allowed to be married to more than one person at a time, under French law foreigners resident in France are in principle governed in family matters by the laws of their own country. Until recently, citizens of Mali, Senegal and other states where polygamy is lawful were therefore allowed to bring more than one wife to France, together with their children, provided the marriages were contracted in the country of origin (Rude-Antoine 1991).

Since 1993, however, the laws governing family reunification have restricted admissions to only one spouse and one set of directly dependent children per resident foreign citizen (Costa-Lascoux 1994a: 29–31). Moreover, even before then immigrants wishing to be joined by their families were required to prove that they had sufficient income and adequate housing to meet the needs of their dependants. As few polygamous Africans had the material resources to satisfy these requirements, their wives often circumvented the regulations by entering France simply as visitors rather than within the framework of the formal procedures governing family reunification. When foreign visitors exceed a stay of three months, they become illegal immigrants liable to deportation. However, prior to the reform of French nationality laws in 1993, the threat of deportation was removed in the case of women originating in ex-colonies such as those in sub-Saharan Africa if they bore children

while in France, for such children automatically held French nationality from birth. By the same token, neither they nor their parents could
be deported from France, even if the mother's status remained that
of an illegal immigrant (Rude-Antoine 1991; Poiret and Guégan
1992: 92–102).

This legal maze has been compounded by the regulations concerning social security and family allowances. While allowing
foreign men to live with more than one wife, the French state has
always restricted social-security cover to only one of the spouses,
unless the others took up employment in their own right, which has
generally proved possible only in a minority of cases. By contrast,
family allowances are paid in respect of all children resident in
France, regardless of the nationality or immigration status of their
parents. The legal and regulatory framework in France has thus
offered positive incentives to child-bearing within polygamous
marriages: children have served as a guarantee against deportation,
and as their numbers have increased so, too, has the income derived
from family allowances. Poiret (1992: 29, 33, 40) has argued that
this situation has perverted the cultural code underpinning polygamy
in the countries of origin. There, the number of wives taken by a
man, and the children born from these unions, serve to mark his
wealth and social status. In France, multiple marriages retain their
value as status symbols, but as most immigrants have very low
incomes the economic base on which polygamy is built in West
Africa is generally lacking; in many cases, instead of symbolizing
wealth children serve to compensate for poverty.

In the highly charged atmosphere surrounding the public debate
over immigration, polygamous families have attracted the ire of
French politicians. In a speech in 1991, for example, the mayor of
Paris and former prime minister, Jacques Chirac, attacked alleged
financial abuses by polygamous families and voiced his sympathy
with those who disliked the 'noise and smell' associated with
immigrants (*Le Monde*, 21 June 1991). As Poiret and Guégan (1992:
8) observe, polygamous families have become one of the most
emotive symbols currently incarnating French fears over immigration. Most polygamous men are poorly educated, unskilled Muslims
with low incomes and large families who in some cases are housed
in dense micro-concentrations. As such, they exemplify French fears
of immigrants as culturally alien people 'taking over' parts of the
country and abusing its regulations.

While it would be foolish not to recognize the cultural clashes associated with multiple marriages and the very real material difficulties to which they give rise, it is likely that the living conditions experienced by polygamous families in France will in the long run serve to discourage this kind of kinship system. These conditions are almost invariably more stressful than those obtaining in Africa, where it is customary for each wife to have a separate home. In France, African immigrants have great difficulty in finding even one affordable home adequate for their needs, and it is rarely large enough to provide a separate room for each spouse. The daily stress of the overcrowding which results from this is frequently compounded by personal rivalries. Although it is often difficult for African women to organize independently of their husbands, the main associations which they have established in France have placed the reform or abolition of polygamy high on their agenda (Barou 1992b: 53–5; Poiret and Guégan 1992: 84–90). While their settlement is still at a relatively early stage, with relatively few second-generation Africans yet of adult age, there is little, if any, evidence to suggest that those whose childhood has been spent in overcrowded and sometimes quarrelsome homes will be keen to perpetuate the polygamous practices of their parents. As French nationals, they will in any case be legally bound to monogamy.

Many parents nevertheless expect their children to retain at least some of the cultural codes inherited from the country of origin. One of the most tangible marks of parental expectations is circumcision, a physical act of cultural initiation performed on children at an age when they are generally too young to control, or in some cases even understand, its significance. Male circumcision is practised throughout the Islamic world, as well as by Jews, and is perfectly lawful in France. Female circumcision is less widespread, being confined principally to sub-Saharan Africa, and although the main countries where it is practised are predominantly Islamic, it is not part of the Islamic religion *per se*. Until the mid-1970s, when families from Mali and Senegal first began to emigrate in significant numbers, female circumcision was unheard-of in France. According to Piet (1992: 190–2), the majority of adult women emigrating from these countries were circumcised during their childhood. With the growth of family settlement in France, many West Africans have arranged for their daughters to be circumcised there. Following the death of a 3-year-old girl on whom the operation was performed in 1982, court cases have been successfully brought against a number of parents charged with aiding in the mutilation of their daughters, and in 1991 a Malian woman hired by parents to circumcise girls was given a five-year prison sentence.

Perceptions of female circumcision vary widely, depending on the cultural context within which it is viewed. The equation of this practice with mutilation in French jurisprudence imputes to parents a malicious motive entirely at odds with their own view of the matter, for in their eyes the operation is designed so as best to prepare girls for adulthood. In their country of origin, uncircumcised girls would be severely handicapped in the matrimonial market. Some analysts argue that the customs on which this market is built are rooted in a project of male domination over female sexuality (M'Barga 1992: 170). Others point out that the practice is largely organized and carried out by women, and note that the associations of immigrant women campaigning against polygamy have been more reserved where female circumcision is concerned (Bourdin 1992: 182–5; Barou 1992b: 62–3). Against this, it is sometimes argued that women have been conditioned into serving as the agents of their own imprisonment within male-dominated cultures.

The extent to which individuals are free to construct their own values independently of the cultural codes which they inherit depends on a host of social and psychological variables. It is not always easy to know whether particular acts have been freely chosen, passively reproduced or grudgingly performed under psychological or even physical coercion. Girls brought up in France by Muslim parents are generally given very little personal freedom once they reach adolescence. Parents feel that their own status in the eyes of other Muslims depends on keeping their daughters insulated from any risk of pre-marital sex and on finding for them suitable husbands who share the Islamic faith. Young women placed in such a situation have very restricted opportunities for finding partners of their own choice, with little chance of their parents being prepared to accept a non-Muslim son-in-law. There are regular press reports of girls running away from home to avoid arranged marriages (*Ouest-France*, 28 November 1985; *Le Monde*, 11 August 1988), and frequent claims that young women of Maghrebi origin have a higher suicide rate than their French-born peers (*Le Monde*, 17 March 1989; *L'Express*, 3 November 1989), though there appear to be no wholly reliable statistics to confirm this. Runaways are often helped by support organizations run by women of immigrant origin who have first-hand experience of their problems (*Hommes et migrations* 1991a). In the face of high unemployment levels, unless they have access to networks of this kind capable of providing material support, many young people have little alternative but to remain in the family home, with marriage to an approved partner the only possible way out. In these circumstances, consent to a proposed partner may sometimes be perceived as the least undesirable available option rather than as a positive preference.

The distinction between acceptance of this kind and genuinely forced marriages is not always easy to draw. Only very rarely have young women succeeded in mobilizing the French courts against marriages into which they were unwilling to enter. One such case involved a Moroccan girl brought up near Nancy, in north-eastern France, under the guardianship of an uncle after her parents were killed in a road accident. Shortly after her sixteenth birthday, she was taken to Morocco and married against her will to the uncle's son. Unusually, the girl was able to secure documentary proof of what had happened, so that when the newly weds returned to France she was able to obtain a court order quashing the marriage (*Le Monde*, 27 October 1989). There is no way of knowing how many marriages are based more on coercion than on consent, and in the absence of firm evidence it would be wrong to over-generalize. There can be little doubt, however, that serious tensions exist in many Muslim families as a consequence of the acculturation of the younger generation.

ISLAM

Most immigrants of European origin, together with those originating in the Caribbean, come from countries with a long tradition of Christian, mainly Catholic, belief. About half of the immigrants from sub-Saharan Africa are also estimated to be Christians. However, the vast majority of immigrants originating outside Europe come from predominantly Islamic countries. Smaller numbers adhere to a variety of other religions ranging from Judaism and Buddhism to Taoism and Confucianism (*Migrants-formation* 1990; *Hommes et migrations* 1993). Research into the development of these faiths within France is very unevenly spread, and it is not possible in the space of this chapter fully to encompass them all. Instead, we shall focus on Islam, which merits particular attention for three main reasons.

One of these is numerical: while precise figures cannot be established with certainty, it is clear that Muslims now far outnumber adherents to other minority faiths in France, placing them second only to Catholics and well ahead of long-standing religious minorities such as Protestants and Jews. Second, unlike other religious minorities, Muslims have in recent years been involved in a number of major disputes concerning their rights within France. Third, these clashes have taken place at a time when Islam has become a much more potent force in international politics than any of the other faiths associated with recent migratory inflows. All these elements, which have become frequent reference points in domestic politics, have combined to induce fears among the majority population that Islam represents a serious threat to social stability in France.

These fears – reflected in a 1992 opinion poll in which two out of three interviewees said they were frightened by the development of Islam in France (SOFRES 1993: 233) – are in my view largely unfounded. The analysis which follows will show that, in at least three respects, the challenge posed by Islam to the existing structures of French society has been greatly exaggerated. In the first place, there is ample evidence to show that religious belief and observance are far weaker among the descendants of immigrants than among first-generation Muslims in France. Second, the organizational structures of the Islamic population are seldom aimed at disturbing the established social order, and most of them are in any case too weak to present a significant threat even if their leaders were so inclined. Finally, we shall see that even the most widely publicized confrontations over the status of Islam have never mobilized more than a tiny minority of Muslims in France.

Religious beliefs and practices

The number of Muslims in France is generally put at about 3 million. This figure is arrived at by totalling up the foreign residents who are nationals of predominantly Islamic countries, and then adding the estimated number of French nationals descended from them (a figure of about 1 million is commonly used) together with the half-million or so *harkis* and their descendants, and 30,000 or more native French converts to Islam (Kepel 1987: 12–13; Leveau 1988: 108–10; Nielsen 1992: 10–11). Maghrebis account for about four-fifths of the total, with sub-Saharan Africans and Turks making up most of the rest. This sort of calculation is open to many criticisms (Kepel 1987: 13–16; Etienne 1989: 51–3, 89–100). While it is safe to assume that the overwhelming majority of immigrants from mainly Muslim countries are of the Islamic faith, there are certainly exceptions to this. Far more questionable is the assumption that all their descendants (who together account for almost half the estimated total of 3 million Muslims) share their faith. In numerous surveys, between one-fifth and one-third of young people from Muslim backgrounds regularly say they are not Islamic believers, and many of the others profess only a weak allegiance to the religion of their parents (Hargreaves and Stenhouse 1991).

Table 3.3 Islamic beliefs and practices among French residents of Algerian origin in Roubaix, 1988–9

Harkis and their descendants

	Age <26	Age 26–30	Age 31–40	Age 41–50	Age >50
Prayers and Ramadan	4	8	12	61	90
Ramadan only	44	20	27	11	10
Neither, but considers self Muslim	26	47	38	28	0
Other	26	25	23	0	0
	100%	100%	100%	100%	100%

Other French nationals of Algerian origin

	Age <26	Age 26–30	Age 31–40	Age 41–50	Age >50
Prayers and Ramadan	3	10	13	75	–
Ramadan only	42	10	25	0	–
Neither, but considers self Muslim	33	60	25	25	–
Other	22	20	37	0	–
	100%	100%	100%	100%	100%

Source: Souida 1990: 62.

The inter-generational erosion of Islam can best be illustrated by examining data from surveys conducted in 1988–9 among the population of Algerian origin in the northern town of Roubaix (Table 3.3). The data cover over 1,000 interviewees, of whom the majority were *harkis* and their descendants, while the remainder were economic migrants or their descendants questioned in exit polls conducted during the presidential elections of 1988. The *harkis* and their descendants are all French nationals, and as the remainder of those questioned were interviewed after participating in French elections, they too necessarily held French citizenship. This makes the sample in some ways untypical of the population of Algerian origin as a whole, for while most of the children of economic migrants automatically acquire French citizenship, the majority of their parents remain Algerian nationals. The absence of any data on 'Other [i.e. non-*harki*] French nationals of Algerian origin' over the age of 50 reflects the fact that no person in that category voted, or at any rate none was interviewed, in the polling-stations where the exit polls were conducted. However, it is not unreasonable to suppose that, like their *harki* counterparts, Algerian economic migrants of that age are all Muslim believers. Among all the other age groups, there are close parallels between the *harki* population and the rest of the sample, and the overall trend is unmistakably towards a much weaker attachment to Islam among the younger generations.

Perhaps the most striking feature is the number of responses corresponding to the category which the survey designers diplomatically labelled 'Other'. As implicitly defined in the context of the alternatives, 'Other' means that the respondent does not consider himself or herself to be a Muslim. While there were no responses of this kind among interviewees over the age of 40, about a quarter of younger respondents replied in this way. A large majority of older respondents said they prayed regularly and fasted during Ramadan. Very few of those aged below 41 prayed. While almost half of those below the age of 26 said they observed Ramadan, it is likely that a large proportion of them were still living in the parental home, where there may have been no practical alternative to following the dietary customs of their parents. Ramadan was observed by far fewer of those aged between 26 and 40, many of whom were likely to have set up their own homes.

Despite their low rates of religious observance, the majority of younger interviewees nevertheless described themselves as Muslims. Other surveys, such as that of Gonzales-Quijano (1988), have shown that young people brought up by Muslim immigrants know very little about Islamic doctrines and often take a negative view of the dietary, sexual and other restrictions associated with it; yet most continue to say they are Muslims. In its most extreme form, the co-existence of affective identification with doctrinal detachment is summed up in a remark uttered by more than one young 'Muslim': 'I am a Muslim atheist' (Bourgeba-Dlchy 1990: 634; *L'Express*, 17 February 1994;

cf. *Panoramiques* 1991: 109). This residual identification with Islam even among young people who consider themselves to be atheists reflects the fact that Islam is inextricably intertwined with their family roots. For many people brought up by Muslim immigrants, it would be impossible to break altogether with Islam without causing profound distress to their parents. Islam is in this sense a primordial attachment, the denial of which is almost literally unthinkable. Yet this is not the same as saying that it is a primary source of values in the life projects of young Muslims. While young activists sometimes evoke their Islamic heritage as part of an anti-racist strategy, the promotion of religious doctrines or institutions seldom features among their objectives. As we shall see later in this chapter, they have been far more concerned to address social, political and economic injustices.

Organizational structures

The doctrinal ignorance of many youngsters brought up in Muslim families is a consequence of the very weak organizational infrastructure which has long characterized the Islamic population in France. Poorly educated and confined to low-income jobs, the vast majority of Muslim immigrants have lacked both the financial resources and the organizational skills necessary for the effective reproduction of their Islamic heritage. In the mid-1970s, there were fewer than fifty places of Islamic worship in France. By the mid-1980s, there were well over 1,000 (Kepel 1987: 229). This exponential growth has sometimes been taken as a sign of awesome power. In fact, it is first and foremost a reflection of the organizational weakness of Islam. Despite the fact that Muslims were to the fore in migratory inflows during much of the post-war period, they had very little organizational infrastructure until the mid-1970s, when a vigorous but late catching-up process began. After a period of rapid growth during the 1980s, there are signs that this is now levelling off (CNCDH 1993: 309).

While Safran (1986) has rightly argued that these organizational developments provide the basis for an enduring Islamic presence in France, they remain limited in their resource base and outreach. Very few of the places of Islamic worship established during the last twenty years are purpose-built mosques complete with minarets; most are simply a room set aside for prayers in an apartment block or hostel for immigrant workers. The main beneficiaries of these initiatives have been immigrants who were initiated into Islam before leaving their countries of origin. Their descendants have remained to a large extent beyond the reach of organized religion, despite growing attempts to draw them into its orbit. In a survey of people attending mosques in Marseille in the late 1980s, Cesari (1989: 64) found that no more than 15 per cent were aged below 36, despite the fact that this age group accounts in theory for roughly half of the 3 million believers commonly attributed to Islam across the country as a whole. Looking back over the last quarter of a century, it is no exaggeration to say that almost an entire immigrant-born generation has been raised in France with little more than a rudimentary knowledge of Islamic values and practices, derived in the main from parents who, by virtue of their illiteracy, were unable to offer any formal instruction, or even direct access to the Koran.

Despite the formal separation of church and state in France, Catholics continue to enjoy a privileged status. Public holidays are still built to a large extent around the Christian calendar, as is the timetable of state schools, most of which leave Wednesday afternoons free in order to permit the children of Catholics to attend catechism classes. Moreover, the state directly funds church-run schools in exchange for a commitment to cover the national syllabus laid down by the Ministry of Education alongside confessional teachings. Across France as a whole, 13 per cent of primary-school children and 20 per cent of secondary-school children are educated in state-funded private schools, 95 per cent of which are Catholic (Conseil Economique et Social 1994: 45). Not one state-funded Islamic school exists in the whole of metropolitan France. Koranic schools attached to mosques are able to offer religious instruction to children on Wednesday afternoons or at weekends, but their availability is patchy.

Islam has been similarly disadvantaged where the media are concerned. Until 1991, when its allocation was doubled to thirty minutes, Islam was given only a fifteen-minute slot in the sequence of religious programmes broadcast on Sunday mornings by one of the state television channels; despite the fact that they are out-numbered by Muslims, Jews have an equal length of time, while Protestants have a longer slot, second only to that enjoyed by Catholics. While local radio stations run by and for Catholics, Protestants and Jews have been licensed in several cities, the authorities have been reluctant to allocate frequencies to stations which are specifically Islamic in character. Practically the only station of this kind, Radio-Orient in Paris, was hand-picked for its religious 'moderation', i.e. opposition to so-called Islamic 'fundamentalism' (*Le Point*, 6 March 1989; *Le Monde*, 13 October 1994).

It is as normal for Muslims to wish to practise their religion with suitable organizational support as it is for Catholics or Jews. There is no incompatibility between the diversity of their beliefs and the fact that they all pay taxes to the same state and, if they are French citizens, vote in the same elections. Just as there is no reason to suppose that practising Catholics or Jews are *ipso facto* plotting with Rome or Jerusalem to overthrow the established social order in France, so it is unreasonable to impute a similar motive to Muslims who have links with outside countries. Because their own resources and skills are limited, many Muslim associations in France have depended on help from their home countries or oil-rich Islamic states such as Saudi Arabia, which have funded the construction of mosques and provided trained personnel. It was not until the early 1990s that the first training facilities for imams (Islamic prayer leaders) were established in France; until then, most associations had no practical alternative to relying on foreign-trained imams (*Migrations société* 1994).

In their internal affairs, almost all the states which have given assistance in this way blend principles based on Islamic law with more pragmatic elements, and they take the view that Muslims living in predominantly non-Islamic countries should respect the laws prevailing there. A few states – most obviously, Iran – and a number of private or semi-private associations take a more fundamentalist line, arguing that Islamic law must be followed in every particular and imposed, if necessary by force, as widely as possible. The Iranian Revolution, which brought the Ayatollah Khomeiny to power in 1979, marked the onset of a more assertive Islamic dimension in international politics than had previously been apparent during the post-war period. It coincided with a sudden rise in the visibility of Muslims in France, who until the beginning of the 1980s had been seen merely as cogs in the chain of economic production ('immigrant workers') rather than as a settled communities with distinct cultural identities ('ethnic minorities') (Hames 1989).

Although these two developments were not directly linked, they became fused in the minds of many politicians and ordinary members of the public, who were inclined to draw a blanket equation between 'Muslims' and 'fundamentalists'. Yet Etienne (1987: 287), who has conducted extensive fieldwork among Muslims in southern France, estimates that less than 1 per cent could be reasonably described as 'fundamentalists'. Most have no desire to challenge France's existing legal order. From time to time, France has served as a place of asylum and/or terrorist activity for Muslims bent on political change in other countries. The Ayatollah Khomeiny lived in exile in France until his return to Iran in 1979. In 1986, pro-Iranian terrorists seeking to influence events in the Middle East staged a series of bomb attacks in Paris. They were aided by a handful of Maghrebis living in the Paris area but had no mass base among the immigrant population at large. Since 1992, when the Front Islamique du Salut (FIS) was banned by the Algerian government, a bitter armed struggle has been waged in Algeria between the security forces and Islamic 'fundamentalists', now commonly labelled 'Islamists'. Although the French authorities have organized several swoops on FIS supporters in France, there is no evidence to suggest that these are at all numerous. Attempts by exiled FIS activists to enlist the support of Maghrebi youths in the *banlieues* (Pellegrini 1992: 105) have met with little success. The overwhelming majority of Algerians in France have remained aloof from or positively hostile towards the FIS, whose political project has little if any relevance to their own daily concerns. According to a survey carried out among Muslims in France in the autumn of 1994, only one in ten has a good opinion of the FIS and would like to see it in power in Algeria, while seven out of ten are hostile (*Le Monde*, 13 October 1994).

The headscarf affair

In the debate over Islam in France, no single incident has generated greater acrimony than the headscarf affair of 1989. It began early in October, when three Muslim girls were suspended from their state school in Creil, 50 kilometres (30 miles) to the north of Paris, because their insistence on wearing headscarves was judged by the headmaster, Ernest Chenière, to be in contravention of French laws on *laïcité* (secularism), a term denoting the formal separation of the state from religious institutions. The teenage girls – two of whom were of Moroccan origin, the other being Tunisian – were wearing the headscarves in line with their understanding of Islamic teachings on female dress. Chenière's decision was brought to the attention of the national media when an anti-racist organization, SOS-Racisme, appealed against it to the Minister of Education, Lionel Jospin, claiming that Chenière was breaking the law by victimizing the girls because of their religion. Another anti-racist organization, the Mouvement contre le racisme et pour l'amitié entre les peuples (MRAP), had already lodged a similar complaint with the education authorities in Creil. Over the next few months, the affair developed into a major political controversy, attracting saturation coverage in the media (ADRI 1990; Perotti and Thépaut 1990; Perotti and Toulat 1990; Siblot 1992).

When Jospin overturned Chenière's suspension order, his decision was likened by a group of leading intellectuals – among them Régis Debray and Alain Finkielkraut – to Munich (*Le Nouvel Observateur*, 2 November 1989), a byword for the feckless appeasement of threatening foreign forces. At the Munich peace conference of 1938, Britain and France had given in to the expansionist demands of Nazi Germany; by implication, the Islamic bridgehead established by the three girls in Creil now represented a comparable threat to the future well-being of France. By December 1989, the controversy had enabled Jean-Marie Le Pen's anti-immigrant Front National (FN) to win a sweeping by-election victory in Dreux, 50 kilometres (30 miles) to the west of Paris, forcing the Socialist government to rush through a series of institutional initiatives aimed at reassuring the public that immigrants and their descendants could be successfully 'integrated' into French society (see pp. 195–6 below).

In assessing the significance of the headscarf affair, it is important to correct two serious misconceptions about it. First, the confrontation in Chenière's school did not arise – as is often mistakenly thought (see, e.g., Fitzpatrick 1993: 121–2) – from a Muslim refusal to obey French law. On the contrary, it was triggered by a particular interpretation of the law on the part of the headmaster which was found by the courts to be untenable. After overturning Chenière's decision, Jospin referred the matter to the Conseil d'Etat, France's highest administrative court, which ruled that the wearing of head-scarves at school did not *per se* infringe the laws on *laïcité* (*Le Monde*, 29 November 1989). By the same token, the Conseil d'Etat upheld the spirit of SOS-Racisme's complaint that it was Chenière (not his Muslim pupils) who had contravened the law, by dis-criminating against the girls on the grounds of their religion.

In state schools throughout France it is common practice to allow Catholics to wear crucifixes; similarly, Jewish boys are permitted to wear yarmulkas. Neither the expression of religious opinions nor the wearing of religious insignia is prohibited. What the law prohibits on the premises of state schools is *proselytism*, i.e. attempts to persuade others to accept particular religious or political opinions. Chenière and others claimed that the wearing of an Islamic headscarf constituted an act of proselytism, whereas the wearing of a crucifix or yarmulka did not. Acknowledging that religious insignia or items of dress might in certain circumstances be used for acts of proselytism – and hence put their wearers in breach of the law – the Conseil d'Etat ruled that it was only usage of that kind (not particular garments or insignia *per se*) that contravened the law. Subsequent jurisprudence arising from disputes in other schools similar to that in Creil confirmed that religious garments or insignia could not be banned as such, although schools have the right and indeed the duty to prevent their being used by teachers or pupils for the purpose of proselytizing.

In the autumn of 1994 François Bayrou, Education Minister in the centre-right government appointed the previous year under the premiership of Edouard Balladur, nevertheless attempted to institute a tougher line by issuing a circular to headteachers asking them to ban 'ostentatious' signs of religious belief, which he equated with acts of proselytism or discrimination (*Le Monde*, 21 September 1994). In a press interview, he made it clear that he intended the ban to apply to headscarves but not to yarmulkas or crucifixes, which he classified as unostentatious (*Le Point*, 10 September 1994). By December 1994, seventy-nine girls had been expelled from school as a result of Bayrou's circular. It remained to be seen whether these actions would be upheld in the courts, to which a number of expellees had appealed. Marceau Long, head of the Conseil d'Etat, which had ruled in 1989 that the headscarf could not be banned *per se*, thought it quite possible that Bayrou's circular and the expulsions resulting from it would be found to be unlawful (*Le Monde*, 20 December 1994).

A second misconception about the headscarf affair lies in the impression that it was a rallying-point uniting France's Muslim population against the code of *laïcité*. Nothing could be further from the truth. As already noted, the wearing of an Islamic headscarf is not in itself incompatible with *laïcité*. No less importantly, the number of girls dressed in that way was and remains small, and they are almost certainly supported by only a minority of the Muslim population as a whole. An IFOP opinion poll conducted among a sample of 516 Muslim interviewees at the height of the original affair found that only 30 per cent were in favour of allowing Islamic headscarves to be worn in state schools, compared with 45 per cent who opposed it (*Le Monde*, 30 November 1989). In a similar survey five years later, the proportion of Muslims in favour of tolerating the headscarf at school had fallen to 22 per cent, while those against remained steady at 44 per cent; 31 per cent said they were indifferent, while 2 per cent made no reply (IFOP poll in *Le Monde*, 13 October 1994). Although poll samples of this size can serve as only a rough guide to Muslim opinion in France, their broad findings are corroborated by the very limited Islamic mobilization in favour of the headscarf.

The organizations which first took up the case of the three girls in Creil – SOS-Racisme and the MRAP – are not Islamic associations at all. SOS-Racisme is a multi-ethnic youth organization which, from its creation in 1984 until 1992, was presided over by Harlem Désir, whose mother (a native of Alsace) and Afro-Caribbean father (from the overseas *département* of Martinique) were both French Catholics. Like the older-established, mainly French-run MRAP, SOS-Racisme has always included anti-Semitism among the forms of racism targeted by its campaigns. These anti-racist movements were neither 'fundamentalist' nor even 'pro-Islamic', but simply opposed to unlawful discrimination against minorities, regardless of their creed or colour.

After SOS-Racisme and the MRAP had taken the initiative, several Islamic organizations began mobilizing in favour of the Creil girls. First into the fray was the Fédération Nationale des Musulmans de France (FNMF), an organization founded in 1985 principally by French converts to Islam, who are hardly typical of the majority of Muslims in France. During the entire affair, the only attempt at a national demonstration by Muslims was a march through Paris on 22 October. It was organized by the Voix de l'Islam, a tiny pro-Iranian group, and the mainly Turkish Association Islamique en France (AIF). In all, out of the 3 million believers commonly attributed to Islam in France, only five or six hundred joined the march (*Le Monde*, 24 October 1989; *Le Point*, 30 October 1989).

This was a far cry from the 100,000 demonstrators who turned out in Paris at the end of the first nationwide March Against Racism, organized by young Maghrebis in 1983 (*Marseille–Paris, je marche, moi non plus* 1984). Most of those who joined the headscarf demonstration were Turks. There was no significant involvement by Maghrebis, who account for the vast majority of Muslims in France, including the three girls in Creil. The most powerful organization representing mainly Maghrebi Muslims, the Algerian-dominated Grande Mosquée de Paris, refused to associate itself with the demonstration, while supporting the right of Muslim girls to wear headscarves if they wished (*Le Monde*, 21 October 1989, 24 October 1989). This was hardly a subversive act. Exactly the same position was taken by both the archbishop of Paris and the chief rabbi of Paris, who no doubt appreciated that it would be morally and legally impossible to ban headscarves without also prohibiting crucifixes and yarmulkas. France-Plus, the foremost national organization of young Maghrebis, favoured a complete ban on all religious insignia in state schools, including the headscarf (*Le Point*, 30 October 1989). Vigorous opposition to the headscarf was also voiced by Djida Tazdaït, President of a leading provincial youth association, Jeunes Arabes de Lyon et sa Banlieue (JALB), and one of two women of Algerian origin elected as members of the European Parliament earlier in 1989 (*L'Express*, 3 November 1989).

While the headscarf affair might appear at first sight to have favoured the emergence of a form of ethnic politics in France (Feldblum 1993), on closer analysis one cannot but be struck by the minimal level of the political mobilization which it sparked among minority ethno-cultural groups. Far from being a trial of strength pitting minority groups against the majority population, the controversy over the headscarf was first and foremost a Franco-French affair, i.e. a struggle between two different camps within the native population. It was they that generated most of the political heat and media coverage. Both camps, it should be noted, wanted to limit the influence of Islam; they differed less in their aim than in the means felt to be appropriate to that end (Berris 1990). Chenière represented those who were determined to impose draconian controls on Islam; Jospin spoke for those who favoured a less confrontational approach, arguing that if girls wearing headscarves were to be excluded from France's secular education system, this would be a certain recipe for pushing them back into an exclusively Islamic milieu (*Le Nouvel Observateur*, 26 October 1989). This Franco-French battle was undoubtly marked by the politicization of ethno-cultural differences in the debate over ethnicized notions of Islam. However, those differences were of far greater significance in the minds of rival French actors than in motivating minority groups.

At the height of the affair, Socialist Prime Minister Michel Rocard pointed out that while three girls in Creil and a handful elsewhere had aroused a storm of controversy because they insisted on wearing headscarves, some 350,000 other girls from Muslim families were attending state schools daily without raising any such problem (*Le*

Monde, 21 November 1989). The IFOP poll conducted at the same time confirmed that Muslims in France had understood and internalized the spirit of *laïcité*. Aware that religious convictions must not intrude into the state educational system, a majority among those interviewed felt the headscarf should be kept out of school – a stricter interpretation of *laïcité* than was required by the letter of the law, as ruled on by the Conseil d'Etat.

The precise number of girls wearing headscarves in state schools is not known. Chenière, who was elected as a Member of Parliament in 1993, wearing the colours of the neo-Gaullist Rassemblement pour la République (RPR), claimed in the autumn of that year that seven hundred girls were involved, while the Education Ministry put the figure at only a few dozen (*Le Monde*, 11 November 1993). Pressure from Chenière and other right-wing MPs nevertheless led Bayrou to issue his ministerial circular in September 1994 aimed at excluding the headscarf from school. Early in October, Bayrou put the total number of schoolgirls wearing headscarves across the country as a whole at 1,143 (*Le Monde*, 12 October 1994). Later, he stated that 2,000 girls had been wearing headscarves just before he issued his circular in September, and claimed that as a result of his action the figure had fallen to only 400 by December 1994. At the same time, uncorroborated estimates leaked to the press by the Interior Ministry put the total as high as 10,000 or even 15,000 (*Le Point*, 24 November 1994; *Le Monde*, 26 November 1994, 20 December 1994). Even if the highest of the Interior Ministry's figures were to prove accurate, it should be noted that this would amount to at the most one in eight Muslim schoolgirls of secondary-school age; on the highest estimate put forward by the Education Ministry, which was probably better informed than the Interior Ministry, it would be less than one in sixty.[5]

Just as Chenière had stirred up the original confrontation in Creil by taking action of doubtful legal validity in 1989, so Bayrou's 1994 circular led to a rash of confrontations in schools where girls refused to remove their headscarves. As in the original affair, small groups of militant Muslims seized on these fresh incidents to demonstrate in support of those excluded from school because of the headscarf. Somewhat incongruously, they were now joined by French Trotskyists seeking to make their own political capital out of what they described as the discriminatory treatment being meted out to young Muslims (*Le Monde*, 6 October 1994). Only very rarely did support groups form inside schools affected by these disputes. When twenty-four girls were threatened with exclusion from their high school in Mantes-la-Jolie, about three hundred classmates demonstrated in sympathy with them. Significantly, they marched behind a banner bearing the republican motto 'Liberty, Equality, Fraternity' (*Le Monde*, 11 October 1994). This kind of opposition to the victimization of a religious minority hardly constituted an assault on the core values of French society.

It is clear that most Muslim immigrants and their descendants have adapted to the framework of law governing religious practices in France. This is not the same as saying that a mechanical process of acculturation has led to the abandoning of their religious faith. Still less does it mean that they have been entirely assimilated into a pre-existing set of cultural norms. Rather, in the field of religion, as in other cultural spheres, immigrants and their descendants are forging new syntheses combining elements drawn from their pre-migratory heritage with a commitment to the overarching norms governing social intercourse in France.

TERRITORIAL BELONGING

'Home is where the heart is': like all folk-wisdom, this adage contains an important element of truth, while inevitably oversimplifying many complex realities. Importantly in the present context, it hints at a tension between primordial affects and instrumentalist calculations, for the maxim is implicitly framed by the unspoken assumption that while a person's 'real' home depends on emotional ties, his or her place of residence may be governed by other necessities. Still more fundamentally, it suggests that 'home' may not be a place at all, but a state of mind and/or set of relationships. These tensions are exemplified in the complex processes of identification which characterize immigrants and their descendants. Most people retain deep emotional bonds with both the family into which they are born and the place where they are brought up. Immigrants who leave the land of their birth in the hope of securing better economic opportunities elsewhere usually expect to return, even if only when they retire, to the place of their primordial attachments. However, this apparently simple polarity between a place of affective origins and a place of instrumentally defined interests breaks down when immigrants begin to raise children.

While living in France, immigrant parents continue to speak of their country or village of origin as 'home', and encourage their children to think in the same terms. Yet the 'home country' of immigrants is not in any directly equivalent sense the 'home country' of children who are born and raised in France.[6] Their earliest affective ties are, of course, forged with the family. Through this, they are encouraged to identify with a distant place of which (by contrast to their parents) they may have little or no first-hand experience (Hargreaves 1995). The topographical fact of the matter is that the family home is in France and, like all children, the descendants of immigrants feel deep affective ties not only with their family but also with the place where their earliest years are spent. As they move into adolescence and adulthood, the choices faced by the children of immigrants are therefore weighted very differently from the apparently simple polar opposites facing their parents.

Their affective ties with their parents' country of origin are real, but seldom as strong as those that bind them to France. Often, their feelings of allegiance to the 'home country' have relatively little to sustain them beyond a sense of loyalty to their parents. As we have seen earlier in this chapter, in crucial cultural spheres such as language and religion, most of the descendants of immigrants lack the competence and/or the commitment necessary to function effectively within the 'home country'. During family holidays there, they are not uncommonly treated as outsiders by the local population. When they reach working age and are theoretically free to settle wherever they wish, very few seek to make a career in the country from which their parents originate. Not surprisingly, most of the immigrant-born youngsters deported to their 'home country' during the presidency of Giscard d'Estaing subsequently sought to re-enter France (Lefort and Néry 1985).

To the extent that their ties with France outweigh those with the 'home country', the descendants of immigrants also complicate the seemingly simple position of their parents. If their own children wish to remain in France, the equation initially drawn by immigrants between the land of their birth and that of the family breaks down. By the same token, the balance of affective and instrumental calculations becomes more complicated than it first appeared.

This mental shift within the older generation is reflected in a number of indicators. Monetary transfers to their home country are one such sign. Immigrant workers without families in France usually send money regularly to the home country, often to support not only members of their immediate family but also a wider village community or network of kinspeople. When family settlement develops, monetary transfers may still continue, particularly if immigrants are planning to retire to a new home in their country of origin built with the aid of their savings. Monetary flows are difficult to calculate with precision, partly because many different methods of transfer may be used, ranging from salary deductions by employers to cash in hand or payments in kind. It is nevertheless clear that while variations in political and economic circumstances are sometimes significant, the dominant trend is for monetary transfers to decline as family settlement lengthens (Garson and Tapinos 1981; Salgues 1988). Thus sub-Saharan Africans, whose settlement is relatively recent, still make substantial transfers (Barou 1992a: 32–3), while remittances by Algerians are now very much lower after a longer period of settlement.

A second indicator of the deepening roots of immigrants within the receiving society is the lack of success of government schemes aimed at inducing them to leave. Between 1977 and 1981, when immigrant workers were under strong pressure to leave, fewer than 100,000 people (including dependants) benefited from the first scheme of this kind. By 1992, the total had risen to about 215,000 (Lebon 1993: 109). Although dependants account for the majority of this figure, it should be noted that immigrant workers unaccompanied by family members heavily outnumber those returning as part of a family unit. Between 1984 and 1992, for example, only about one-third of the foreign workers repatriated with government aid were accompanied by dependants. Immigrant parents know that most of their children would find it very difficult to resettle in the 'home country'; hence the relatively small numbers of family units 'returning' there.

For young people born and brought up in France, resettlement in the 'home country' would not in fact be a 'return' at all, but an act of emigration tearing them away from their deepest roots. Because few of their descendants are inclined to leave the country where they were raised, most immigrants wishing to remain close to their children find themselves facing the prospect of remaining permanently in France even after their retirement. The myth of return is thus pushed to its ultimate point and beyond: only after death, with a burial-place in the land of their birth, will many immigrants finally accomplish the return journey of which they have dreamed since their initial departure (Chaïb 1994).

Despite being more or less permanently resident in France,

immigrants are often reluctant to take French nationality. In some cases there are important practical reasons for this. Many states refuse to recognize dual nationality, forcing immigrants to renounce their citizenship rights in their country of origin if they take the nationality of the country in which they have settled. For citizens of countries such as Turkey, this means forfeiting inheritance and other rights. Affective ties with the country of origin also weigh against a change of nationality, for the symbolic status of such a step fits ill with the myth of return. Ideological factors may also play a part, for no territory can be entirely separated from the political complexion of the state which exercises sovereignty over it. In the eyes of many Algerians, for example, the ideological legacy associated with the founding myths of Algerian statehood render the taking of French nationality almost literally unthinkable (Sayad 1987).

Table 3.4 Proportion of immigrants having acquired French national-ity, by selected national origins, 1990

Current or previous nationality	% of immigrants now French nationals	% of immigrants aged >64
EC	40.2	24.2
Spanish	54.0	31.6
Italian	57.4	40.6
Portuguese	16.7	3.4
Polish	68.3	64.4
Algerian	12.7	6.7
Moroccan	11.3	2.3
Tunisian	25.8	7.4
Ex-French sub-Saharan Africa	18.9	0.7
Ex-French Indo-China	42.0	7.5
Turkish	7.7	3.9
Chilean	33.4	3.7
Haitian	21.6	1.1

Source: INSEE 1992a: Tables 11, 12.

As a general rule, the rate of naturalization among immigrants increases with the length of settlement, but there are marked differences between different national groups (Table 3.4). Among Europeans, the correlation between naturalization rates and length of settlement is fairly constant. Mass migration from Poland ceased several decades ago. Almost two-thirds of the immigrants from that country are now aged 65 or over, and more than two-thirds have acquired French nationality. At the opposite end of the scale, only 3.4 per cent of Portuguese immigrants are of retirement age, with 16.7 per cent now French nationals. Although Algerian immigrants of retirement age are, proportionately, almost twice as numerous as those originating in Portugal, a much smaller percentage has taken French nationality. The ideological legacy of colonization weighs less heavily on immigrants from former French sub-Saharan Africa, less than 1 per cent of whom are aged over 65; already, almost 19 per cent have taken French nationality. Similarly, immigrants from former French Indo-China have extremely high naturalization rates. In part, this reflects the fact that a large proportion of them are refugees who feel no allegiance to the state as presently constituted in their country of origin, making a return even more mythical than it is for many economic migrants. A similar point applies to Chileans and Haitians.

Until the 1993 reform of the French nationality code, most children born in France to immigrant parents automatically became French nationals on reaching the age of majority. In principle, they were free to decline French citizenship, but very few actually did so (Catani and Palidda 1989). The position of children born to Algerian immigrants was rather different, and remains largely untouched by the 1993 reform. Those born before Algerian independence in 1962 held French nationality until then, but lost it that year unless they or their parents specifically requested to keep it. They can, if they wish, resume French citizenship, and some have exercised this right. Somewhat paradoxically, children born to Algerian immigrants since independence are automatically French from birth. At the same time, however, they are considered by the Algerian state to be Algerian nationals. This is because the nationalists who successfully fought to obtain Algerian independence refused to acknowledge the legitimacy of French sovereignty during the colonial period. As Algerian nationality law is based on *jus sanguinis*, Algerian nationals automatically pass on citizenship to their descendants, regardless of where these are born. Children born to Algerian immigrants in France since 1962 are therefore *de facto* bi-nationals from birth, for both the French and the Algerian authorities regard them as citizens of their respective states (Costa-Lascoux 1983).

Because of the bitter legacy of the war of independence (Stora 1991), the nationality status of these youngsters is a matter of acute sensitivity on all sides. Almost 3 million Frenchmen fought in the

Algerian War, leaving deep scars of suspicion and resentment towards those of Algerian origin who now live in France. The automatic acquisition of French citizenship by children whose parents supported the nationalist cause is considered by a significant part of the majority population to be unacceptable. According to the official Algerian version of events, 1 million Algerians died during the war (a lower but still fearsome figure is given by most historians). Their sacrifice makes the tenure of French citizenship by modern-day Algerians an equally unacceptable proposition in the eyes of those with first-hand memories of the war.

The conflicting claims of France and Algeria concerning the descendants of immigrants are nowhere more sensitive than in the matter of military service, which is often regarded as the most potent symbol of national allegiance. When they began to reach their late teens at the end of the 1970s, young men born to Algerian immigrant parents after 1962 found that, as nationals of two states, they were called upon to do military service in both France and Algeria. Failure to fulfil this duty rendered them liable to imprisonment, as some discovered to their cost when they visited Algeria after ignoring or never receiving their call-up papers. In 1983, France and Algeria signed an agreement under which military service performed in one country enabled the young men concerned (though still not formally recognized by Algeria as bi-nationals) to be dispensed from being drafted by the other (Babadji 1992). According to a French Defence Ministry report issued in 1990, at the most three in ten Franco-Algerian bi-nationals were reporting for duty in Algeria; the rest chose to serve in France (Biville 1990; Faivre 1990: 33).[7]

Bearing in mind the symbolic significance of military service in the eyes of immigrant parents, and the psychological pressure often brought to bear on their children as a consequence of this, the high proportion of Franco-Algerian bi-nationals opting for France is quite striking. It should not be assumed, however, that military service has the same symbolic status in the eyes of the younger generation. For many, it is simply a legal obligation, like paying taxes or carrying an identity card; for practical purposes, it is necessary to comply in order to enjoy the benefits of citizenship, but that is not the same as saying that draftees automatically feel patriotic. The high proportion opting for France may simply be a reflection of the greater practical difficulties associated with Algeria, where military service is longer, material conditions are poorer and the prevailing cultural codes are less familiar.

Opponents of *jus soli* often argue that it allows the descendants of immigrants to enjoy the benefits of citizenship without feeling
a true allegiance to the French state. Fears of an 'enemy within'
reached a paroxysm during the Gulf War of 1991, when France
joined the mainly Western coalition against Iraq's occupation of
Kuwait. Even allowing for the fact that a sizeable proportion of
Maghrebi immigrants are Berbers, France has by far the largest Arab
population of any country in Western Europe. During the early stages
of the war, the French media engaged in near-hysterical speculation
over the possibility of immigrants and their descendants serving as
a Fifth Column in support of Saddam Hussein (Hargreaves and
Stenhouse 1992; Rachedi 1994). On the day the allied coalition
forces launched their air attack against the Iraqis, *Le Monde* (17
January 1991), France's most respected newspaper, reported that
'four out of five Beurs are thought to be admirers to a greater or lesser
extent of Saddam Hussein'. In an opinion poll conducted a fortnight
into the war, 70 per cent of French interviewees said they thought it
likely there would be serious incidents involving the country's
Muslim population (SOFRES 1992: 138). It was widely feared that
there might be fighting between France's Arab and Jewish populations. In the event, no such disorders occurred, and when public
opinion polls were conducted among the Muslim population they
found that only one in five (exactly the opposite of the ratio claimed
by *Le Monde*) backed Saddam Hussein; two out of three said they
were opposed to his policies (SOFRES poll in *L'Express*, 8 February
1991; cf. IFOP poll in *Le Figaro*, 29 January 1991).

No less remarkably, in a poll conducted among young Maghrebis
almost three years later, two-thirds said that if France came under
military attack they would be willing to defend the country (SOFRES
poll in *Le Nouvel Observateur*, 2 December 1993). Only one in five
– a proportion similar to that opting for the draft in Algeria and
expressing support for Saddam Hussein – said they would refuse to
defend France. As the poll did not include a parallel sample of young
people of French descent, no direct comparison can be made, but it
is by no means impossible that a significant number of them, too,
would have reservations about military engagement.

Nation-states can no longer claim to exercise a monopoly of rights
over the territorial identification of their citizens. That monopoly was
never complete, and it is being steadily eroded by powerful trans-
national forces, of which international migration is but one example.
At the same time, local particularisms are reasserting themselves in

new ways. These sub- and trans-national currents are vividly combined in the gang cultures which have recently blossomed among youths of immigrant origin in the *banlieues* of many French cities. Modern urban spaces have long been marked by gang-style assertions of local territorial control by young men (women are seldom involved) experiencing difficulty in establishing a secure place in the socio-economic hierarchy. What is new in France is the prominence of young men from immigrant families displaying highly visible markers of ethnic differentiation. Most come from ethnicized groups suffering high levels of discrimination and socio-economic exclusion: above all, Maghrebis, sub-Saharan Africans and DOM-TOMiens.

Gangs are not necessarily criminally-orientated. While some commit violent acts, many infringe no laws more serious than those prohibiting excessive noise or the unauthorized painting of public buildings. Firearms, the scourge of American gang life, are seen relatively little in the French *banlieues*. Excluded from socio-economic incorporation by high levels of unemployment, gang members seek self-esteem and solidarity by reappropriating anony-mous urban spaces at a neighbourhood level. Their assertion of territorial control over parts of the *banlieues* may seem at first sight to confirm French fears of ghettoization. Yet such an interpretation is in many ways misguided. Gangs of this kind seldom recruit from a single ethnic group, and they never mobilize more than a small minority of the population in a given area (Dubet 1987; Jazouli 1992: 139–50).

During the disorders which broke out in several French cities in 1990–1, police were occasionally given instructions to limit their presence and/or turn a blind eye to certain offences in order to reduce tension. This led to talk of 'no-go' areas beyond the control of the state emerging in certain *banlieues*, but the authorities were quick to reassert themselves, ensuring that no districts were closed to them (*Le Monde*, 30 May 1991, 18 June 1991). The dominant forms of territorial appropriation practised by most gangs are more symbolic in nature. They function visually (by marking territory with a type of graffiti known as *tagging*), verbally (using particular forms of slang to establish linguistic in-groups) and musically (through loud performances of rap and other imported idioms) (Kokoreff 1991).

The lingua franca of all these groups is French. While their cultural codes also draw substantially on elements originating outside metropolitan France, they are not in any substantive way engaged in the mobilization of pre-migratory cultures. Maghrebi gang-members, for example, speak little if any Arabic, know virtually nothing of Islam and, if they refer to their parents' religion at all, do so almost solely as a provocation, knowing that it causes consternation among the majority population (Roy 1991, 1994: 65). The trans-national cultural codes on which these gangs draw most heavily originate in what Gilroy (1993) has called the Black Atlantic, a cultural archipelago stretching from sub-Saharan Africa through the Caribbean and into the black ghettos of the United States; the Maghreb (where most young people of Third World origin in France have their ancestral roots) offers certain parallels but is not directly part of this space.

The most influential model for youth gangs of immigrant origin in France is the Zulu Nation, founded in New York in 1975 by the black American activist Africa Bambatta. Since the mid-1980s, its example has been followed in many of France's *banlieues*. Most of these gangs, who refer to themselves generically as Zulus, have chosen American–English names such as Black Dragon, Criminal Action Force and Fight Boys (*Le Nouvel Observateur*, 9 October 1990). They dress in the stylized fashion of young black Americans, incorporate liberal doses of American English into their linguistic codes, and have adapted the rhythms of rap into newly inflected forms of French. While physically confined to small localities within particular *banlieues*, in their signifying practices they are part of a global post-colonial culture. As Kokoreff (1991: 36) puts it: 'The Zulus [in France] live in a world situated somewhere between Manhattan, Dakar and Saint-Denis [a northern Paris suburb].' There is here a certain kind of ethnicity. Gang members share linguistic and other codes and identify with particular territories, both concrete and mythical. Gang cultures do not, however, represent a con-tinuation of the cultural traditions imported by immigrants. They owe far more to the youth cultures of France and the Black Atlantic, with which they interface through the mass media (Roy 1993).

While only a minority of immigrant-born youths are gang mem-bers, there is among them a much wider identification with the trans-national nexus at the heart of gang cultures. This does not necessarily imply hostility towards French cultural norms. Many youths of French descent have also assimilated elements of both black Atlantic and white American culture through the US-dominated mass media. Although not of French origin, these are now *de facto* parts of the culture of France. In identifying with them, young people of immigrant origin leave far behind the cultural heritage of their parents while not ostensibly melting into a specifically French cultural mould. These cultural cross-currents traverse the many rock bands formed by young musicians of immigrant origin (Moreira 1987). They are perhaps best summed up in the rendering of 'Douce France' (Sweet France) recorded by Carte de Séjour, one of the top bands formed by immigrant-born Maghrebis. The song, with its chorus 'Sweet France, my dear childhood home', was first made famous by the archetypal French crooner Charles Trenet. As re-recorded by Carte de Séjour in 1986, the words are sung with intermittent Arab tonalities over an American-inspired disco beat picked out in a combination of African and Western instruments. There are many deliberate ironies in this, but also a deep underlying seriousness, for in the hearts of countless immigrant-born youths France is indeed home, in the fullest sense of the word.

POLITICAL MOBILIZATION

Because people of immigrant origin identify strongly with cultural codes which are not co-terminous with French national boundaries, they are often mistrusted by members of the majority population, who suspect them of harbouring projects of ethnic separatism. Pushed to their ultimate extreme, such projects might theoretically threaten the political integrity of the French state. Yet if we define political mobilization as collective actions designed to influence the constituent elements and decision-making machinery of the state, there is little evidence to suggest that minority ethnic groups are mobilizing in a separatist direction.

In an analysis of minority ethnic groups in Britain, Miles and Phizacklea (1977) usefully distinguish between three main modes of political mobilization: class unity, black unity, and ethnic organ-ization. Class unity brings together people of majority and minority origin in pursuit of common socio-economic interests. As understood at that time in Britain, 'black' unity signified the organizational coalescence of diverse minority ethnic groups (including Asians as well as Afro-Caribbeans) in pursuit of goals defined by their shared minority status. In the present context, it might better be termed 'minority ethnic' unity. Ethnic organization, by contrast, is char-acterized by separate forms of mobilization on the part of each minority group. Applying this typology to France, we shall see that no single form of mobilization dominates.

Ethnic organization

As noted earlier in this chapter, there are many thousands of
associations run by people of immigrant origin in France. The
majority serve particular ethno-cultural groups, rather than minority
ethnic people as a whole. However, this is obviously not the same
as saying that they are engaged in political separatism. Most exist to
serve either the welfare needs or the cultural interests of particular
groups. French nationals who give voluntary help to medical research
charities or local drama societies or who are active in their local
church are engaged in activities which are separate from and wholly
compatible with any political activities which they might wish to
pursue within the normal framework of the law. The same applies to
immigrants and their descendants who set up advice centres, language
classes or places of worship catering for members of particular ethno-
cultural groups.

Even supposing that a separatist project existed, few minority
groups control an autonomous resource base sufficient to sustain it.
As noted in Chapter 2, there are few if any cases of self-contained
economic enclaves. Most minority groups are dependent on native
employers and/or markets. Were it not for their ready access to the
benefits of the welfare state, minority groups suffering from high
rates of unemployment might perhaps have developed more extensive mutual support networks than those which actually exist. Yet
even Schmitter Heisler (1986: 82), who has argued that groups of
recent immigrant origin are unusually resistant to the processes of
acculturation and assimilation, acknowledges that their inclusion in
the system of material support afforded by the welfare state has to a
large extent stunted the growth of autonomous financial institutions.

First-generation members of minority ethnic groups – particularly
those who have come to France as political refugees – sometimes
work for radical political change in their countries of origin.
Expatriates from countries such as Portugal and, until recently,
Morocco have been allowed by their home country to elect Members
of Parliament to represent them in the national legislature. Sending
states pursuing such a policy have seen it as a means of retaining the
loyalty of their citizens (Miller 1981: 30–82). Such activities have
little direct bearing on French political life. As foreigners, most
immigrants are excluded from electoral or governmental participation within France. Consultative mechanisms have been established
by a number of local councils. Since 1985, half a dozen towns have

gone as far as allowing foreign residents to elect 'associate councillors', but the turn-out has often been low, probably because those
elected in this way have no voting rights within the city council
(Centre des Cultures Méditerranéennes 1989: 167–227). While the
Maastricht Treaty, signed in 1992, gives citizens of European Union
(EU) member-states the right to vote in local and European (but not
national) elections, the implementation of local voting rights in
France appears likely to be delayed until the year 2001 (*Le Monde*,
12 July 1994). As the majority of foreign residents in France are from
non-EU states, they remain wholly excluded from the electoral
process.

This has suited sending states wishing to retain the active identification of their citizens. However, those states have found it
virtually impossible to sustain a comparable grip on the descendants
of immigrants. Until recently, for example, Algeria urged second-
generation members of the expatriate population in France not to use
the political rights which were theirs under the terms of French
nationality laws, but this approach proved wholly ineffectual. By the
second half of the 1980s, growing numbers of young Franco-
Algerian bi-nationals were registering as voters and standing as
candidates in French elections. Realizing that they were acting
completely independently of its own concerns, the Algerian government belatedly backtracked on its advice and encouraged the
descendants of immigrants to exercise their rights as French citizens
under the aegis of a newly created youth organization run by its own
front organization in France, the Amicale des Algériens en Europe.
The initiative failed almost completely, and the Amicale itself is now
virtually defunct (Hargreaves 1990).

Minority ethnic unity

Attempts to unite all residents of immigrant origin in concerted
political action are hampered not only by the lack of voting rights
among non-citizens but also by deep differences between, and indeed
within, different minority groups. Why should Spanish or Italian
immigrants share the concerns of Turks or other Muslims who feel
moved to demonstrate over matters such as the headscarf affair? In
its organizational structures, the Muslim population as a whole has
itself been characterized by deep national and ideological divisions
(Kepel 1987; Etienne 1989). Since the early 1980s, several attempts
have been made at establishing an all-embracing federation of

Islamic associations in France; all have foundered on irreconcilable differences between rival organizations (Nielsen 1992: 18–19; Roy 1994: 57). Nationally defined ethnic groups such as the Turks or Vietnamese are also split by major ideological rifts (Gokalp 1992; Le Huu Khoa 1985).

Potentially, the strongest basis on which to make a common cause is probably anti-racism, for this is in principle an interest shared by many minority groups. However, by no means all groups of immigrant origin feel equally threatened. There is a wealth of evidence to show that Europeans now suffer comparatively little racism. The main victims are visible minorities, above all Maghrebis. Afro-Caribbeans and sub-Saharan Africans also suffer to a significant degree, whereas South-East Asians are less affected (see pp. 151–7 below for further details). Since the beginning of the 1980s, young people of immigrant origin have led a series of anti-racist initiatives. The earliest of these was Rock Against Police, a series of concerts organized in 1980–1 (*Questions clefs* 1982). A nationwide March Against Racism in 1983 was followed by several similar demonstrations over the next few years (Jazouli 1986: 113–99). In the autumn of 1984, SOS-Racisme was launched. It quickly gained widespread media coverage by enrolling well-known figures from the world of entertainment in support of its anti-racist message, and although it is now less forceful than it once was, it continues to exert considerable influence (Désir 1985; Malik 1990). While young people of French descent have given support to some of these initiatives, particularly SOS-Racisme, relatively few of European immigrant origin have done so. Only a handful of young Asians joined the 1983 march and a similar one held the following year (Le Huu Khoa 1987: 78–81). Even young Afro-Caribbeans, who unquestionably suffer serious discrimination, have sometimes hesitated to join in, for as French nationals they are reluctant to associate themselves publicly with what are seen as 'immigrant' initiatives (*Le Monde*, 11 December 1991).

Theoretically broad anti-racist fronts have therefore mobilized in practice rather more narrow ethnic constituencies. Like Rock Against Police, the 1983 march was dominated by young Maghrebis. Though oficially called the *Marche pour l'égalité et contre le racisme* (March Against Racism and for Equality), it was retitled by the media the *Marche des Beurs* (March of the Beurs). In the follow-up march, *Convergence 84*, a conscious effort was made to involve Asian, Portuguese and sub-Saharan African youths alongside Maghrebis

(Rodrigues *et al.* 1985), but the demonstration was plagued by internal dissension, and the overall turn-out was less than half that achieved by the 1983 march.

SOS-Racisme has always emphasized its multi-ethnic membership, but it has been hampered from the outset by deep suspicions on the part of Maghrebis, who feel it has unfairly taken the limelight off them and dislike its willingness to co-operate with Jewish anti-racists (Hargreaves 1991b). The rift between SOS-Racisme and leading Maghrebi activists finds its most visible expression in the rivalry between it and France-Plus, which was founded in 1985. The primary purpose of France-Plus is to mobilize young Maghrebis as an electoral force based on the citizenship rights enjoyed by the descendants of immigrants. Its leader, Arezki Dahmani, has often spoken of the organization as an ethnic lobby, the potential power of which lies in the demographic importance of Maghrebis, who, if taken together, constitute the largest single minority ethnic group in France. Unlike SOS-Racisme, which seeks minority ethnic unity, France-Plus is based on the principle of ethnic organization. As will be shown below, however, in its practical achievements France-Plus appears to be furthering the class interests of a small elite rather than a collective ethno-cultural project.

Class unity

Opinion surveys and exit polls conducted among people of immigrant origin consistently show very high levels of political support for the Left, particularly the French Socialist Party (PS) (see, for example, the exit-poll data in Leveau and Wihtol de Wenden 1991: 4–9, and the SOFRES polls in *L'Express*, 30 March 1990; *Le Nouvel Observateur*, 13 May 1993). As minority ethnic groups are heavily concentrated at the lower end of the socio-economic hierarchy, these findings are not especially surprising, for most French voters of a similar socio-economic standing also favour the Left. There are two notable exceptions to this pattern. The first concerns the *harkis*, who are much more conservative than economic migrants in their political loyalties; the children of both groups, however, display similar Leftist sympathies, which suggests that their underlying class position outweighs the peculiar political heritage of the older generation (Souida 1990: 63). Asians are the other main exception. Among those expressing an opinion in the 1990 SOFRES survey, sympathies were evenly divided between the Left and the Right. Again, this is consistent with the higher levels of self-employment and entre-preneurship among people of Asian origin as compared with the majority of immigrants.

The triumph of class interests over ethnic origins appears to be confirmed by the poor showing of candidates campaigning on minority ethnic tickets. Very few have succeeded in mobilizing even the financial resources necessary to stand as candidates. In the 1986 regional elections, for example, which were fought under a list system in each *département*, a slate of minority-ethnic candidates was fielded in just one *département*, Val-de-Marne, where it took less than 0.5 per cent of the vote. In those elections, all the main parties had included for the first time a few candidates of Maghrebi origin on their lists. However, they were tiny in number and none was placed in a winnable position under the system of proportional representation used in those elections. In the run-up to the 1989 municipal elections, France-Plus fixed its sights on persuading the main parties to include Maghrebis in winnable positions on their lists of candidates. It proved quite successful in this, helping to secure the inclusion of about a thousand Maghrebi candidates, several hundred of whom won seats on town councils (Hargreaves 1991b: 362–4).

Research into candidate-selection procedures suggests, however, that many of those put forward by France-Plus had little experience of grass-roots activism among the Maghrebi population (Geisser 1992; Poinsot 1993). Unlike the majority of Maghrebis, whose sympathies are heavily to the Left, the candidates who won council seats were fairly evenly spread across the party lists of the Left and Right. There appear to have been no negotiations over the policy platforms of different parties: Maghrebis accepted as candidates simply fell in line with pre-defined manifestos (Bouamama 1989). France-Plus has never pursued a distinctive ethno-cultural agenda, such as the promotion of Islam. The organization's watchword is in fact 'integration' (*Etre Français aujourd'hui et demain* 1988: I, 467–8), principally by the provision of better opportunities for Maghrebis who, as an ethnicized group, suffer severe discrimination and disadvantage. In socio-economic terms, those elected with the support of France-Plus are generally of higher status than the mass of Maghrebis. Their election as town councillors has given them additional status without necessarily bringing any tangible benefits to Maghrebis at large. In line with its own class interests as part of the upwardly mobile segment of Maghrebis, this small elite appears to have been moving steadily away from its supposed ethnic base (Cesari 1992). The urban disorders seen during the early 1990s have been widely interpreted as expressions of frustration by the most disadvantaged sections of that base, who feel that those in authority have abandoned them to chronic unemployment and unacceptable housing (Begag 1991; Hargreaves forthcoming).

For young people of immigrant origin hoping to escape from the low socio-economic status to which most of their parents were confined, education is of pivotal importance. In the autumn of 1986, and again in 1990, nationwide demonstrations by high-school and university students were marked by the very visible participation of immigrant-born activists alongside those of French descent (Bryson 1987; Mestiri 1988; Jazouli 1992: 151–2). On both occasions, the protests were against government policies which were felt to be disadvantaging poorer sections of the population, particularly in the *banlieues*, in the struggle for access to high-quality education. The headscarf affair prompted no comparable mobilization among the student population of immigrant origin. The handful of girls con-fronting school authorities on a matter of Islamic conviction were almost completely isolated; support groups organized by classmates were few and far between and tended to be motivated more by anti-discriminatory than by pro-Islamic sentiments.

While it is clear that socio-economic interests and anti-racism have generally outweighed the promotion of ethno-cultural dif-ferences in mobilizing people of immigrant origin, Ireland (1994: 76, 85) has correctly pointed out that the younger generation is often reluctant to identify with traditional working-class organizations such as the French Communist Party (PCF). During the 1990 student demonstrations, for example, SOS-Racisme and the Young Com-munists pursued similar objectives but through competing organ-izational structures. The PCF, like the PS, has often behaved in an ambivalent way towards immigrants and their descendants, partly because working-class people of French descent have been far from immune to racism. The anti-immigrant Front National (FN) has, indeed, drawn a significant measure of support from working-class voters (Mayer 1987). Thus while real or perceived class interests are certainly significant in shaping the political behaviour of immigrants and their descendants, class unity between them and members of the majority population is far from assured (Tripier 1990; Gallissot, Boumaza and Clément 1994).

CONCLUSION

Events such as the headscarf affair and the Gulf War have brought to the fore French anxieties over the social incorporation of people of recent immigrant origin. Physically visible in ways that earlier immigrants were not, those from Islamic countries are incapable of 'melting' anonymously into the social fabric. As the coming-of-age of their descendants has coincided with a more strident political posture by Islamic states such as Iran, it has been easy to assume that France is faced within her own borders by potentially explosive tensions generated by the presence of new ethno-cultural minorities. In fact, all the evidence examined in this chapter points in a very different direction. While some immigrants do adhere to cultural codes which clash in certain respects with the prevailing norms in France, there is little evidence to suggest that clashes of this kind are being reproduced by succeeding generations. In the overwhelming majority of cases, the descendants of immigrants – whether they come from Europe, Africa or Asia – identify more closely with France's dominant cultural norms than with those of their parents.

This is not to say that minority ethno-cultural norms cease to exert any influence at all or that the role-models of immigrant-born citizens – any more than those of the majority population – are purely French. On a per capita basis, the Portuguese population is believed to have a denser network of voluntary associations than any other minority group in France (Wihtol de Wenden 1988: 364; Hily and Poinard 1987). This, together with the relatively generous provision of state support for mother-tongue teaching and the geographical proximity of Portugal, which makes it easy for families to pay regular visits to the home country, has enabled the Portuguese to maintain closer cultural ties than many other groups of recent immigrant origin. There is no incompatibility between this and what is universally judged to be the successful incorporation of the Portuguese into French society. Their unemployment rates are lower than those of the native population, they are seldom the victims of racial discrimination, and they are virtually invisible in contentious parts of the political arena.

The spatial distribution of minority groups in France is such that mono-ethnic neighbourhoods are extremely rare and never at all extensive. The densest micro-concentrations are probably those of South-East Asians, particularly ethnic Chinese, in areas such as the Choisy Triangle. It is often said that the Chinese function as a more self-enclosed community than any other minority group. Yet South-East Asians – large numbers of whom are ethnic Chinese – have exceptionally high rates of naturalization, acquiring full citizenship after only a few years of residence. It is seldom suggested that there is any contradiction between the relatively high level of economic and cultural self-sufficiency sustained by the Chinese and their rapid admission to full rights within the political community of France.

Suspicions of separatism or malevolent intentions towards French norms are reserved primarily for Muslim immigrants and their descendants. As these groups are very much larger than those originating in South-East Asia, it is theoretically conceivable that dense concentrations might provide the basis for a significant separatist project. Concentrations of that kind do not exist. No less importantly, there is no evidence to indicate that a political project inimical to the integrity of the French state is seriously harboured by anything other than the tiniest of minorities. Far from being a serious attempt at severing their links with the rest of society, the challenge to local police thrown down by young people involved in recent urban disorders is first and foremost a distress signal: by attracting the attention of the media, those concerned hope to force the authorities to redress the lack of opportunities open to ethnicized groups relegated to the *banlieues* (Hargreaves forthcoming).

Only one in five of the young Maghrebis questioned by SOFRES for *Le Nouvel Observateur* (2 December 1993) said they felt closer to the culture of their parents than to that of the French. Seven out of ten said the opposite. Nine out of ten young people from Muslim families questioned in the survey by Muxel (1988: 928) expressed a strong desire to be integrated into French society, as did eight out of ten from Catholic immigrant backgrounds. If young Maghrebis have been more assertive politically than young Iberians, this is not because they are less acculturated but because, on the contrary, they share to a very large extent the values and aspirations of their French peers but are denied a fair chance of fulfilling their amibitions as a consequence of social and economic discrimination by members of the majority population (Lapeyronnie 1987). The biggest long-term obstacle to 'integration' lies not in the cultural heritage of recent immigrants and their descendants but in the barriers placed in their way by the French themselves. These pressures, which reached a symbolic peak in the reform of French nationality laws, are examined in the next chapter.

Chapter 4

National identity, nationality and citizenship

IMMIGRATION AND NATIONAL IDENTITY

In the modern world, the most potent forms of ethnic identification are generally those associated with nationhood. So powerful and omnipresent are the signs of national belonging that majority populations seldom refer to themselves as ethnic groups at all. National identity is apt to be seen as the 'natural' condition of the majority, while ethnic belonging is an exceptional condition ascribed only to minorities. In reality, nations are simply ethno-cultural groups which acquire or aspire to the legitimacy associated with statehood, i.e. political sovereignty over a territory whose boundaries are recognized in international law. The extent to which immigrants and their descendants are incorporated into nation-states depends not only on socio-economic processes of the kind examined in Chapter 2, together with the values and aspirations of minority ethnic groups, considered in Chapter 3, but also on the attitudes and behaviour of the majority population both in civil society and at the level of the state. This chapter considers how far immigrants and their descendants are accepted, both formally and informally, as part of the French national community.

If individual members of the receiving society are hostile towards people of immigrant origin, this self-evidently makes their incorporation more difficult. Barriers of this kind are all the more potent if they have the backing of the state. Some of the ways in which the state discriminates against non-nationals are considered below (pp. 197–201). After an analysis of mass attitudes towards minority groups, the main focus of the present chapter falls on the rules governing the formal dividing-line between French nationals and foreigners. As generally understood today, French nationality is

virtually synonymous with French citizenship, and the two expressions are used more or less interchangeably, though in the past
they have often diverged (Borella 1991). Nationality, and the
citizenship embedded in it, consists of a range of rights and duties
which are reserved for those who are recognized in law as members
of the nation-state. In a formal sense, citizenship is associated
particularly with political rights. Broader concepts of citizenship,
pioneered by Marshall (1950), have now been stretched so wide that
they sometimes embrace almost any form of social participation
(Martiniello 1994). In the present context, citizenship is to be
understood in the narrower sense of formal national membership,
including the right to participate in the political processes through
which the state is governed.

Nations have played and continue to play a crucial role in
structuring the modern world, not least because of an unresolved
tension between their cultural and political axes. If we define nations
as cultural entities, their boundaries are contingent on subjective
relationships binding together groups of individuals who may or may
not constitute a spatially distinct whole. If we define nations as
political units, their boundaries are marked by the territorial limits
within which states exercise sovereignty. Defined thus, the cultural
and political boundaries of nations seldom coincide exactly. The
urge to make them coincide has, however, been a major force in
modern history. Cultural communities have sought to fulfil their
sense of nationhood by constructing and defending state boundaries
against outsiders, while states have frequently attempted to control
or in some cases eliminate cultural diversity within their borders.

By their very nature, immigrants cut across this homogenizing
imperative, for they are born without the citizenship of the country
in which they reside, and the cultural norms internalized in their
country of origin differ from those prevailing in the receiving
society. Depending on the circumstances, however, immigrants and
their descendants may be accepted or even positively welcomed,
while at other times they may be shunned or forcibly expelled.

In formal terms, there are two main ways in which non-nationals
may be incorporated into a nationally defined society. One is by
granting residence and other rights within the national territory, but
not the political rights associated with formal citizenship. The other
is by granting full citizenship to people of foreign origin. The extent
to which national boundaries are open on either or both of these
levels varies from one state to another and also across time.

Compared with many other states, France has traditionally been relatively open in both respects, but since the early 1970s she has become more exclusionary. During the 1970s, stricter controls on residence and work permits were introduced with the aim of limiting, and if possible reducing, the foreign population. In the mid-1980s, the laws governing access to French nationality became the subject of intense political debate, culminating with the passage of restrictive legislation in 1993.

Since the early 1980s, it has become commonplace in France to claim that immigration is a threat to national identity.[1] Two-thirds of those questioned in a 1985 opinion poll said France was in danger of losing her national identity if nothing was done to limit the foreign population (BVA poll in *Paris-Match*, 29 November 1985). By 1989, that view was shared by three-quarters of respondents (BVA poll in *Paris-Match*, 14 December 1989). The theme of national identity was brought into the political limelight by the rise of the extreme right-wing Front National (FN), campaigning on a vigorously anti-immigrant platform. Responding to this shift in the political agenda, the traditional parties of both Left and Right organized major debates on the theme of French identity in the spring of 1985 (Espaces 89 1985; Club de l'Horloge 1985); a few months later the neo-Gaullist Rassemblement Pour la République (RPR) and centrist Union pour la Démocratie Française (UDF) announced joint proposals aimed at restricting the access of foreigners to French nationality.

While political and cultural factors have certainly played a significant role in these changes, the most fundamental force pushing in this direction has been economic. Growing acceptance of immigrants during the post-war period was largely attributable to the perceived need to meet labour shortages by importing foreign workers. It is no accident that more restrictive attitudes have become dominant since the mid-1970s in a context of growing concern over unemployment, which has been sustained at levels which are almost without precedent this century. As economic circumstances have changed, the state has attempted to improve conditions in the labour market by opening or closing access to it by non-nationals.

Even formal incorporation is not enough to ensure that immigrants and their descendants enjoy genuine equality of opportunity. As was seen in Chapter 2, people of foreign descent, particularly those of Third World origin, frequently experience discriminatory treatment even when they are French nationals. Discrimination of this kind has been amply documented not only in relation to young French nationals born of African parents originating both north and south of the Sahara but also in relation to first- and second-generation DOM-TOMiens, whose ancestors have in many cases been formally French for centuries (CNCDH 1992: 40–2; Galap 1993). While cultural differences sometimes help to account for discriminatory behaviour, cruder exclusionary reflexes are often involved. In cultural terms, many of those who suffer discrimination differ little, if at all, from the mass of the population. Their exclusion arises, rather, from competition in the fields of employment or resource allocation, where some members of society seek to rig markets against vulnerable sections of the population, notably those with non-white skins, who are easily branded as 'outsiders'.

Just as the formal and informal construction of the national community is conditioned by changes over time, so it is also shaped by the particularities of the outsiders with whom its members find themselves in contact. National identity derives its content from implicit or explicit dividing-lines which are taken to separate the nation from those who stand outside it. The significance attached to particular others depends on the contingencies of geography and history and the way in which these are reworked in the light of current preoccupations. If some outsiders are seen as more alien than others, their incorporation into the national community is likely to appear particularly problematic. A substantial body of data exists to show that among the French at large immigrants are viewed through the prism of a long-established ethnic hierarchy. The hierarchy itself has changed relatively little in the course of the twentieth century, but its practical implications have varied considerably as a consequence of political, economic and demographic changes affecting french society.[2]

Current perceptions of different ethnic groups are typified by the results of a 1989 public opinion poll in which respondents were asked to state which out of four groups of immigrants would be the most difficult to integrate into French society. For 50 per cent of respondents, the single most problematic group consisted of Maghrebis; 19 per cent were mainly concerned by sub-Saharan Africans, 15 per cent by Asians, and 2 per cent by Europeans (BVA poll in *Paris-Match*, 14 December 1989). Half a century earlier Georges Mauco, who was to become an influential figure in French immigration policy, had conducted a survey among employers asking which ethnic groups were the best foreign workers. The classification which emerged was headed by workers from neighbouring European states such as Belgium and Italy; Central Europeans were concentrated in the middle ranks; while the Chinese, Greeks and Arabs filled the last three places (1937 survey, cited in Weil 1991: 35, 360).

Immediately after the Second World War, Mauco and others argued for the official adoption of a similar ethnic hierarchy through the application of quotas in French immigration policy. While not formally adopted in law, this hierarchy structured many important administrative practices (Weil 1991: 53–75), though for the reasons noted above (pp. 11–12), the authorities proved unable to prevent the main sources of migratory inflows shifting from Europe to Africa and Asia. The absence of sub-Saharan Africans from Mauco's company survey reflected their numerical insignificance in pre-war and early post-war France. In a large-scale public opinion survey conducted in 1951 by the Institut National d'Etudes Démographiques (INED), Maghrebis[3] were the only non-European group cited in a list of ten ethnic groups on which respondents were invited to comment. Asked to say how readily the different groups were capable of adapting to the French way of life, interviewees placed Belgians and Italians at the top of the list, Central Europeans lower down and Maghrebis last of all except for Germans. An almost identical ranking emerged in response to a question on which groups were most liked (Girard and Stoetzel 1953: 144).

The close parallel between levels of personal liking and the evaluation of the capacity of different groups to fit into French society, which recurs in more recent surveys, raises an important question: are certain ethnic groups liked more than others because they fit in easily, or do they appear to fit in more easily because they are made more welcome? This is linked in turn to the question of whether hierarchical ethnicization of this kind is a reflection of significant cultural differences or the product of political or other circumstances. The low regard for Germans recorded in the 1951 survey is undoubtedly a reflection of the unhappy political relationship between France and Germany, which had reached its nadir in the Nazi occupation of France during the Second World War. Similarly, while the low ranking of Asians and Arabs in the Mauco and INED surveys may well arise in part from a greater cultural distance separating them (compared with Europeans) from the native French population, it is probably also conditioned by the political fact of colonization. The ideology of colonial domination was built on the alleged inferiority of non-Europeans. The widespread view that colonized peoples differed from the French to a far greater degree than Europeans helped to underpin the colonial system, and was reinforced by it in turn.

Less than thirty years after the end of the Second World War, an INED survey showed that the Germans had risen markedly in French esteem, while Maghrebis and sub-Saharan Africans (who had now been added to the list of groups mentioned in the questionnaire) scored the lowest rankings (*Population* 1971). The healing powers of time are not in themselves sufficient to explain this evolution. Today, well over thirty years after the final phase in the liquidation of France's overseas empire, marked by Algerian independence in 1962, people originating in former colonial territories still occupy the lowest positions in French perceptions of different ethnic groups. Since 1957, France and Germany have been political partners in the construction of what was initially known as the European Economic Community; in addition, under the terms of a Treaty of Friendship signed in 1963, the highest authorities in both countries have actively sought to overcome past enmities through bilateral programmes of co-operation involving the public at large. There has been no comparable investment aimed at overcoming the divisive memories and attitudes inherited from the colonial period.

This legacy is clearly visible in the results of a survey conducted in 1984 asking whether different groups were perceived as well or badly integrated into French society (Table 4.1). The hierarchy which emerges is very similar to that seen in pre-war and and early post-war surveys, with West Europeans at the top, Central and East Europeans in the middle, and Africans at the bottom. Algerians, whose struggle for independence left deep scars in the French national psyche, are seen as by far the least well-integrated group. Moroccans and Tunisians, who are culturally similar to Algerians but gained their independence at the cost of relatively little violence, score less badly. The relatively favourable evaluation of Asians probably reflects the political sympathy enjoyed by refugees who fled to France from south-east Asia after the fall of Saigon in 1975. Memories of the Indo-China war of decolonization, which ended in French defeat in 1954 and which might have left an enduring legacy of enmity, appear to have been effaced subsequently by two decades of war between South and North Vietnam, at the end of which anti-Communist middle-class South-East Asians were welcomed as victims of the Cold War rather than as former adversaries associated with anti-colonial nationalism.

While some variations of this kind have occurred, the broad

Table 4.1 French perceptions of minority ethnic groups, 1984

Question: Here is a list of communities living in France. For each of them, can you tell me whether they are on the whole well or badly integrated into French society?

	A Well %	B Badly %	C No reply %	D A–B
Italians	81	9	10	+72
Spanish	81	9	10	+72
Poles	75	8	17	+67
Portuguese	70	18	12	+52
Pieds-noirs	66	21	13	+45
West Indians	57	20	23	+37
Jews from E. Europe	49	16	35	+33
Yugoslavians	43	20	37	+23
Asians	47	25	28	+22
Armenians	37	28	35	+9
Tunisians	37	42	21	−5
Black Africans	36	48	16	−12
Moroccans	33	48	19	−15
Turks	19	43	38	−24
Gypsies	21	64	15	−43
Algerians	21	70	9	−49

Source: SOFRES opinion poll for MRAP 1984: 22.

hierarchical ordering of ethnic categories by the French public has remained fairly stable during the post-war period. There have, however, been marked changes in the perception of immigration and its effects on French society. In INED's 1951 survey, 45 per cent of respondents felt that foreign residents would always remain foreign, while 36 per cent thought them capable of gradually mixing in with the mass of the French population. When the same question was asked in the winter of 1973–4, only 35 per cent felt that immigrants would remain permanently foreign, whereas 56 per cent thought they would gradually mix in (*Population* 1974: 1061). This greater confidence in the capacity of French society to absorb immigrants clearly reflects the rising prosperity experienced during the boom decades of the 1950s and 1960s. The economic utility of Maghrebis,

who had by then become dominant in migratory inflows, clearly
outweighed any misgivings associated with the cultural and political
heritage of non-Europeans.

In 1951, only 50 per cent of respondents had felt that foreign
residents in France performed useful services; by 1973–4, the figure
had risen to 80 per cent (*Population* 1974: 1059). An almost identical
proportion of interviewees (79 per cent) said foreign workers were
doing jobs which the French themselves did not wish to do; only 14
per cent considered that immigrants were competing against French
nationals in the labour market. At the same time, 65 per cent felt that
if a severe rise in unemployment were to take place, foreigners
should be sacked before French nationals. Thus ticking away beneath
the surface of this greater acceptance of immigrants was a time-bomb
set to explode in the event of an economic downturn, the first signs
of which began to appear not long after the 1973–4 survey.

With unemployment rising sharply in the late 1970s and the 1980s,
the repatriation of immigrant workers was regularly ranked in
opinion polls as the best solution to the problem (SOFRES 1984:
221, 1991: 120). In the early 1990s, annual polls consistently showed
that those who thought immigrant workers were a burden on the
French economy were twice as numerous as those who regarded them
as beneficial. In 1993, for example, the figures were 60 and 28 per
cent respectively (CNCDH 1994: 457). There was now great uncertainty as to whether immigrants could be integrated into French
society, as well as deep divisions over the desirability of this. In the
late 1980s, interviewees were split almost exactly down the middle
between those who wished to prioritize the repatriation of immigrants and those who wished to integrate them into French society
(SOFRES poll, in *Le Nouvel Observateur*, 23 November 1989). By
1990, the proportion favouring repatriation stood at 46 per cent,
against 42 per cent wishing to prioritize integration (SOFRES 1991:
125). In 1985, 42 per cent of respondents thought most immigrants
were too different for it to be possible to integrate them into French
society, while 50 per cent thought integration would eventually be
possible; five years later the proportion declaring integration to be
impossible had risen to 49 per cent, against 43 per cent who were of
the contrary view (ibid.: 122).

As noted earlier, Maghrebis are the main source of concern among
those who doubt whether immigrants can be successfully integrated
into French society. Maghrebis have the double misfortune of
occupying the lowest ranking in the ethnic hierarchy prevalent in

France and of having emerged as by far the most visible component in the population of immigrant origin at precisely the time when the expansionary climate which had favoured the recruitment of foreign workers in the early post-war decades was giving way to more difficult economic circumstances. It was therefore almost inevitable that the increased hostility towards immigrants and their descendants resulting from this economic downturn would focus on the Maghrebi population (Naïr 1988). Even before the first oil crisis of 1973, an outbreak of violence against Algerian immigrants in the summer of that year (Giudice 1992: 93–103) led the Algerian government to halt further emigration to France, almost a year before the blanket ban on non-EC entrants imposed by France in July 1974. Recorded cases of racist violence rose sharply during the 1980s. In the period between 1980 and 1993 Maghrebis, who represented less than 40 per cent of the foreign population, accounted for 78 per cent of all those injured and 92 per cent of those killed in attacks officially classified by the authorities as racist (CNCDH 1994: 23).

Islam is usually cited as the main obstacle to the integration of Maghrebis. Some 49 per cent of those questioned in a 1991 poll said Islam was so different from the prevailing norms in French society that it made the integration of Muslim immigrants impossible; only 40 per cent thought Muslims could eventually be integrated (CSA poll in *La Vie*, 28 November 1991). These figures match up closely with the pattern noted above in the responses made to a less ethnically specific question about the chances of integrating immigrants; behind this seemingly general question, respondents had clearly sensed that they were being invited to comment primarily on Maghrebis. Similarly, when 45 per cent of interviewees agreed in another poll that Maghrebis had a 'way of life' which could not be integrated into French society, compared with 42 per cent who disagreed (CSA poll in *Le Journal du dimanche*, 18 March 1990), they were no doubt thinking principally of Islam.

There are at least three possible explanations for this apparent decline in confidence among the French public concerning the chances of successful integration. One is that it reflects an objective shift in the cultural complexion of immigrants and their descendants, making them more difficult to incorporate when compared with earlier migratory inflows. It is certainly true that the mainly non-European cultures which have come to the fore during the last twenty years differ markedly from those associated with earlier, European migrants. Yet, as we saw in Chapter 3, direct conflicts with the norms prevailing in French society are the exception rather than the rule, and it is by no means certain that they now occur more frequently than when immigrants were mainly Europeans. Moreover, there is overwhelming evidence to show that the inter-generational trend is towards the reduction of cultural differences when the descendants of recent immigrants are compared with the majority of the population. Their acculturation flies in the face of those who claim that integration is impossible.

An alternative explanation for those claims is that they are based on mistaken but sincerely held beliefs concerning the population of immigrant origin. Two-thirds of French respondents questioned in recent surveys say there are too many immigrants in France; an almost identical proportion say they have never had any significant personal dealings with immigrants (SOFRES 1991: 121–2). It is clear that the negative images associated with immigrants in general and with certain ethnicized groups in particular owe more to second-hand information and impressions than to direct personal experience. The mass media play a central role in this process. Research on the representation of minority ethnic groups on French television has shown that they are mainly visible as 'problems' in news and current-affairs broadcasts. It is in the nature of journalism to highlight conflicts and difficulties rather than ordinary or benign occurrences. An understanding of the native French population based solely on news and current-affairs programmes would no doubt conclude that the French as a whole were riddled with conflicts and problems. News and current affairs are, however, only one part of total broadcasting output. Many other programmes, such as game shows, sitcoms and variety shows, present a far more convivial picture of 'ordinary' people. Because recent immigrants and their descendants have been largely absent from these programmes, viewers tend to gain a very lopsided and unattractive idea of how they fit into French society (Hargreaves and Perotti 1993). In the absence of a wider media presence, Muslims in particular suffer as a consequence of the high-profile coverage given to news stories such as the Islamic headscarf affair, for the deeply disturbing images generated by what in fact are exceptional events come to be perceived as the norm.

A third explanation for the widespread view that immigrants can no longer be integrated into French society is that those who argue in this fashion are influenced less by defective information than by their own exclusionary reflexes. The steady rise of non-Europeans in migratory inflows during the post-war period did not prevent the

French from expressing growing acceptance of immigrants as long as there was rising economic prosperity and a favourable labour market. To claim now that cultural differences make integration impossible is a convenient way of blaming immigrants themselves for the alleged necessity of excluding them from French society at a time when this is also widely seen as a solution to the country's economic difficulties. During the economic downturns of the 1890s and 1930s, similar arguments were advanced concerning the alleged unassimilability of Italians and Poles, who are often held up today as examples of easily integrated immigrants in contrast with more recent arrivals from Third World countries (Schor 1985; Milza 1985: 5–6; Noiriel 1988: 247–94).

In a 1990 poll, the proportion of respondents (49 per cent) who held that immigrants were too different to be integrated into French society was almost identical to the level of support (46 per cent) expressed for repatriation in preference to integration (SOFRES 1991: 122, 125). Many respondents would no doubt argue that the second proposition followed from the first, but another reading might reverse the causal chain. While it is impossible to prove that calculations of self-interest outweigh unprejudiced analysis in shaping attitudes of this kind, it is certainly arguable that the principal obstacles now blocking the social incorporation of immigrants and their descendants lie not in their cultural particularities but in the unfavourable conditions prevailing in the labour market and the exclusionary attitudes found among the French themselves.

What is beyond doubt is that the ethnicized categories against which French images of national identity are constructed are seriously at odds both with the *de facto* participation of immigrants and their descendants within French society and with their own sense of belonging. Seven out of ten young Maghrebis interviewed in a 1993 survey said they identified more closely with the lifestyle and culture of the French than with their parents' norms (SOFRES poll in *Le Nouvel Observateur*, 2 December 1993). French perceptions are quite different: in a 1990 poll, only three out of ten saw second-generation Maghrebis as mainly French, while five out of ten regarded them primarily as Arabs (CNCDH 1991: 210). Eight out of ten thought it would be difficult or impossible to integrate young Maghrebis born in France. Yet most of those concerned are in a formal sense already French, for French nationality has been automatically bestowed upon them under the terms of the French nationality code (CNF).[4] This disjunction between popular perceptions of the ethnicized boundaries defining French national identity and the juridical contours of French nationhood emerged as a major issue in French politics during the mid-1980s. The debate over the CNF became symbolic of the anxieties and exclusionary pressures traversing French society in the face of minority groups of immigrant origin. Before examining the details of that debate and the reform to which it led in 1993, it is important to understand first of all its historical and ideological foundations.

THE REPUBLICAN TRADITION

The prevailing conceptions of nationality and citizenship in France are rooted in the revolution of 1789. Breaking with the system of privileges associated with the division of society into rigidly stratified estates or orders, the revolution wrested sovereignty (i.e. legitimate political authority) from the monarch and invested it in the nation, all of whose members were proclaimed equal before the law. The republican values which are now most commonly associated with the revolutionary heritage include universalism, unitarism, secularism and assimilationism, though not all these terms were in use at the time of the revolution. Universalism has both an external and an internal face. The Rights of Man proclaimed in August 1789 were held to be valid not only for every individual in France but also for the whole of humanity. Within the republican tradition the nation, including its political incarnation in the form of the state, is indivisible: no intermediary orders are recognized between the individual and the unitary state of which he or she is a member. The principle of *laïcité* (secularism), a term which entered currency only in the later part of the nineteenth century, includes both freedom of conscience, already proclaimed during the revolution of 1789, and the formal separation of the state from any religious order (Brubaker 1992: 35–49).

The revolutionary period was shot through with tensions and contradictions, some of which were already implicit in the declaration of 26 August 1789, the formal title of which was the Declaration of the Rights of Man and of the Citizen. The fields embraced by the two terms joined together through the word 'and' co-existed but were not coterminous. While some rights belonged inalienably to all human beings, others – including, in particular, the right to share in the exercising of political sovereignty – were reserved solely for citizens. As all authority emanated from the nation, citizens were by definition members of the nation, but as the revolution unfolded gaps opened up in the apparent symmetry between citizenship and membership of the national community.

The Constitution of 1791 confirmed that citizenship was reserved exclusively for members of the nation but distinguished between 'active' cizitens, who had political rights, and 'passive' citizens, including all females and poorer members of society, who were not allowed to participate in the political processes governing the state, though they remained subject to its jurisdiction. Admission to the French nation came automatically, through a mixture of *jus soli* and *jus sanguinis*, to anyone born on French soil and resident there or descended from a French father. In addition, foreigners who wished to become French citizens were eligible to do so after five years' residence provided they satisfied other criteria indicating that they were incorporated into the life of the nation. The Constitution of 1793, which granted citizenship rights to most foreigners after a year's residence, was never applied. Not until 1794 did the revolutionaries declare slavery – the very antithesis of citizenship – to be abolished, but it was reinstated in the colonies under Napoleon (Borella 1991).

Most of the monarchical or authoritarian regimes which have exercised power in France at various times during the last two hundred years, including that of Napoleon, have restricted access to French nationality by prioritizing *jus sanguinis* over *jus soli*. Republican regimes, by contrast, have adopted more liberal measures. In 1851, the Second Republic determined that third-generation residents of foreign origin would be French from birth provided they and one of their parents were born on French soil. Under the Third Republic, a law passed in 1889 lowered the threshold for the second generation by conferring French nationality automatically on children born in France when they reached the age of majority. In 1927, first-generation foreigners were given easier access to French nationality when the conditions governing naturalization were liberalized. Further inclusionary measures were introduced by the post-war provisional government in 1945 and under the Fifth Republic in 1973. Except for the late stages of the revolutionary period, the 1993 reform, which ended the automatic acquisition of French nationality by the children of immigrants at the age of majority, was the first under a republican regime to move in an exclusionary direction.[5]

At the heart of the arguments advanced by those who favoured this reform was the conviction that the assimilationist assumptions on which a liberal nationality code was based were no longer well founded. The assimilationist tradition, like other aspects of the revolutionary heritage, is double-sided and steeped in ambiguity. From a political perspective, it appears universalist and egalitarian; in cultural terms, it is particularist and intolerant (Silverman 1992: 19–33). Historically and ideologically, as Brubaker (1992) has shown, the French and German constructions of nationality and citizenship differ profoundly in the relative weight accorded to political and cultural considerations. In France, a unitary state existed well before the cultural unification of those resident within its borders. Before and since the revolution of 1789, the state has pursued policies aimed at promoting cultural uniformity based on the norms prevailing among the political and social elite. In Germany, by contrast, the sense of a shared national culture preceded and to a considerable extent motivated the drive towards political unification. When a unified German state was established, nationality laws were designed to exclude those originating outside the German ethno-cultural nation. Membership of the French polity was relatively open to outsiders, whose incorporation was assumed to be facilitated by a process of acculturation. This openness was partly motivated by demographic concerns, for throughout the nineteenth century and most of the twentieth France has been characterized by a much lower birth rate than most of her European neighbours, notably Germany. The incorporation of people of foreign origin helped to redress this demographic imbalance, which was widely perceived as a threat to France's international standing and military security.

In theory, the principle of assimilation was extended beyond the borders of metropolitan France into the overseas empire. Officially designated as the ultimate objective of the colonial project, assimilation appeared to promise equal political rights to the indigenous inhabitants of the overseas territories (Betts 1961). In practice, political equality would have destroyed the very foundations of the colonial system, and it was refused to all but a tiny elite among the indigenous populations on the grounds that the broad masses were insufficiently acculturated to justify the granting of citizenship (Guillaume 1991). Their low level of cultural assimilation was the inevitable consequence of the minimal or completely non-existent educational provision made available by France to the majority of her colonial subjects. In metropolitan France, by contrast, primary education was publicly funded, compulsory and universal from the

1880s onwards. Under the terms of French nationality laws, as codified in 1945, the state held the right to block the automatic acquisition of French nationality by second-generation foreigners if they were judged to be insufficiently assimilated on reaching the age of majority (Brubaker 1992: 224), but the national educational system, extended after the war into compulsory secondary schooling, effectively rendered this provision unnecessary. In the early 1980s, when more than 15,000 people a year were automatically acquiring French nationality at the age of 18, the number refused each year on the grounds of inadequate assimilation averaged less than one (Lebon 1987: 12–13).

Tainted by its colonial connotations, the word 'assimilation' fell into general disuse with the collapse of the overseas empire in the early post-war decades, but it retained a juridical existence in the CNF, where assimilation was formally enshrined as as a prerequisite for the acquisition of citizenship by people of foreign origin. The concept (if not the term) continued to underlie the debate over immigration, where it resurfaced during the 1980s as one of the meanings attached to the word 'integration'. When advocates of a reform of the CNF justified their proposals on the grounds of an alleged breakdown in the traditional processes of integration, more often than not they meant that immigrants and their descendants were no longer being culturally assimilated. Almost invariably, this claim was illustrated by pointing to the rise of Islam in France. Other cultures originating outside Europe were seldom if ever mentioned, while European immigrants were regularly cited as examples of successful 'integration' and by implication, therefore, assimilation (Taguieff 1990; Silverman 1992: 140–7). It is certainly true that first-generation residents originating in Islamic countries generally remain deeply attached to the faith which they internalized during their formative years prior to emigrating. It is no less clear, however, that most of the children born in France to Muslim parents have a much weaker attachment to Islam and are far more committed to the values and aspirations commonly found among their French-born peers. On the evidence reviewed in Chapter 3, claims that 'integration' (in the sense of cultural assimilation) is no longer operative simply do not hold water.

Other arguments advanced by those wishing to limit access to French nationality were more political in nature. Again, Algerians were at the heart of these concerns. The low naturalization rates of first-generation Algerians in France were read, with some justification, as a sign of their unwillingness to accept formal membership of the French national community because of the political legacy of decolonization (Sayad 1987). Most second-generation Algerians in France automatically hold French nationality and have practical reasons to value the rights associated with this, but, influenced no doubt by their parents, they often appear indifferent, distrustful or positively hostile towards the French state. As they also hold Algerian nationality, their loyalty to France appears open to question. Stora (1990) has convincingly argued that, at root, historically conditioned political factors of this kind have been more significant than cultural differences in shaping the debate over contemporary immigration and the reform of the CNF:

> The difference, compared with earlier [i.e. European] immigrants, resides not in religious history but in the history of France and of French colonization. This is why the institutions designed to produce assimilation or integration suddenly seem to be misfiring. The children born from these more recent migratory waves, whose parents asserted the right to a nationality which was denied, rejected and forced underground [during the colonial period], are marked by this history. . . .
>
> In France, the debate is clouded by an unreal vision of Islam, which is equated with politically motivated Islamic fundamentalism; behind this phantasm lurks once again the settling of old colonial scores; people want revenge for the Algerian war.
>
> (Stora 1990: 38–9)

While it would be going too far to characterize the reform of the CNF as an act of revenge committed out of spite because of events that took place more than a quarter of a century earlier, it is certainly true that a lack of trust on all sides inherited from that period has been a potent factor in focusing public disquiet over immigration on the population of Algerian origin. As the largest national group of Third World origin, as Muslims and as former adversaries in a bitter war of decolonization, Algerians more than any other group have come to symbolize in French eyes all the problems associated with immigration (Silverman 1992: 70–94). As Brubaker (1992: 139) has observed, they have been at the centre of the most symbolic struggle of all – over the formal boundaries of French nationhood – though, as we shall see, for technical reasons the reform of the CNF enacted in 1993 left them virtually unscathed.

NATIONALITY AND CITIZENSHIP

The main forces seeking to restrict access to French nationality have been on the Right of the political spectrum. While those efforts have to a large extent set the terms of the debate since 1985, minority ethnic groups and sympathizers on the Left had been arguing since the late 1970s for no less radical but very different changes. In 1978, the Socialist Party (PS) promised that if elected to government it would amend the constitution so as to allow foreign residents to vote in local elections without first acquiring French nationality. This was seen as a way of allowing immigrants to participate in public affairs without directly confronting the symbolically charged issue of formal national membership. The proposal was included in Mitterrand's manifesto for the presidential elections of 1981. After Mitterrand's victory and that of the PS, allied with the Communist Party (PCF), in the parliamentary elections held immediately afterwards, Foreign Minister Claude Cheysson announced during a visit to Algiers that the government was planning to implement this proposal. His announcement was met by such a hostile reaction on the Right and such a lukewarm response on the Left that it was followed in less than forty-eight hours by a government climbdown. While Mitterrand remained on record as personally favouring local voting rights for foreign residents, the PS said it would not proceed with the proposal in the foreseeable future on the grounds that public opinion would not accept it, and the necessary parliamentary majority was also unlikely to be forthcoming (Wihtol de Wenden 1987: 52–73; Weil 1988: 193–5).

Critics of the proposed reform said that it was not only unconstitutional but also fundamentally at odds with the republican values inherited from the revolution. Within the tradition of 1789, political sovereignty was indivisible and was vested solely in the nation. Seen in this light, nationality and citizenship were inseparable. Historically, this was at best no more than half true. It is certainly true that, as a general rule, nationality has been a prerequisite for citizenship. While foreigners granted citizenship rights during the revolutionary period also became by the same token French nationals, between 1889 and 1983 naturalized foreigners had to wait several years before being allowed the political rights enjoyed by the rest of the nation (Wihtol de Wenden 1994a: 45–6). Moreover, nationality has not automatically entailed citizenship. Political rights were denied to a full half of the French nation (i.e.

the female half) until 1944, and the vast majority of people in the overseas empire, while officially classified as French subjects, were also excluded from citizenship (Borella 1991).

It is no accident that Cheysson made his announcement during a visit to Algeria, for the colonial legacy was nowhere more sensitive than in former French North Africa. The denial of Algerian nationhood throughout more than a century of colonial rule – during most of which Algerians were told that they were French nationals though not French citizens – and the bitter eight-year war that preceded independence made Algerians extremely reluctant to accept any outward sign of French domination (Sayad 1987). The PS's proposal to facilitate partial citizenship for immigrants without their being required to take French nationality would have made it easier for Algerians and other former colonial subjects to participate in French public life while avoiding formal allegiance to the French state.

Similar considerations led senior PS figures to consider revising Article 23 of the CNF, which attributes French nationality at birth to anyone born in France at least one of whose parents was also born on French territory. Despite Algerian independence in 1962, children born since then to Algerian immigrants in France have automatically been given French nationality, because Algeria was officially regarded as French territory at the time of their parents' birth. Since independence, Algeria has refused to recognize these claims, on the grounds that to do so would be to legitimize France's former colonial domination. Under Algerian law, the children of emigrants are Algerian nationals. In practice, therefore, they are bi-nationals, although Algeria does not formally acknowledge French claims. In the early 1980s, Socialist ministers examined possible changes to Article 23 so as to enable the children of Algerian immigrants to choose whether or not to accept French nationality instead of having it automatically imposed on them. However, technical difficulties were encountered: it appeared impossible to change Article 23 without adversely affecting *rapatriés* (i.e. former colonial settlers of European descent) and the change might also pose administrative problems in relation to the mass of French nationals originating in metropolitan France. By 1984 the emergence into the political limelight of the FN, calling for radical restrictions on access to French nationality, led the Left to abandon any thoughts of revising the CNF (Weil 1988: 195–6, 1991: 165–6; Brubaker 1992: 141–2).

France and Algeria did, however, sign an agreement in 1983 under which Franco-Algerian bi-nationals who performed their military service in either country would be exempted by the other (Babadji 1992). Until then, as nationals of both France and Algeria, the sons of Algerian immigrants had been subject to the draft in both countries. Military service is one of a range of rights and duties – some of them highly symbolic, others of great practical import – associated with nationality and citizenship. Others include the right of access to the national territory and protection from expulsion, access to employment in the public sector, and the right to participate in the exercise of political sovereignty by voting and standing as a candidate in elections to the local and national institutions of government.

In the post-colonial period, French nationality and citizenship have formed a virtually indissoluble whole. The Franco-Algerian military-service agreement was no more than a small crack in this amalgam. The Socialists' flirtation with the possibility of making political rights unconditional on nationalty was all but abandoned by the mid-1980s, but the idea has continued to circulate among minority groups as well as anti-racist and human-rights associations (Wihtol de Wenden 1987: 64–73; Balibar 1988). The project of what has become known as a New Citizenship (Bouamama, Cordeiro and Roux 1992) attracted considerable attention during the bicentenary celebrations of the French Revolution. Several campaigns and conferences were organized by intellectuals and grassroots activists with the aim of advancing the cause of local voting rights for foreign residents. This was presented not as a break with French republican-ism but as its true fulfilment, with the language and ideals of 1789 constantly to the fore, together with plentiful references to the Constitution of 1793. A petition in favour of local voting rights for immigrants organized by SOS-Racisme brought together dozens of associations in a collective called 89 for Equality. Shortly after-wards, hundreds of associations joined a similar collective called Here I Am and Here I Vote, run by the League of Human Rights, whose founding fathers had been directly inspired by the ideals of 1789 when setting up the organization in the late nineteenth century at the height of the Dreyfus affair (Oriol 1992: 104–7).

The emphasis of grassroots activists has been on the local dimension of the New Citizenship. By focusing on the sub-national level, they have sought to open to minorities from former colonial territories a political space uncompromised by the emotional and ideological baggage inherited from the struggle for national libera-tion. Following the Single European Act of 1986, however, there has been a growing realization that some of the most powerful arguments at their disposal are trans-national in nature. The act, which provided for a complete end to internal border controls between member-states of the European Community (EC) by the end of 1992, highlighted the steady erosion of national sovereignty with the development of economic and political integration in Western Europe. Two EC member-states, Denmark and the Netherlands, had recently granted local voting-rights to foreign residents. Similar rights had existed in Ireland since 1963, while in the United Kingdom all citizens of Commonwealth (i.e. ex-colonial) countries have always enjoyed full political rights at the national as well as the local level. In 1985, the European Parliament called for reciprocal voting rights in local elections for citizens of EC states residing in any member-country; if implemented, this proposal would break the link between citizenship and nationality across practically the whole of Western Europe, thereby demolishing the claims of those who argued that such a link was sacrosanct (Oriol 1992: 109–36).

The Maastricht Treaty of 1992 made a legal reality of this project by creating, in Article 8, a European citizenship enjoyed by the nationals of all member-states, who were given voting rights in local and European elections, no matter where they resided within the common frontiers of what now became known as the European Union (EU). The partial dilution of national sovereignty implied by this and other provisions of the treaty, particularly those dealing with economic and monetary union, required a constitutional amendment in France. This was approved by only a whisker in a referendum held in September 1992 after a· vigorously fought campaign which split most of the main parties from top to bottom. The main centre-right parties, the RPR and the UDF, were particularly divided over Maastricht. After returning to power in 1993 they announced that France was unlikely to implement local voting rights for EU nationals before the year 2001 (*Le Monde*, 12 July 1994). Local voting rights even for Europeans were thus conceded only grudgingly. While a precedent has certainly been set, the prospects for extending those rights to non-EU nationals are poor. For people of African and Asian origin, in the foreseeable future the only means of access to political rights in France lies in the acquisition of French nationality. Far from smoothing their path, however, the Right has placed new obstacles in their way through its reform of the CNF.

THE REFORM OF FRENCH NATIONALITY LAWS

The reform of French nationality laws was placed firmly on the political agenda in 1985, when the RPR and UDF included it in their joint manifesto for the 1986 parliamentary elections. In a more draconian form, such a reform had long been advocated by the FN (Le Gallou and Jalkh 1987), but little attention had been paid to this extreme right-wing party until it began to score significant electoral successes in 1983–4. Anxious to staunch the loss of their supporters to the FN, the traditional centre-right parties hardened their policy platform on immigration and related issues. After gaining a narrow election victory in March 1986, they formed a government under the premiership of RPR leader Jacques Chirac, who announced that the government would introduce legislation ending the automatic acquisition of French nationality by people of foreign origin.

This would require the reform or abolition of Articles 23 and 44 of the CNF. However, when the government began drafting the necessary legislation it found that Article 23 could not be changed without running into unwanted and unacceptable side-effects. If Article 23 were to be abolished, this would remove the simplest mechanism open to the mass of French citizens for proving their nationality. The production of two birth certificates – that of the person concerned and that of at least one parent – showing that both births had taken place on French soil sufficed to prove that the person was French, and the government was advised that it would be unwise to tinker with this. If the provisions of Article 23 were to be declared inoperative only with reference to Algeria and other former colonies, this would be tantamount to denying the historical legitimacy of French colonization; it would also raise difficulties for the *rapatriés*. For these reasons, the government reluctantly left Article 23 in place and focused instead on Article 44 (Brubaker 1992: 151–2).

As it stood, Article 44 gave French nationality automatically to people born on French soil of foreign parents when they reached the age of majority. Certain conditions applied: it was necessary to have resided in France during the five years prior to this procedure; French nationality could not be acquired by any person who had committed certain criminal offences; and the state could in principle refuse French nationality to a person judged to be of unacceptable morals or inadequately assimilated. However, these latter provisions were almost never invoked, and none of the conditions attached to Article 44 altered the central point that those acquiring French nationality in this way did so without having to request it. The centrepiece of the Chirac government's draft legislation was the revision of Article 44 in such a way as to require those covered by it to request French nationality instead of receiving it automatically.

One of the justifications advanced by the government in favour of this reform was that it would give more freedom to young people of immigrant origin: instead of having French nationality forced upon them, they would be free to choose whether or not to take it. This voluntarist argument was unconvincing for two main reasons. In the first place, second-generation foreigners were already permitted to decline French nationality in the year leading up to their eighteenth birthday if they so wished. Thus freedom of choice already existed, · and the proposed reform did nothing to widen it. On the contrary – and here was the second reason for doubting the government's liberalist claims – in its revised form Article 44 added important new conditions on the basis of which applicants could be refused access to French nationality. The range of criminal convictions disqualifying applicants was greatly extended, and it would in future be necessary to swear an oath of allegiance to the French Republic before being admitted to citizenship (Brubaker 1992: 152–3).

The latter provision was openly acknowledged by the government to be aimed at weeding out people of foreign origin whose loyalty to France might be open to doubt. At a more subtle level, the very fact of forcing the children of immigrants to request French nationality instead of receiving it passively was calculated to have a similar effect. The prime targets of these measures were the children of immigrants from former colonies who, because of parental influences, might be more reluctant than those of European origin actively to request French nationality. Because the government had found itself compelled to leave Article 23 intact, there was a certain amount of shadow-boxing involved in all this. Had the government had its wish, young Franco-Algerians, whose loyalty was doubted more than that of any other group, would have fallen under the terms of the revised version of Article 44. As it turned out, they were protected from this by the retention of Article 23, which ensured that they automatically held French nationality from birth. However, throughout the debate over the CNF, perceptions of practical realities were frequently obscured from view by gestures of highly charged political symbolism.

The outcry against the proposed reform voiced by opposition parties on the Left, trade unions, church leaders, anti-racist and

National identity   171

human-rights associations, grassroots activists and others of both
immigrant and native origin was so strong, and came at a time when
the government was already vulnerable on other fronts, that a tactical
retreat was soon ordered (Wayland 1993). Even the before the bill
was formally tabled in Parliament in November 1986, Justice
Minister Albin Chalandon announced that while second-generation
foreigners would still have to request French nationality, they would
not, after all, be required to swear an oath of allegiance. A month
later, faced with the prospect of massive demonstrations against the
bill, Prime Minister Chirac said the reform would not be brought
forward in the next parliamentary session. In January 1987 the
prospective legislative timetable was slowed down still further by
the decision to set up a special commission to conduct a comprehensive review of the CNF as a whole.

Composed essentially of experts from outside the field of party
politics, the Nationality Commission was encouraged to look beyond
the government's existing proposals and to make whatever recommendations it considered appropriate for the modernization of
French nationality laws. Given *carte blanche*, the Commission was
free to explore all the issues currently exercising public opinion as
well as a range of technical issues brought to its attention by civil
servants and jurists. Not surprisingly, Muslims in general and
Algerians in particular occupied centre-stage in the Commission's
deliberations. Their resonance was greatly increased by the Commission's decision to hold public hearings which, quite uniquely by
French norms, were broadcast live on French television (Hargreaves
1988). Only as an afterthought did the Commission add an extra
session so that it could hear evidence from activists and academics
of Asian and Portuguese origin; by then, the television cameras had
been switched off. One of the Commission members, Dominique
Schnapper, later acknowledged that they had been particularly
concerned to

> examine head-on the problems preoccupying public opinion,
> including the most sensitive issues. There is particular public
> concern over dual nationality, military service and Islam, so we
> prioritized those problems and perhaps went a bit far. It was only
> in the final public session that we heard evidence from Asian and
> Portuguese contributors.
>
> (Schnapper 1988: 15)

Bearing in mind the alarmist atmosphere in which the Commission had been set up, the expert evidence which it heard was surprisingly reassuring. Dual nationality, including arrangements covering military service similar to those agreed by France and Algeria, was shown to be commonplace. France had bilateral agreements on military service with no fewer than fourteen states and had signed a multilateral agreement with a dozen others under the auspices of the Council of Europe; among Franco-Algerian bi-nationals (the only specific group for which the Commission requested detailed figures), no more than one in five was opting to do military service in Algeria (*Etre Français aujourd' hui et demain* 1988: I, 211–21, II, 259–61).[6] Where Islam was concerned, the tone was set during the first televised hearing by a leading researcher, Bruno Etienne, who pointed out that it had taken France three hundred years to manage successfully the presence of a Protestant minority, and a hundred and fifty years to do the same for Jews; he thought it not unreasonable to aim to accomplish something similar in relation to Muslims within a mere half-century. 'French identity strikes me as being far more threatened by the globalization of culture and by Europe than by the Beurs [i.e. second-generation Maghrebis]', Etienne told the Commission (ibid.: I, 131).

The Commission presented its report, including a full transcript of the hearings, in January 1988 (*Etre Français aujourd' hui et demain* 1988). While agreeing that Article 44 should be revised so as to require a positive decision to opt into French nationality, its recommendations were in most other respects far more liberal than the abortive proposals which had been put forward by the government. Assent to the acquisition of French nationality would be as simple as ticking a box and adding a signature; no oath of allegiance would be required. People born in France of foreign parents would be able to benefit from these procedures between the ages of 16 and 21. While certain criminal offences would disqualify them if they applied after reaching the age of 18, between the ages of 16 and 18 their right to French nationality would be absolute, subject only to the condition of their having resided in France during the five years preceding the application. The Commission not only ruled out the extra conditions which the government had wished to impose on Article 44 candidates but also recommended abolishing the state's right to refuse French nationality on the grounds of poor morals or inadequate assimilation, powers which were regarded as unnecessary in the light of the period of socialization spent in France.

In line with the desire to establish a closer harmonization between

acculturation and political incorporation, the Commission also recommended a limited revision of Article 23. This rested on a
distinction between former colonies which had been officially
classified as fully fledged French *départements* (Algeria being the
most important instance) and those which had had the status of
French overseas territories (which included most of French sub-
Saharan Africa). No change was envisaged in relation to Algeria and
other ex-*départements*, but it was recommended that Article 23
should no longer apply to other former colonies, on the grounds that
these had not been as fully subject to French cultural influences as
Algeria. The effects of this recommendation were, however, partially
cancelled out by the Commission's proposal that there should be
easier access to French nationality for applicants originating in
independent states (among which were many former colonies) where
French was now the official language.

By the time the report appeared, it was too late for legislation to
be brought forward before the presidential elections due to be held
in the early summer of 1988, but Chirac indicated that if he were
elected in place of Mitterrand, he would hold a referendum to reform
the CNF in line with the Commission's recommendations. In the
event, Mitterrand won a second term of office, and the centre-right
parties lost their majority in the parliamentary elections held immediately afterwards. When they returned to office five years later
under the premiership of Edouard Balladur, the first significant
legislative text submitted to Parliament was the reform of the CNF.
Almost simultaneously, two other pieces of legislation were introduced, providing for tougher immigration controls and more widespread identity checks by the police.

Balladur was pushed into prioritizing the CNF reform by pressure
from hard-line RPR deputies. As Justice Minister, the UDF centrist
Pierre Méhaignerie assumed formal responsibility for the bill, but it
had in fact been drafted by RPR deputy Pierre Mazeaud, who served
as its *rapporteur* (i.e. principal spokesperson) (*Le Monde*, 15 April
1993, 12 May 1993). Méhaignerie had opposed the reform originally
proposed by the Chirac government in 1986, but said he favoured
the new bill because it was based solely on the recommendations of
the Nationality Commission, which had been widely praised when
first published in 1988. The minister claimed that the purpose of the
legislation was to foster integration, but Mazeaud offered a more
revealing insight into the thinking behind it when he told the
Chamber of Deputies that citizenship should be acquired only by

those willing to make an act of commitment to the French nation, and added: 'The role of Islam stands out more and more – Islam, and particularly the fundamentalist threat, which refuses all adherence to our society' (*Le Monde*, 13 May 1993).

With the hard-liners still not satisfied by the bill, the government introduced a number of amendments which went well beyond the Nationality Commission's recommendations. The most politically symbolic of these was an amendment to Article 23. In addition to ending its application to ex-colonies such as those in sub-Saharan Africa, as suggested by the Commission, the government now proposed to impose a residence qualification on Algerians. Children born in France to Algerian parents would be French from birth only if one of their parents had lived in France for at least five years prior to the birth. Méhaignerie justified this on the grounds of the need to combat the fraudulent use of Article 23 by Algerian mothers allegedly travelling to France with no other purpose than to gain residence rights for themselves and their children by giving birth there. No figures were given to indicate the extent of this 'fraud', but it seems unlikely to amount to more than a few hundred cases a year at most (Wihtol de Wenden 1994a: 51). Once again, the symbolic weight of the gesture outweighed its practical significance.

The revised bill was adopted by Parliament in June 1993 and took effect on 1 January 1994. Its practical consequences cannot be predicted with certainty, and as young people of immigrant origin have several years in which to opt into French citizenship, it may be some time before a clear pattern emerges. Some of the provisions adopted in the reform may well impact harshly on limited numbers of individuals. Foreigners marrying French nationals, for example, must now wait two years before applying for French citizenship; limitations on their residence rights may effectively render such a marriage inoperative, which will in turn disqualify them from citizenship. Where the bulk of immigrant-born youngsters is concerned, however, the right to French nationality is, as recommended by the Nationality Commission, absolute between the ages of 16 and 18; the state is obliged actively to invite those concerned to exercise this right, and the procedures for opting into French citizenship are relatively simple. For these reasons, it would not be surprising if the net outcome were to differ little from the pattern of automatic incorporation which existed prior to 1994.

The speedy passage of the 1993 reform was in marked contrast to the débâcle of 1986–8. In his analysis of the Chirac government's initiative, Brubaker attributed its failure to 'the prevailing idiom of nationhood' among French political and cultural elites, and thought it unlikely that a future government of the Right would succeed in enacting an exclusionary citizenship reform (Brubaker 1992: 162–4). On this view, while mass opinion was more attached to a narrow ethno-cultural vision of nationhood, the majority of French intellectuals, politicians and civil servants were deeply committed to 'an open, inclusive definition of citizenship' (ibid.: 164). How, then, are we to explain the adoption of exclusionary legislation by the traditional centre-right parties so soon after their withdrawal of a similar project only a few years earlier?

Wayland (1993) has underlined important differences in the political opportunity structure prevailing at the time of the Chirac and Balladur governments, as well as differences in resource mobilization by those opposed to the reform. In 1986, the RPR and UDF held only a wafer-thin majority in Parliament, and there were known to be dissensions within its ranks on the issue of the CNF. The government's loss of nerve following massive demonstrations in the autumn of 1986 against its educational reform proposals, combined with the very broad front successfully mobilized against its CNF reform project, led Chirac to pull back rather than risk another humiliating defeat. In 1993, by contrast, Balladur had a landslide parliamentary majority, the opposition parties were beset by internal feuds, and the old alliance of anti-racist and other pressure groups was able to generate far less momentum than in 1986.

On both occasions, the Right was playing to the gallery of public opinion which, as was seen above (pp. 151–6), has been preoccupied by the issue of immigration since the early 1980s. Yet while mass opinion has been strongly influenced by the feeling that 'something needs to be done' about immigration, the evidence yielded by opinion polls on the question of nationality laws has not indicated an overwhelming desire for exclusionary legislation. Certain polls have indicated support for the general idea of a reform of the CNF (CSA poll in *L'Evénement du jeudi*, 12 May 1988), but when more precise questions have been asked, respondents have not usually favoured tougher laws. In particular, when asked specifically if children born to immigrants should automatically acquire French citizenship on reaching the age of majority, those in favour of retaining this provision have generally outnumbered those against by two to one (SOFRES poll in *Le Nouvel Observateur*, 13 September 1990; SOFRES poll in *Le Figaro Magazine*, 21 September 1991).

A very similar ratio – but this time of a hostile nature – is regularly recorded in polls asking whether non-nationals resident in France should be allowed to vote in local elections (BVA poll in *Le Figaro Magazine*, 4 November 1989; SOFRES poll in *Le Nouvel Observateur*, 13 September 1990).

It is clear from these findings that the republican-inspired idiom of nationhood described by Brubaker is strong not only among French elites but also among the public at large. There is a wide consensus in favour of the view that citizenship is to be reserved for members of the nation, and that the nation should be open to people of foreign origin who have internalized its norms, as have most young people born and socialized in France. While open at the level of political incorporation, the assimilationist aspect of this idiom is closed to cultural difference. This is true at both the elite and the mass level. Few politicians or civil servants are prepared to endorse the concept of multi-culturalism. In opinion surveys, those who say immigrants must adapt or wholly conform to French cultural norms regularly outnumber by three to one those who feel they should be allowed to retain the traditions of their country of origin (IPSOS poll in *Le Point*, 30 October 1989; CSA poll in CNCDH 1994: 465).

The 1993 reform of the CNF was calculated to serve as a symbolic gesture of the government's intent to 'do something' about immigration without fundamentally infringing the values associated with France's republican tradition (cf. Weil 1994: 268–9). In particular, it was designed to appeal to the sizeable minority among the electorate which was tempted by the more exclusionary arguments of the FN. Had it not been for the rise of the FN in the mid-1980s and the threat this posed to the electoral base of the RPR and UDF, it is doubtful whether the traditional centre-right parties would have implemented or even proposed the changes which have now been made in the CNF. The debate over French nationality laws is thus symptomatic of a party-political contest in which, since the mid-1980s, a large part of the agenda has been set by the anti-immigrant platform of the FN. The dynamics of party politics and their impact on public policy formation are considered in more detail in the next chapter.

Chapter 5

Politics and public policy

FROM *LAISSEZ-FAIRE* TO STATE INTERVENTION

The reform of French nationality laws in 1993 represents in many ways the symbolic culmination of a much longer process which has held immigration at the forefront of party politics for more than a decade. The politicization of immigration in recent years is all the more striking when contrasted with the marginal position of this issue in political debate during most of the post-war period. The present chapter has two main aims: to delineate and account for the emergence of immigration as a key issue in party politics, and to analyse how this has translated into substantive changes in the field of public policy. First, however, we need to understand something of how immigration was handled by political elites prior to the 1980s.

It is a remarkable fact that, with the exception of a 1972 law against racial discrimination, no legislation relating to immigration was passed by the French Parliament at any point in the post-war period before 1980. The fundamental lines which were to guide public policy during most of this period were laid down in an ordinance (an executive order having the force of law) issued in November 1945 by the provisional government installed the previous year under the leadership of General de Gaulle pending the organization of France's first post-war parliamentary elections, which took place with the creation of the Fourth Republic in 1946. The marginal role of Parliament in shaping immigration policy until the end of the 1970s is partly a reflection of the relatively limited powers enjoyed by the legislature compared with the executive under the constitution of the Fifth Republic, the terms of which were set by de Gaulle in 1958. Yet even under the Fourth Republic, which gave much more extensive powers to the legislature, immigration seldom attracted parliamentary attention (Verbunt 1985: 156–60).

At root, the absence of parliamentary debate reflected the relatively uncontroversial nature of immigration policy at a time of labour shortages, as well as the executive's preference for dealing with potentially sensitive aspects in a technocratic fashion away from the glare of party politics (Freeman 1979: 99–130). As noted above (pp. 10, 153), an important debate took place within the provisional government immediately after the war over the relative importance of demographic and economic considerations in the recruitment of immigrants, together with the desirability of setting ethnic quotas (Weil 1991: 53–62). The 1945 ordinance empowered the state to control the overall level of recruitment according to economic and demographic needs but did not set out any formal ethnic preferences since it was felt these might appear too reminiscent of Nazi ideology, from which Europe had only just been liberated. An ethnic hierarchy favouring Europeans over Africans and Asians nevertheless commanded wide assent and, while never formally codified in law, underlay the actions of successive governments to the extent that they pursued a pro-active recruitment policy.

However, state control over the recruitment process was in practice undercut by three main forces: unexpectedly low inflows from European countries such as Italy, the exemption of Algerians from formal immigration controls, and the reluctance of French employers to comply with the procedures laid down by the 1945 ordinance. Under the terms of that ordinance, employers were required to request from the state-controlled Office National d'Immigration (ONI) advance authorization for the entry of each would-be immigrant. While ONI offices established in Italy failed to secure the anticipated number of recruits, entirely separate developments in colonial policy gave Algerians complete freedom of movement in and out of France beginning in 1947, thereby removing them from immigration controls. From the mid-1950s onwards, economic expansion and labour shortages were such that ONI's procedures were increasingly flouted by employers anxious to hire foreign workers as quickly as possible. By the late 1960s, the overwhelming majority of new entrants were technically illegal immigrants before being regularized *ex post facto* by ONI after they had found jobs in France. Government ministers acquiesced uncomplainingly in these developments. In 1966, for example, the Minister for Social Affairs, Jean-Marcel Jeanneney, stated: 'Illegal immigration has its uses, for if we adhered rigidly to the regulations and international agreements we would perhaps be short of labour' (quoted in Wihtol de Wenden 1988: 161).

A *laissez-faire* approach thus came to dominate official policy on migratory inflows, which were effectively left to the free play of the labour market.[1] A similar lack of intervention characterized to a large extent public policy concerning the welfare of immigrants once they had arrived in France. In principle, ONI's procedures required employers to make suitable arrangements for the housing of immigrant workers; in practice, most were left to fend for themselves. There was an acute housing shortage in post-war France. Many immigrant workers were employed in construction projects designed to remedy this shortage, but they were not among the planned beneficiaries of these programmes. Instead, they faced severe discrimination in the housing market and, with low disposable incomes, were relegated to its most marginal sectors, such as inner-city slums and *bidonvilles* (shantytowns) thrown up illegally on vacant land. The Fonds Action Sociale (Social Action Fund – FAS), a public agency created in 1959, invested significant sums in hostel accommodation initially designed specifically for Algerians; its terms of reference were extended in 1964 to include all immigrants. This programme made only a limited impact on the overall housing problem, however, and in other respects social assistance for immigrants was left largely to voluntary agencies.

By the late 1960s, the public authorities were increasingly troubled by two main consequences of the *laissez-faire* approach: their loss of control over the ethnic composition of the foreign population, and the appalling social conditions in which many immigrants were living. Beginning in 1968, a series of measures was introduced aimed at reducing inflows of Third World, especially Algerian, immigrants while continuing to facilitate migration from Europe, notably Portugal. Circulars issued by Interior Minister Raymond Marcellin and Labour Minister Joseph Fontanet in 1972 made regularization contingent on more stringent employment and housing criteria, with deportation orders being served on those unable to satisfy them. At the same time, the state began to take a more interventionist role in matters relating to the welfare of immigrants, particularly housing. The twin principles of controlling primary inflows and integrating immigrants legally resident in France, which were to become the leitmotif of public policy,[2] thus began to emerge during this period. Both trends became sharply accentuated in 1974, when the admission of non-EC labour migrants was halted altogether and for the first time a wide-ranging social policy was developed for the population of immigrant origin.

If we define ethnic politics as political behaviour conditioned to a significant degree by conscious processes of ethnic differentiation, it was not until the mid-1970s that stirrings of this kind became apparent in mainstream party-political activities, and it is only since the early 1980s that they have played a sustained role in French national politics. The absence of ethnic politics prior to the mid-1970s is attributable to three main factors: the insulation of policy-making in the field of immigration from parliamentary debate; the largely non-interventionist role of the state prior to 1968, particularly where the social welfare of immigrants was concerned; and, above all, the conditions of full employment and rapid economic growth which prevailed until the oil shocks of the 1970s. The ethnicization of French politics which has been witnessed since then has its roots in radical changes in all three respects.

THE ETHNICIZATION OF POLITICS

The government habit of treating immigration as an almost private affair in which parliamentarians had no rightful role was challenged during the second half of the 1970s by a series of legal rulings, the most important of which emanated from the Conseil d'Etat, France's highest administrative court. Major immigration controls imposed by executive order (circulars, decrees, etc.) were declared to be un-lawful, forcing the government to amend the measures and/or submit them to Parliament in the form of draft legislation open to analysis and argument from all sides of the political spectrum. The party-political divisions revealed by the parliamentary debates of 1979–80 were so deep that the legislation passed in January 1980 amounted to little more than a shadow of the draconian measures which had been initially proposed by the government with the aim of forcing the mass repatriation of Third World immigrants (Wihtol de Wenden 1988: 232–43). Every government elected since 1981 has brought forward important legislative proposals in the field of immigration, as a consequence of which parliamentary debate of this issue has become a standard feature of French politics.

The state has become more active not only in the field of immigration controls but also in measures designed to assist in the settlement of people of immigrant origin. These measures, discussed in greater detail later in this chapter, have included initiatives designed to reduce some of the chronic socio-economic disadvantages suffered by minority groups. As Crowley (1993: 629–31) has observed, improvements of this kind became increasingly visible from the mid-1970s onwards, particularly in the field of social housing. At the same time, groups of recent immigrant origin were becoming greater consumers of other welfare services as a consequence of family settlement. With unemployment rising, members of the majority population exposed to increased social insecurity have been inclined to see minority groups as competitors for scarce resources to a greater degree than when they were confined to the outer margins of housing and other markets. Competition over resource allocation at a time of growing socio-economic insecurity has been the single most important force pushing towards the ethnicization of French party politics.

Where mass opinion is concerned, resistance to immigration has always existed among certain sections of the population but, as was seen above (pp. 155–6), this hostility declined during the post-war boom before gathering strength with the onset of a more difficult economic climate beginning in the mid-1970s. Even before the economic downturn seen in the later part of the decade, Algerians were the target of considerable racial violence during the early 1970s (Giudice 1992: 55–103). This prompted the Algerian government to suspend emigration by its citizens to France in 1973, a year before the introduction of France's blanket ban on non-EC labour migrants. However, ethnic tensions of this kind were not generally exploited by mainstream political parties during the early post-war decades. A very different pattern began to emerge after 1973. While the structural change conditioning this shift lay in the macro-economic situation, the particular forms in which it manifested itself owed much to the tactical contingencies of inter-party rivalry (Schain 1988).

At the national level, the centre-right governments presided over by Valéry Giscard d'Estaing between 1974 and 1981 argued unsuccessfully but ever more stridently for the reduction of the immigrant population as a response to unemployment among the native population, which by the late 1970s had become the single most important preoccupation of the French electorate (Weil 1991: 108). The Left was by no means immune to the temptations of ethnic politics. At the local level, minority ethnic groups are concentrated in poorer districts, where the French Communist Party (PCF) is traditionally strong. Schain (1985) has shown that from the mid-1970s onwards a growing number of Communist-run municipalities recast disputes over the allocation of social resources (particularly housing) around the division between natives and immigrants, rather than presenting them within the party's habitual ideological mould, based on the antithesis between capital and labour. It thus championed one part of the working class (white French nationals, who could vote) against another (visible minorities, most of whom lacked political rights). During the campaign for the 1981 presidential elections, the ethnic card was also played by the PCF's national leadership, most notoriously through its support for the Communist mayor of Vitry, in the south-eastern suburbs of Paris, when he ordered the demolition of a hostel housing African immigrant workers on Christmas Eve of 1980.

Socialist Party (PS) leaders, too, have sometimes resorted to ethnicized representations of social issues. During the winter of 1982–3, the French automobile industry was hit by a wave of strikes arising from massive job losses among unskilled immigrant workers, mainly from Islamic countries. Exasperated by the difficulties he faced on the economic front, Socialist Prime Minister Pierre Mauroy claimed that the strikers were being 'stirred up by religious and political groups motivated by factors which have little to do with labour relations' (interview in *Nord-Eclair*, 27 January 1983). Interior Minister Gaston Defferre and Labour Minister Jean Auroux lent support to this view, claiming that the culprits were Islamic fundamentalists (Kepel 1987: 253–4). Yet there was no evidence to support these claims, in which a classic conflict between capital and labour was grotesquely misrepresented as a struggle between ethno-cultural groups.

Shortly afterwards, in the final stages of the campaign for the municipal elections held in March 1983, Defferre and his centre-right opponent for the mayoralty of Marseille, Jean-Claude Gaudin, vied with each other in their claims as to who would be toughest in dealing with the city's Arab population. The election campaigns in many other localities were marked by similar rhetoric highlighting the alleged dangers of immigration.

It was against this backdrop that the extreme right-wing Front National (FN) emerged from almost total obscurity into the political limelight in a series of local elections held in 1983. The most notable of these took place in Dreux, 30 miles (50 kilometres) to the west of Paris, where the party scored 17 per cent of the vote in September 1983 (Gaspard 1990). The FN had been founded under the leadership of Jean-Marie Le Pen in 1972. During the first ten years of its

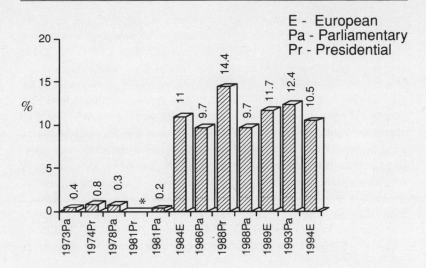

Figure 5.1 Front National's percentage share of vote in nationwide
           elections, 1974–94
* No candidate

existence, it failed to score even 1 per cent of the vote in any
nationwide election; since the European elections of 1984, when it
was supported by 11 per cent of voters, it has consistently taken
between 10 and 14 per cent of the national vote (Figure 5.1). Le Pen's
party has long stood on a vigorously anti-immigrant platform, with
the mass repatriation of non-Europeans, the restrictive reform of
French nationality laws and the exclusion of non-nationals from
social-security benefits foremost among its aims.[3] Its sudden electoral successes cannot be explained by a shift in FN policies or tactics.
They reflect, rather, the growth of insecurity among a significant part
of the electorate during a period of rising unemployment, and a shift
in the terms of political debate towards ethnic scapegoating for
which the mainstream parties of both Left and Right had already
paved the way (Schain 1987; Shields 1991).[4]

The heightened salience of immigration in French politics is
clearly visible in a variety of indicators ranging from agenda-setting
by political elites to public opinion polls and voting-patterns at a
mass level. Increased media coverage of immigration and minority
ethnic groups (Bonnafous 1992; Gastaut 1994) has served as an
important relay in this process. While the mainstream parties had
already begun to talk up the issue before the FN's electoral

breakthrough, the sudden, highly publicized emergence of Le Pen's party placed immigration at the centre of political debate, for it forced the other parties to react to his agenda. The way in which the initiative had been seized by the FN was encapsulated in a remark made in 1985 by Socialist Premier Laurent Fabius, who stated that Le Pen was asking some of the right questions even though he was giving the wrong answers (*Le Monde*, 29 October 1985). Fear of appearing 'soft' on immigration in the face of the FN contributed to a toughening of the policy platforms not only of the traditional centre-right parties but also of the Socialists. The Left's reintroduction of repatriation assistance and tighter restrictions on family reunification in 1984 were in part a response to the FN's initial electoral breakthrough. Similarly, the FN's parliamentary by-election victory in Dreux in December 1989 in the wake of the Islamic headscarf affair (Roy 1990) prompted Socialist Premier Michel Rocard to announce tougher controls against illegal immigrants.

Since 1977, unemployment has been the single most important issue named by voters when asked to explain their party preferences (Duhamel and Jaffré 1987); while immigration has not generally featured as the overriding issue, it has often ranked close behind. FN supporters are alone in consistently identifying immigration as their prime concern. They also express higher levels of insecurity than those found among the supporters of any other party (Mayer 1995). While economic insecurity is only one element in a much wider network of anxieties ranging from concern over law and order, commonly associated with the *banlieues*, to fears about the erosion of French national identity, linked like the problems of the *banlieues* to people of immigrant origin, it would be a mistake to underrate the significance of economic concerns among FN voters. In an exit poll conducted during the first round of voting in the 1993 parliamentary elections, 72 per cent of FN supporters (compared with 31 per cent of voters as a whole) said immigration had been an important consideration when casting their vote. At the same time, 64 per cent of FN voters said unemployment was an important concern, a figure practically identical to the 68 per cent of all interviewees attaching importance to this issue (CSA poll in *Le Parisien*, 22 March 1993). While inclined to perceive economic problems as the symptoms rather than the causes of a wider national malaise, FN voters nevertheless see a close connection between immigration and un-employment. In their eyes, minority ethnic groups are both the cause and – if migratory flows were to be reversed – the potential solution to practically every difficulty facing the nation, including un-employment.

The FN regularly takes a larger share of the national vote than the PCF, which in the early post-war period enjoyed greater popularity than any other party. It is particularly noteworthy that Le Pen's party is more popular than the PCF among the young as well as among manual workers and the unemployed (BVA poll in *Libération*, 23 March 1993; CSA poll in *Le Parisien*, 22 March 1993; SOFRES 1994: 144), groups to whom the Communists traditionally looked for strong support. Platone and Rey (1989) have shown that there is little evidence to suggest that large numbers of former Communist voters have defected to the FN. The PCF appears by and large to have retained the allegiance of voters who entered the Communist fold before the mid-1970s, but while these have advanced in years the party has failed to replenish its electoral base by recruiting among young voters from disadvantaged social backgrounds who in earlier decades might have been its natural supporters, and who instead are voting for the FN. High levels of job insecurity and long-term unemployment have placed many young voters beyond the reach of organized labour, which in the past was a key recruitment ground for the PCF.

The biggest transfer of votes to the FN has come not from the PCF but from former supporters of the traditional centre-right parties, the Union pour la Démocratie Française (UDF) and more particularly the Rassemblement pour la République (RPR). This has presented the RPR and UDF with a troubling dilemma: in order to win back their lost supporters, should they argue against Le Pen's ideas, make deals with the FN, or try to undercut its electoral appeal by stealing some of the party's programme? Since the mid-1980s, RPR and UDF leaders have veered between these different approaches, and in so doing have further accentuated the ethnic dimension in political discourse.

In September 1983, senior party figures gave their blessing to a local pact between the FN and the traditional centre-right parties which enabled them to win power in Dreux (Gaspard 1990). A commitment to reform French nationality laws, included in the joint RPR–UDF manifesto for the 1986 parliamentary elections, was clearly inspired by the FN's proposals in this area. While RPR leader Jacques Chirac officially refused to countenance a national deal with Le Pen and just secured enough seats to form a government in 1986 without the support of the extreme Right, he turned a blind eye to local alliances forged at the same time which enabled his party and the UDF to gain control of several regional councils with the support of the FN. Another senior RPR figure, Michel Noir, declared that he would prefer to see the centre-right parties lose the 1988 presidential election, rather than their own soul by making a pact with Le Pen (*Le Monde*, 15 May 1987). While no such pact was made nationally, there were again local deals in the south of France during the parliamentary elections held in the summer of 1988 immediately after François Mitterrand's successful bid for a second presidential term. In the early 1990s, the mainstream centre-right parties appeared to turn their backs on deals of this kind (none was made in the 1992 regional elections), but the barrage of legislation relating to immigration introduced when they returned to power nationally following the parliamentary elections of 1993 (Costa-Lascoux 1994a)[5] was clearly designed to enable them to recapture the initiative in the struggle for voters attracted by the FN.

The alternation of the Left and Right in government during the 1980s and early 1990s did nothing to halt the seemingly inexorable rise in unemployment, which has been the foremost concern of most voters throughout this period. Less than 0.5 million in 1973, the total number of unemployed stood at 1 million in 1977, 1.5 million in 1980, 2 million in 1982, 2.7 million in 1987, and 3.3 million at the end of 1993. During most of the post-war period, the rhetoric of political debate in France was dominated by the division between Right and Left over how to manage relations between capital and labour. The Left came to power in 1981 promising to tilt the balance against private capital after almost a quarter of a century of centre-right rule. After only two years, it abandoned the attempt to break out of recession by reflationary policies and fell back on orthodox austerity measures. Unhappy with the open acceptance of capitalist economics, the Communists, who had served as junior partners in the administration formed in 1981, stood down in 1984, leaving the Socialists to govern alone.

In 1981, 43 per cent of those interviewed by SOFRES found the distinction between Left and Right a valid framework for understanding French politics, compared with 33 per cent who thought it out of date. Three years later, only 37 per cent felt the distinction was still valid, while 49 per cent said it was out of date. By 1991, the proportion finding it valid had fallen to 33 per cent, against 55 per cent who considered it out of date (SOFRES 1992: 59). By the late 1980s, a large majority of survey interviewees felt that in practically every policy field there were few differences between Left and Right. Immigration had become – and in the 1990s still remains – the only policy issue where a majority consider the Left and the Right to be divided by major differences (1988 and 1989 polls in SOFRES 1990: 18; 1992 poll in SOFRES 1993: 223).

When respondents were asked in 1991 to rank key words indicating *ideas* most commonly associated with the Left, welfare protection topped the list. By contrast, when the same respondents were asked about 'the *reality* of the Left during the last ten years' (SOFRES 1992: 68; emphasis in the original), anti-racism emerged at the top of the list, ahead of the construction of Europe and social welfare, in second and third places respectively. The identification of the Left's policies with the protection of a relatively small minority of the population – that of immigrant origin – more than with its classic role as the guarantor of welfare protection for all in need is a striking development. It tells us much about the ethnicization of political debate but relatively little about the substance of public policy. As we shall see in the remainder of this chapter, after a series of liberal measures enacted by the Left during the early 1980s, policy differences between Left and Right in the field of immigration have often been more apparent than real. Summarizing the present section, however, three important points should be noted: the centrality of socio-economic insecurity in shaping mass opinion during the last two decades; the ineffectiveness of public policy in addressing that issue; and the growing tendency among political elites and the public at large to focus on ethnic differences within French society rather than on the traditional cleavage between capital and labour.

DIVISION AND CONSENSUS IN PUBLIC POLICY

A consensus among political elites to keep immigration out of inter-party rivalry has to a large extent prevailed in Britain since the mid-1960s, and a similar truce obtained in France until a decade later (Freeman 1979: 99–130), but it has long since broken down. The point was graphically illustrated when independent Leftist Bernard Tapie faced the FN's Jean-Marie Le Pen in a 1994 television debate in which the presenter suggested that the two men should don boxing gloves (*Le Monde*, 5–6 June 1994). Mainstream politicians, too, have tended to emphasize their differences rather than their common ground where immigration and ethnic relations are concerned.

A rare exception to this came in a televised debate in October 1985 between Socialist Premier Laurent Fabius and RPR leader Jacques Chirac. Fabius' insistence that he agreed to a large extent with Chirac in the field of immigration policy was heavily criticized by the Left and generally judged to have cost him the debate (Weil 1991: 191, 203–4). Cross-party talks organized by Prime Minister Rocard in the spring of 1990, with the aim of defusing immigration as a political issue following the FN's capitalization on the headscarf affair, ended inconclusively, with the Right clearly unwilling to sacrifice the tactical advantage derived from the Left's poor opinion-poll ratings in this field (Schain 1993: 69–70). Yet while important differences certainly exist on a number of questions, behind the bluster of political rhetoric there is substantive agreement among the mainstream parties on some of the most fundamental policy issues. For over a decade there has been almost universal agreement on three key points: firm controls against fresh inward migration, the provision of assistance to migrants willing to return home voluntarily, and the social incorporation of those who wish to remain permanently in France.

Since the formal end of non-EC labour migration in 1974, none of the main parties has questioned the principle of this ban. The two most divisive issues have concerned the degree to which people of immigrant origin already in France should be encouraged or even forced to leave, and the extent to which those permanently settled in the country should be allowed to live in culturally distinct ways. The Right has generally taken a tougher line on both questions, while the Left has been identified with a more sympathetic attitude towards the population of immigrant origin. Both issues generated intense controversy during the late 1970s and early 1980s. The first was effectively settled by a unanimous National Assembly vote in 1984 granting more secure residence rights to most immigrants, while the second became the object of a broad consensus during the late 1980s and early 1990s, when the concept of 'integration' became the watchword of all the main parties, except for the FN. This *de facto*, though seldom acknowledged, consensus has been facilitated by the Right's renunciation of mass repatriation as a policy goal, together with the Left's decision to pull back from a flirtation with multiculturalism in the early 1980s (Vichniac 1991; Weil 1991: 187–204).

Broadly speaking, seven main phases may be distinguished in the evolution of public policy since 1974. Throughout this period, firm immigration controls have been in place, though the Right (and sometimes the Left) has always tightened them further whenever it has been in power:

- Between 1974 and 1977, the centre-right governments headed initially by Jacques Chirac and then by Raymond Barre under the presidency of Valéry Giscard d'Estaing displayed considerable ambivalence over the long-term future of non-European minorities already resident in France.
- From 1977 to 1981, the emphasis fell firmly on measures designed to encourage or force the repatriation of non-Europeans.
- When the Left came to power in 1981 with the election of François Mitterrand as President and the appointment of Pierre Mauroy as Prime Minister, it ended the official pursuit of repatriation and introduced liberal measures designed to improve the rights and living-conditions of minority groups.
- By the end of 1984, however, Laurent Fabius had replaced Mauroy as Prime Minister, this liberalizing phase was largely over, assistance for voluntary repatriation had been reintroduced, and family reunificaton had been made more difficult.
- On returning to government under the premiership of Jacques Chirac in 1986, the RPR and UDF attempted unsuccessfully to reform the French nationality code (CNF), but mass repatriation no longer featured as a policy goal.
- While the Socialist-led governments headed successively by Michel Rocard, Edith Cresson and Pierre Bérégovoy between 1988 and 1993 proved more cautious than those of 1981–6 in their attitude towards minority groups, the main thrust of their policies lay in measures designed to facilitate integration.
- The centre-right administration which took over in 1993 under the premiership of Edouard Balladur brought in new immigration controls, easier police identity checks and a restrictive reform of the CNF, but the principle of integration was officially retained.

Thus despite periodic changes in the political complexion of governments and important differences of emphasis associated with these, public policy has been characterized for over a decade by the twin principles of control (externally) and integration (internally). The way in which these principles have been applied is examined in more detail below.

Control

In attempting to control migratory flows, states have at their disposal a range of levers. Some of these regulate the admission to the national territory of would-be entrants, while others limit the duration for which residence is authorized and the terms under which the repatriation of foreign residents may be facilitated or required. The centre-right governments which held office prior to 1981 took vigorous action on each of these fronts. They sought to end not only labour migration from non-EC countries, but also the entry of family members of migrants already in France. Although the principle of banning family reunification was declared to be unlawful by the Conseil d'Etat, the government continued to place administrative obstacles in the path of dependants seeking to join their breadwinner in France. From 1977 onwards, financial inducements known as *aide au retour* (repatriation assistance) were offered in a largely unsuccessful attempt to encourage immigrants to return to their countries of origin. At the same time, executive orders were drawn up by Interior Minister Christian Bonnet and the minister responsible for immigrant affairs, Lionel Stoléru, with the aim of reducing the number of immigrants holding work permits and deporting those who were unemployed. When the Conseil d'Etat ruled that these orders were unlawful, the government attempted to implement the same policy by draft legislation brought before Parliament in 1979. While the Bonnet Law of January 1980 tightened up on entry and residence rights, Stoléru's failure to secure parliamentary backing for the wide-scale non-renewal of work permits rendered impossible the deportation of hundreds of thousands of immigrants already living in France, as had been intended. On a very much smaller but symbolically significant scale, the Ministry of the Interior nevertheless used its executive powers to deport thousands of foreigners who were deemed to be a threat to *l'ordre public* (public order),[6] mainly because of criminal convictions (Wihtol de Wenden 1988: 189–275; Weil 1991: 89–138).

On taking office in 1981, the Left called a halt to administrative expulsions of this kind. Court orders would in future be required for most deportations, and certain categories of foreigners – particularly young people who had spent most or all of their lives in France – were protected altogether from expulsion. The procedures governing family reunification were eased, and an amnesty was declared for illegal immigrants. While the latter move helped to create an image of the Left as 'soft' on immigration, it is important to note that those eligible for regularization had to prove both that they had entered the country before 1981 and that they held a job. The 132,000 who were regularized in this way were thus a legacy from the period when the

Right had been in office, and their work record was a clear sign of their economic utility. Simultaneously with this amnesty, the new government brought in stiffer penalties for employers, whom it hoped to dissuade from hiring illegal immigrants in future.

The most enduring liberal initiative taken by the Left in the field of immigration controls was a law passed in July 1984 granting automatically renewable ten-year combined work and residence permits to the majority of foreigners legally settled in France. The law, which enjoyed all-party support in the National Assembly, put an end to much of the complexity and insecurity which had until then been associated with the renewal of permits. Its acceptance by the Right was a clear signal that mass deportations linked directly to conditions in the labour market were no longer on the agenda of any electorally significant party, except for the FN. The rise of Le Pen nevertheless led the Left to toughen its stance in other respects. Deportations justified on the grounds of threats to public order began to rise again in 1983, voluntary repatriation assistance (now called *aide à la réinsertion*) was reintroduced in the spring of 1984, and at the end of the year family reunification was made conditional on stringent housing conditions which many immigrants were unable to meet (Wihtol de Wenden 1988: 276–305; Weil 1991: 138–86).

When the Right returned to power in 1986, Interior Minister Charles Pasqua brought forward legislation which gave back to the executive control over deportations, on the grounds of threats to public order, and widened the categories of those liable to be expelled; access to the ten-year residence and work permit was also made subject to certain restrictions. His Socialist successor, Pierre Joxe, reversed some of these provisions in 1989 (Harris 1991), but they were reinstated and indeed toughened by Pasqua in 1993 (Costa-Lascoux 1994a). While regulations of this kind are a grave matter for the individuals affected by them, the number of deportations resulting from them – on average, less than a thousand a year during the 1980s (Weil 1991: 260)[7] – is very small when compared with the hundreds of thousands which the Bonnet-Stoléru package had been designed to facilitate (ibid.: 197).

Since the mid-1980s, the member-states of the European Community have moved increasingly towards a common policy concerning the entry of non-EC nationals. This has been necessitated by plans to abolish internal border controls between member-states. The Schengen Agreement, initially negotiated by France and four other member-countries in 1985, is due to take effect in most EU states in

1995. In 1990, all twelve EC member-states signed the Dublin Convention harmonizing procedures for handling asylum applications. Following the closure of EC borders to labour migrants in the mid-1970s, it was widely felt that the increase in asylum applications during the 1980s arose from abuses by would-be economic migrants. The 1993 Pasqua Law included provisions limiting the rights of asylum-seekers in line with the Schengen and Dublin agreements. It necessitated a constitutional revision, which was passed by Parliament in November 1993. Although the Socialists voted against it (*Le Monde*, 20 November 1993), they had in fact signed both the Schengen and the Dublin agreements. They had also introduced administrative reforms in 1990 which speeded up the processing of applications, the great majority of which were rejected, leading to a sharp fall in the overall number of requests for asylum (Wihtol de Wenden 1994b). Thus, here too, overt displays of discord belied an underlying consensus in favour of tight border controls.

Integration

While admission to EU states is increasingly managed at a multilateral level, policy relating to the social welfare of immigrants, especially those who are not EU nationals, is decided almost entirely by each national state. Although the French state is in this sense master in its own house, many of the issues thrown up by the settlement of immigrants and their descendants are fundamentally similar in all receiving countries. Despite historical, cultural and institutional variations which have given European states contrasting starting-points in the rhetoric and sometimes the substance of their policies, a *de facto* process of convergence is visible in many areas (Schnapper 1992; Lapeyronnie 1993). After phases of marginalization or exclusion, the realization that settlement is now permanent has led most states to embrace policies designed to incorporate minority ethnic groups into the receiving societies. In France, a clear consensus in favour of integration emerged during the mid-1980s, after a decade of division and uncertainty.

The *laissez-faire* approach that characterized immigration controls prior to the 1970s was replicated in the field of social policy by a minimal level of state intervention in favour of immigrants and their families (Tapinos 1975). Not until 1974 was a ministry created with specific responsibility in this field. Antoine Postel-Vinay was appointed Minister of State for Immigrant Workers[8] in June 1974. He

immediately proposed an end to further labour recruitment, coupled
with an ambitious programme designed to improve the living-
conditions of immigrants already resident in France, particularly
their housing. The suspension of labour recruitment was implemented early in July, but Postel-Vinay resigned a few weeks later
when it became clear that his housing proposals would not receive
the required funding. He was replaced by Paul Dijoud, who announced a wide-ranging package of measures in October 1974. Until
his own replacement by Lionel Stoléru in March 1977, Dijoud
pursued a policy which was characterized by deep ambiguity over
the long-term future of immigrants. On the one hand, improvements
in housing, which implicitly favoured the settlement of immigrant
families, were facilitated by a major increase in funding in 1975; on
the other hand, immigrants and their descendants were encouraged
to retain close contact with the cultural systems of the sending
countries in the hope that repatriation would remain a practical
possibility.

The most important initiative in the field of housing was the
decision to earmark part of a payroll tax for the specific purpose of
assisting immigrants. Since 1953, companies with more than ten
employees had been required to pay 1 per cent of their total salary
bills to public bodies which invested the money in new housing. In
1975, one-fifth of the money raised by this tax was earmarked to
assist in the housing of immigrants, and a new body, the Commission
Nationale pour le Logement des Immigrés (National Commission for
the Housing of Immigrants – CNLI), was set up to supervise the
use of these funds. Some of the money was to be spent on the
construction or refurbishment of hostels for foreign workers whose
families were still in the country of origin, but most of the funds were
invested in social housing (HLMs) for family occupation. Although
this source of funding was later reduced, the net effect was greatly
to increase the number of immigrant families living in social
housing. As many had previously been housed in slum properties or
shantytowns, this represented a significant improvement in their
living conditions (Barou 1989).

At the same time, a number of initiatives was taken to facilitate
the distinctive cultural traditions of minority ethnic groups. Agreements were signed with sending states permitting them to fund
limited amounts of mother-tongue teaching for the children of
immigrants within French state schools. A weekly television programme for immigrants entitled 'Mosaïque', launched in 1977,

placed a strong emphasis on the cultural traditions of Third World sending states, which supplied a considerable proportion of the broadcast material. Despite France's constitutional commitment to *laïcité* (i.e. the separation of the state from religious organizations), public bodies facilitated the installation of Islamic places of worship in hostels for foreign workers, HLM blocks housing immigrant families, and factories of state-controlled companies such as Renault, which employed large numbers of Muslims (Weil 1991: 245–9).

Under Dijoud, the aim of these initiatives was to keep open repatriation as a policy option. That option became a positive preference when Stoléru replaced Dijoud in 1977. In parallel with his plans for forced repatriation, Stoléru set up an advisory commission called Culture et Immigration with instructions to consider the cultural needs of minority ethnic groups, who, he said, were 'legitimately asking for the right to be different and to choose their own future' (letter from Stoléru dated 13 November 1979, in *Culture et immigration* 1980: 99). The seemingly liberal connotations of *le droit à la différence* ('the right to be different') were of course undercut by the executive orders and draft laws prepared by Stoléru with the aim of ensuring that many people of immigrant origin would be anything but free to choose their own future. If they were found to be surplus to the requirements of the French labour market and did not choose the 'right' way, Stoléru intended to ensure that they were deported. The maintenance of their cultural heritage was thus conceived as the very antithesis of integration (Sayad 1978).

For different reasons, the concept of *le droit à la différence* commanded widespread support on the Left, particularly among members of the Socialist Party. Decolonization and the near-revolution of May 1968 had led many on the Left to adopt a favourable attitude towards cultural pluralism. Mitterrand explicitly endorsed the principle of *le droit à la différence* during his campaign for the 1981 presidential elections (campaign statement, in *Droit de vivre* 1981: 17). In abolishing repatriation assistance and halting deportations, the administration installed at the beginning of his first presidency made it clear that minority ethnic groups of recent immigrant origin were now expected to settle permanently in France.[9] New measures were introduced to improve the housing, employment and educational prospects of minority groups. They were also allowed the free right of association (previously, the prior approval of the Interior Ministry had been necessary if foreigners wished to establish their own organizations), and substantial state funding was made available to support such initiatives.

The word most favoured at this time in official circles to describe the social incorporation of people of immigrant origin was 'insertion'. It featured, for example, in the title of a report on measures designed to improve the social and economic welfare of second-generation members of minority groups (Marangé and Lebon 1982). It implied that those concerned could be 'inserted' into the social fabric of France while still retaining a distinctive cultural identity. 'Insertion' was thus implicitly contrasted with 'assimilation', a term felt to have been tainted by its association with colonial policies which had denigrated non-European cultures. Although the word 'multi-culturalism' was almost never used, this was implicitly the direction in which the policies of the Left seemed to point during their early years in office.

The rise of the FN, campaigning on a platform claiming that immigration threatened not only employment and law and order but also national identity itself, led the Left to pull back from its apparently multi-culturalist posture. References to *le droit à la différence* all but disappeared, and a separate junior ministry with specific responsibility for immigrants was abolished when Laurent Fabius replaced Pierre Mauroy as Prime Minister in 1984. Issues relating to the social incorporation of minority groups were subsumed within the Ministry of Social Affairs, headed by Georgina Dufoix. This reflected the Socialists' desire to play down the notion of immigrants as distinct socio-cultural groups. Since then, whether the Left or the Right has been in power, no ministry has carried an explicit reference in its title to the population of immigrant origin.

Massive media coverage of the Islamic headscarf affair in the autumn of 1989 led to a spurt of institutional initiatives designed to reassure the public that people of recent immigrant origin were being successfully incorporated into French society. It was at this point that 'integration' became officially consecrated as the watchword of public policy relating to minority groups, though in practice it had already been structuring the policies of both the Left and the Right for several years. In December 1989, only days after the FN's by-election victory in Dreux, Rocard created a new administrative post, that of Secretary-General for Integration, within the Prime Minister's office. Hubert Prévot, the senior civil servant appointed to this post, was given the task of co-ordinating government policy aimed at sections of the population who were in danger of being socially excluded. To generate relevant policy proposals, Rocard set up a think-tank called the Haut Conseil à l'Intégration (High Council for Integration – HCI), which subsequently produced a series of reports and recommendations. In theory, Prévot and the HCI were concerned with integrating into mainstream society all those threatened by marginalization, including members of the native population. In practice, they focused almost exclusively on the population of immigrant origin.

The extreme sensitivity associated with any suggestion of ethnic separatism was apparent in the terminological coloration of Rocard's initiatives. Although fears over the cultural 'threat' associated with Islam had triggered these moves, there was no explicit reference to immigration in their formal designation. Instead, the whole thrust of the preferred term, 'integration', was to suggest that any differences separating minorities from the majority population were being reduced or eliminated by enlightened public policy. For the same reason, Rocard refused to set up a separate ministry responsible for minority groups.

His successor, Edith Cresson, did appoint a Minister of State for Integration, Togolese-born Kofi Yamgnane. The appointment of Yamgnane, who as a Catholic championed the cultural norms dominant in France and displayed a frosty attitude towards Islam, was clearly calculated to demonstrate that people of immigrant origin could be integrated into the very heart of the French state without this threatening the cultural integrity of the nation (Quemener 1991; *Le Monde*, 10 October 1991).

The rapidity with which the Balladur government tightened entry and residence rights for foreigners and reformed the French nationality code (CNF) in 1993 signalled its determination to take a tough stance on immigration (Costa-Lascoux 1994a). Had the CNF reform made it impossible for large numbers of people of immigrant origin to acquire French citizenship, this might have served as an indirect method of facilitating mass deportations. In practice, relatively few would be barred from citizenship, and there was no substantive deviation from the core objective of integration inherited from the Socialist-led administrations of 1988–93.

Integration remains in many ways an ambiguous concept. For many on the Right, it is little more than a euphemism for assimilation, while some on the Left see it as a more palatable term for something akin to insertion. No less importantly, however, as Weil and Crowley (1994: 113–16) have pointed out, the consensus now surrounding this word has removed other ambiguities attaching to earlier terms which helped the FN to establish its political legitimacy during the early 1980s. The concepts of insertion and of *le droit à la différence* were adaptable to the most extreme and opposed of policy positions, ranging from unbridled multi-culturalism to mass deportations. The extreme Right was only too glad to acknowledge cultural differences – and to infer from them the right of one ethno-cultural group to exclude another. For all its ambiguities, integration presupposes the irreversibility of the settlement of minority groups. By the same token, its widespread adoption during the late 1980s and early 1990s came to differentiate at a symbolic level all the older-established political parties more clearly from the FN than had previously been the case.

DISCRIMINATION, ANTI-DISCRIMINATION AND POSITIVE DISCRIMINATION

The FN's policy platform is encapsulated in what the party calls *la préférence nationale* (priority to French nationals). If implemented, this policy would legitimize systematic discrimination against foreigners in practically every area of social life, from employment and housing to education and welfare. There are in principle enormous legal obstacles to a policy of this kind. All EU nationals, for example, enjoy legal protection from this type of discrimination, and the FN has said it will respect these obligations, while the nationals of many other states enjoy certain rights under bilateral treaties negotiated with France which cannot be unilaterally abrogated. The seemingly universal principle of non-discrimination is enshrined in a 1972 French law prohibiting discrimination on the grounds of ethnic origins, nationality, race or religion (Costa-Lascoux 1994b).

Yet in practice very few prosecutions have been successfully brought under this law, while the French state has, like many other receiving states, discriminated both officially and unofficially against foreign residents on a massive scale (Lochak 1992). The formal rights of foreigners have been limited not only with regard to political citizenship, discussed in Chapter 4, but also in many other spheres, particularly employment. In unofficial ways, public authorities have often discriminated against minority ethnic groups, notably in the allocation of housing.

The system of work permits which operated until 1984 enabled the state officially to limit the geographical areas and types of jobs in which most foreigners were allowed to work. They were thus prevented from competing on a wholly equal footing within the national labour market. The relatively small number of foreigners working as tradespeople before 1984 was one of the consequences of this system (Ma Mung 1992: 40). Even today, foreigners are formally excluded from most public-sector jobs, which tend to be among the most secure in the whole economy. Almost all states exclude foreigners from areas where national security could be said to be involved (the army, the police, the senior civil service, etc.), but France draws exceptionally wide boundaries around public-sector employment, so that non-nationals are generally unable to work in state-owned sectors such as public transport, the postal service, education and healthcare, except for temporary and usually low-grade posts (Costa-Lascoux 1989: 53–70). Taking the private and public sectors together, Lochak (1992: 403) has estimated that about one-third of the 18 million wage-earning jobs in France are reserved for French nationals.

In mainly unofficial ways, the authorities responsible for publicly funded housing have discriminated against people of immigrant origin in many cities. In theory, the system of earmarking funds supervised by the CNLI, formally instituted in 1975, came close to a form of positive discrimination, since the money was to be used specifically for the housing of immigrants. Weil (1991: 249–56) has shown that in practice these funds were frequently misused. Substantial sums were awarded to HLM authorities in exchange for agreements to house set numbers of immigrant families. Often, the money was spent on constructing or refurbishing homes which were then offered to members of the native population. The homes given to immigrants were concentrated in decaying parts of the public housing-stock. In some cases, no extra immigrants were housed at all, since the authorities claimed that they were meeting their obligations if they undertook to replace an existing immigrant family with another one. Partly because of these abuses, the proportion of payroll tax funds earmarked for the housing of immigrants was gradually reduced before being virtually abolished in 1987 (ibid.: 274–5).

Despite the fact that ethnic quotas are in principle prohibited by the 1972 law against racial discrimination, they have in practice been applied by public housing authorities in many French cities. Those targeted have been 'visible' minorities (i.e. groups perceived as non-Europeans), including in many cases DOM-TOMiens, despite the fact that they are French citizens. Because the authorities are not obliged to make public their reasons for accepting or refusing individual housing-applications, it is only rarely that documentary proof of discrimination can be brought before the courts (Blanc 1990: 86). Compelling evidence that a general policy of ethnic quotas has been applied on a wide scale has nevertheless been adduced by researchers such as Schain (1985: 176–82), Weil (1991: 254–6) and Villanova and Bekkar (1994: 47–89).

This has often involved a consensus between national and local arms of government, even when these have been controlled by parties of different political persuasions. Many of the poorer municipalities containing substantial areas of social housing are controlled by the Left, particularly the PCF. During the second half of the 1970s, many Left-controlled municipalities sought to limit the number of housing-units allocated to visible minorities, notably Maghrebis, Africans and DOM-TOMiens. They were often assisted in this by the local representatives of the central state, which at that time was under the control of the centre-right parties. Since 1981, when the Left introduced a policy of decentralization, mayors have often used their increased powers to refuse construction permits for new social housing liable to bring into their locality additional minority ethnic families; at the same time, rigid quotas have been applied to existing housing-stocks (Weil 1991: 270–6).

This approach has often been justified on the grounds of the so-called *seuil de tolérance* (threshold of tolerance), a level of immigrant concentrations beyond which the process of social incorporation is held to be threatened (Grillo 1985: 125–7). It is claimed that if this threshold – often put at between 10 and 15 per cent of the population – is crossed in a given locality, the capacity of the native population to absorb minority ethnic groups would be stretched beyond breaking-point. There is no reliable evidence to indicate that such a threshold exists. While fears of ethno-cultural 'ghettos' may have inspired some of those who pursued this policy, anxieties over a possible electoral backlash among native voters were probably a primary concern. One of the ironies of the pattern which developed is that, because housing authorities tended to allocate their least desirable properties to immigrant families, relatively dense micro-concentrations of minority ethnic groups often arose despite the imposition of lower overall limits across given localities (Weil 1991: 254–6).

In attempting to redress the inequalities resulting from past and present discrimination, some states have implemented policies designed to favour disadvantaged groups. In the US, affirmative action programmes sometimes involve the appointment or promotion of people from disadvantaged groups who are less well qualified than candidates or employees from other ethnic backgrounds. That kind of affirmative action would be unlawful in Britain, where successive Race Relations Acts have prohibited any form of discrimination, including so-called 'positive discrimination' in favour of disadvantaged groups. However, the Commission for Racial Equality (CRE), which was established under the terms of the 1976 Race Relations Act, encourages companies and other organizations to engage in ethnic monitoring as a check against racial discrimination as part of a policy approach known as positive action. This involves comparing the ethnic composition of personnel within the organization with that of qualified applicants or the population as a whole, and if necessary instituting measures (such as additional training programmes) designed to achieve a fairer balance. In France, such approaches are almost universally condemned as Anglo-Saxon devices leading to quotas, ghettos and *communautarisme* (communitarianism), i.e. ethnic separatism.

There are at least three main reasons for the official French rejection of affirmative or positive action. One is a deep attachment to the republican tradition of refusing to recognize differences based on separate origins. While originally grounded in opposition to the hereditary transmission of socio-economic privileges, which the revolutionaries of 1789 set out to abolish, the principle of egalitarianism is widely understood to require that, in their dealings with the state, individuals should be treated without regard for their religious, national or ethnic origins (Noiriel 1992a: 70–1). A second factor is the widespread fear of strengthening ethno-cultural differences by giving state recognition and/or state funds to minority groups, thereby undermining national cohesion. Finally, there are painful memories associated with the Vichy regime, which during the Second World War used state-compiled registers listing Jews and other minorities to collaborate actively in Nazi Germany's extermination policies. With the extreme Right in the ascendancy since the early 1980s, it has seemed to many liberal-minded French nationals that the ethnic categorization of the population – which is essential to the success of affirmative or positive action programmes – would create a body of information which in the wrong hands might be used against (rather than in favour of) disadvantaged groups.

It is also true that a proper system of ethnic monitoring would make it impossible for the state to discriminate in the allocation of social housing, an unofficial policy which has been widely practised with the aim of dispersing minority groups, thereby reducing the risk of ethnic ghettos. Ironically, however, in applying housing quotas (an allegedly Anglo-Saxon invention) and concentrating immigrant families in poor-quality properties, public authorities have at time comes close to creating something akin to the very ghettos that they profess to abhor.

While formally rejecting positive discrimination and sometimes practising negative discrimination, French policy-makers have nevertheless instituted a range of programmes which in many respects parallel those adopted in Britain (Lapeyronnie 1993). Some of these are based directly on ethnic criteria, though that expression is never used. The most important institution funding programmes of this kind is the Fonds d'Action Sociale pour les Travailleurs Immigrés et leurs Familles (Social Action Fund for Immigrant Workers and Their Families – FAS). Although the word 'ethnic' is systematically avoided by the FAS – which, at the level of nomen-clature, remains caught in something of a timewarp, alluding to spouses and descendants as mere appendages of 'immigrant workers' – it is required by law to target people of immigrant origin, with the central aim of integrating them into French society. The train-ing programmes which are included among the FAS's spending-programmes are similar to those that the CRE encourages in Britain with the aim of improving the qualifications of disadvantaged groups. Because France refuses to institute ethnic monitoring, the effectiveness of these programmes is difficult to gauge,[10] but the underlying principle is similar in all but name to the British concept of positive action. Bearing in mind that the FAS has a budget ten times larger than that of the CRE (Lapeyronnie 1993: 198), and that the whole of it is designated for the exclusive benefit of immigrants and their descendants, the *de facto* commitment of the French state to positive action is not inconsiderable.[11]

The *Zones d'Education Prioritaires* (Educational Priority Zones – ZEPs) introduced by the Left in 1981 parallel similar initiatives taken in Britain under section 11 of the 1966 Local Government Act. In both cases, additional state funding is made available to schools which have high concentrations of immigrant-born pupils. French schools most likely to benefit are those which have 30 per cent or more foreign pupils. However, ZEP funding is not reserved for minority ethnic groups. An ethnic element is included in the criteria by which schools are designated for ZEP status, because concentrations of minority groups are statistically one of the surest indicators of social deprivation. Although the ZEPs are often seen as a camouflaged 'immigrant' programme, they are not in any sense designed to promote ethnic diversity. On the contrary, their prime aim is better to prepare young people from disadvantaged backgrounds, whatever their ethnic origins, to function effectively in French society. Extra teachers and other facilities are provided with the central aim of improving the delivery of mainstream teaching-programmes, thereby countering high drop-out rates and poor examination results (Costa-Lascoux 1989: 91–5; Lorcerie 1994c).

A similar principle has informed a long succession of government initiatives designed to remedy poor housing and the wider problems of urban decay afflicting many French cities. These are similar to the Urban Programme launched in Britain in 1968 during a phase of so-called 'colour-blind' policy-making, the effect of which was to assist minority ethnic groups within the framework of wider programmes tackling the problems of socio-economically disadvantaged areas. Since 1977, when a government committee called Habitat et Vie Sociale (Housing and Social Life – HVS) was created, the institutional framework of French initiatives in this field has undergone various transformations and gained an ever more prominent position in the machinery of government, culminating in the creation of a Ministry for Urban Affairs in December 1990. Rocard's decision to set up such a ministry was prompted by the disorders which had taken place a few months earlier in Vaulx-en-Velin, a suburb of Lyon typifying the problems of the French *banlieues*: high unemployment, poor-quality housing and neighbourhood infrastructure, and difficult relations between the police and local inhabitants, particularly those of minority ethnic origin.

A key plank of the policy pursued by the ministry and its institutional predecessors was a system of contracts under which central and local government agreed to provide additional funding for areas suffering high levels of social disadvantage (Champion, Goldberger and Marpsat 1993). Although these jointly aided districts contain relatively dense concentrations of minority ethnic groups (see pp. 72–4 above), who have often been to the fore in disturbances such as such as those in Vaulx-en-Velin, the difficulties they face are grounded primarily in socio-economic circumstances rather than ethnic particularities. By the same token, the aid granted to these areas is designed to improve the living-conditions of all those in need, regardless of their ethnic origins.

In 1991 Michel Delebarre, who had been appointed head of the new Urban Ministry, piloted through Parliament what the media called an 'anti-ghetto' law. This was designed to force local authorities to accept in the future a more even distribution of social housing, thereby reducing concentrations of the kind seen in Vaulx-en-Velin and Mantes-la-Jolie, where further disturbances had taken place immediately before the new legislation was adopted. Despite the ethnic connotations of the nickname given to this law by the media, the central aim was to address socio-economic disparities rather than ethnic differences *per se*.

The state has nevertheless recognized that in certain fields significant ethnic differences require specific policy initiatives. As we shall see in the next section, the acknowledgement of ethnic diversity has been an important element in the formation of cultural policy.

PLURALISM, EXCLUSION OR CO-OPTION?

Broadly speaking, three alternative policy approaches may be distinguished in the treatment of cultural minorities. A pluralist approach allows or positively fosters the co-existence of diverse cultural systems, with no real attempt at reducing differences. An exclusionary approach seeks to eliminate differences either by forcing minorities to assimilate totally into the dominant culture or by expelling them from the national territory. A policy of co-option tolerates differences but seeks to ensure that minorities limit their distinctive patterns of behaviour in ways that are compatible with the dominant cultural norms. While pluralist or exclusionary tendencies have sometimes been apparent, the dominant approach in French public policy, particularly since the mid-1980s, has been that of co-option.[12]

The Right has consistently shown itself to be more tempted than the Left by exclusionary reflexes. Ironically, it has also been responsible for some of the most pluralist initiatives taken by the state. During the presidency of Giscard d'Estaing, minorities of recent immigrant origin were encouraged to retain their distinctive cultural traditions. While pluralist in its effects, this approach was to a large extent motivated by exclusionary considerations, which dominated public policy from 1977 onwards, when mass repatriation of Third World immigrants, particularly Maghrebis, became a prime objective. If immigrants and their descendants were to be lured or forced into repatriation, it appeared desirable that they should feel at home with the cultural norms prevailing in the sending states. It was in this spirit that the Right encouraged the teaching of Langues et Cultures d'Origine (Homeland Languages and Cultures – LCO) in state schools during the second half of the 1970s.[13]

However, the effects of this policy should not be exaggerated. While hoping that minority groups would retain sufficient competence in homeland cultures to make repatriation feasible, Giscard and those who served under him were firmly committed to the domination of French cultural norms as long as immigrants and their descendants remained in France. The LCO programme was in every respect half-hearted when compared with the overall educational experience of immigrant-born children within state schools. France did not invest a penny in LCO provision. The recruitment and funding of teachers were the responsibility of sending states, which generally lacked the resources to provide tuition for more than a small proportion of their expatriates' children (see pp. 101–2 above). On average, no more than one in five children has received tuition of this kind (Costa-Lascoux 1989: 92; Boyzon-Fradet 1992: 158). Even if more teachers were to be supplied, the time available for LCO classes is in any case limited to three hours a week, a quite marginal proportion bearing in mind that the rest of the week is devoted to the standard French curriculum.[14]

The LCO programme turned into a political boomerang during the 1980s, when it was frequently attacked by the Right for weakening cultural cohesion in France.[15] During the headscarf affair of 1989, media reports suggested that some of the teachers recruited by sending states were using their classes to spread Islamic fundamentalism, in violation of the secular principles governing the state education system. There was little documentary evidence to support these claims (Lorcerie 1994b), but they were indicative of the widespread anxieties generated by what was now perceived to be the permanent settlement of cultural minorities of immigrant origin.

The Left had appeared more genuinely committed to pluralism when it came to power in 1981. By granting freedom of association to foreigners, it made it easier for minority groups to mobilize around projects which diverged from the cultural norms dominant in France. Additional funds were made available to support minority associations, principally through the FAS, and for the first time people of immigrant origin were included in its decision-making machinery. Similarly, the Conseil National des Populations Immigrées (National Council of Immigrant Populations – CNPI), created in 1984, gave representatives of minority ethnic groups a consultative role in the formation of government policy.

Between 1980 and 1986, the FAS's budget doubled, and the number of organizations receiving financial assistance from it increased fourfold (Weil 1991: 176). By 1991, it was funding more than 4,000 associations serving minority ethnic groups, compared to only a few hundred in 1981. Again, however, it is important to keep a sense of perspective in assessing the significance of these changes. Noting that the FAS has an annual budget of around 1,200 million francs, McKesson (1994: 28) states that much of it is spent assisting ethnically based associations which promote communitarianism, thereby undermining the official project of integration. In fact, over two-fifths of the total budget is allocated to housing, more than a quarter is spent on training designed to improve the employment prospects of immigrants and their descendants, and scarcely one-tenth is devoted to culturally based associations, of which no more than a small proportion might arguably be described as communitarian (Costa-Lascoux 1989: 96–7).

In its allocation of funding to minority-based associations, the fundamental aim of the FAS has been to co-opt people of immigrant origin who, while retaining certain differences, basically respect the cultural and legal norms prevailing in France. That principle has guided the FAS consistently despite the alternation of the Left and the Right in government since the mid-1980s. In line with this, generous funding has been given to organizations such as the Maghrebi-dominated France-Plus and the multi-ethnic SOS-Racisme (*Passages* 1989), which have explicitly committed themselves to the project of integration, understood as a process of constructive participation within French society by people of diverse origins. The same principles have governed the distribution of FAS subsidies to organizations active in radio, television and other media productions, discussed in Chapter 3.

It should not be forgotten, moreover, that simultaneously with its pluralist initiatives the Left instituted in 1981 the ZEP programme, which aims at improving mainstream educational provision in French schools containing dense concentrations of minority ethnic groups. The ZEPs are currently funded by the Ministry of Education alone to the tune of 1,360 million francs; in addition, other ministries and government agencies are estimated to contribute four times as much, making a total budget of around 7,000 million francs (Lorcerie 1994c: 35–6). Granted that the children of immigrants represent at least 30 per cent of those benefiting from this programme, (equivalent to about 2,000 billion francs on a pro rata basis), and that this is an extra layer reinforcing the much larger budget allocated to the basic education programme, state investment in the acculturation of immigrant-born children clearly dwarfs the sums spent by the FAS on cultural activities of all kinds.

Since the Islamic headscarf affair of 1989, a clear policy commitment, shared by Left and Right, has emerged in favour of co-opting organizations representing the Muslim population in France into a constructive dialogue with the state. The aim is to weaken the potential for Islamic fundamentalism by fostering organizational structures and religious practices which are compatible with French law and the spirit of *laïcité*. The French state has long recognized similar organizations as representatives of Catholics, Protestants and Jews (CNCDH 1992: 193–6). Organizations of this kind enjoy tax and other advantages, while serving as consultative channels between religious communities and the state, and as authorized intermediaries in such matters as the admission of spiritual counsellors to hospitals, prisons and other public establishments, as well as in the regulation of certain commercial activities (the preparation of ritually slaughtered meat, for example).[16]

The first government initiative aimed at establishing comparable channels of communication with Muslims was taken in 1990 by Socialist Interior Minister Pierre Joxe, who invited leading members of Islamic organizations to form a Conseil de Réflexion sur l'Avenir de l'Islam en France (Deliberative Council on the Future of Islam in France – CORIF). CORIF was entrusted with the task of advising Joxe on how relations between the state and the Muslim population might best be organized. The hope was that a unified representative organization acceptable to the state, similar to those already recognized for other religious faiths, would emerge from these discussions. Dissensions between rival groups of Muslims prevented this outcome, and when the Right returned to power in 1993 Pasqua attempted to work instead through the Algerian-dominated Grande Mosquée de Paris, traditionally the largest single Islamic organization in France, which sought to federate with other groups by setting up the Conseil Consultatif des Musulmans de France (Consultative Council of Muslims in France) (*Le Monde*, 23 November 1993). Early in 1995, this was transformed into the Conseil Représentatif des Musulmans de France (Representative Council of Muslims in France – CRMF), and Pasqua formally recognized it as the official voice of Muslims *vis-à-vis* the French state (*Le Monde*, 12 January 1995).

The representativeness of the CRMF was immediately challenged by rival federations such as the Union des Organisations Islamiques de France (UOIF) and the Fédération Nationale des Musulmans de France (FNMF) (*Le Monde*, 12 January 1995, 13 January 1995). The Left, too, had been sharply critical of the Right's support for the Grande Mosquée de Paris, but this was a disagreement over means rather than ends.[17] Their common long-term objective is an Islamic community organized as far as possible independently of foreign institutions. While the current level of dependence on foreign assistance (see pp. 122–4 above) makes it impossible to move directly to a 'purely French' Islam, a first step in this direction is being taken by favouring local or national organizations whose foreign connections are judged to be the least inimical to French interests. An important element in this strategy concerns the training and recruitment of imams (Islamic prayer-leaders), who at a grassroots level serve as the spiritual leaders and principal figureheads of local Muslim communities. Until very recently, there were no formal training-facilities for imams in France. As a consequence of this, practically all the imams active in France were trained and recruited abroad, where it was impossible for the French authorities to exert any significant influence. Shortly before leaving power in 1993, the Socialists signalled their wish to reduce this reliance on foreign-trained spiritual leaders by refusing visas to dozens of Algerian and Egyptian imams, extra numbers of whom were normally allowed into France during the month of Ramadan (*Le Monde*, 28 February 1993). They also attempted to exert tight control over the recruitment of staff and students in the first training-institute for imams in France, which was set up in 1991 by the UOIF. Two other such institutes were founded in 1993, one at the initiative of the FNMF and the other under the auspices of the Grande Mosquée de Paris (*Migrations-société* 1994). Because the last of these was regarded by the Balladur government as the most moderate, it received the support of Pasqua and of his colleague in the RPR, Jacques Chirac, who as Mayor of Paris had already provided a subsidy for the renovation of the Grande Mosquée de Paris (*Le Monde*, 30 July 1994).

In September 1994, Pasqua turned out in person to inaugurate a new mosque in Lyon, whose leaders, like those of the Grande Mosquée de Paris, were regarded as politically moderate. This, it should be recalled, was the same minister who, little more than a year earlier, had promised the French public 'zero immigration' and who during the intervening period had instigated several round-ups of alleged Islamic fundamentalists, some twenty of whom were deported by Pasqua only a month before he opened the Lyon mosque (*Le Monde*, 2 September 1994). His speech in Lyon included a revealing statement of government policy:

> We need to treat Islam in France as a French question instead of continuing to see it as a foreign question or as an extension into France of foreign problems. . . . It is no longer enough to talk of Islam in France. There has to be a French Islam. The French Republic is ready for this.
>
> (*Le Monde*, 1 October 1994)

In sketching this vision of a 'French Islam' independent of foreign forces, Pasqua was effectively inviting Muslims to participate in the conjuring-trick through which France has traditionally sought to minimize or efface public recognition of the diverse ethnic origins from which the population is descended (cf. pp. 2–5 above). Those whom the minister had expelled a few weeks earlier could have no place in this scheme of things, since they were alleged to be aiding terrorist networks set up in Algeria after the government there banned the fundamentalist Front Islamique du Salut (FIS). By supporting institutions such as the Grande Mosquée de Paris, whose leadership was appointed by the fiercely anti-fundamentalist Algerian government, Pasqua hoped to foster among the broad mass of Muslims in France a moderate form of Islam compatible with the republican tradition of *laïcité*.[18]

Although this is considerably less than the full-blown policy of multiculturalism once apparently favoured by some on the Left, it also falls a long way short of the intolerant mono-culturalism for which right-wing nationalists have traditionally argued. In pursuing a strategy of co-option, governments of both Left and Right have effectively accepted that cultural differences associated with recent migratory inflows are to be accommodated in France provided they are not felt to threaten the basic principles of republicanism and *laïcité*. The evidence examined above (pp. 118–31) suggests that those principles are indeed being internalized by Muslims. Hugely publicized confrontations between small numbers of Muslims and public agencies, such as those seen during the Islamic headscarf affairs of 1989 and 1994, have masked this underlying trend.

Similarly, behind the divisive rhetoric generated by the tactical exigencies of party-political rivalry, French policy-makers reflecting most shades of the political spectrum appear now to be committed to the social incorporation of minorities who continue to display cultural particularities derived from their pre-migratory past.

Conclusion

Since the suspension of labour recruitment from non-EC countries in 1974, French perceptions of immigration and its social consequences have changed radically. A process which was once seen as narrowly economic has now become highly politicized, and its cultural dimensions have raised searching questions about French national identity. Anxieties over the degree to which people of immigrant origin can or should be incorporated into French society have crystallized in the debate over 'integration' (Wieviorka 1990). Among politicians and the public at large, there is a widely held view that integration has become more difficult because recent immigrants and their descendants are both more different in their cultural traditions and more resistant to cultural change than were earlier minority groups. It is true that the cultural roots of today's minorities, which are predominantly of African and Asian origin, are often more distant from the norms prevailing in France than are the traditions in which most European immigrants were raised. Yet if recent immigrants and their descendants appear less well incorporated than earlier minority groups, the evidence examined in the course of this study suggests that this is due far more to socio-economic and political changes which have taken place within the receiving society than to differences in the cultural complexion of the minority population.

Marked contrasts in the pattern of ethnic relations frequently emerge when periods of economic expansion and labour shortages are compared with times of high unemployment and job insecurity (Milza 1985; Noiriel 1988: 247–93). After being welcomed during the labour shortages of the 1920s, the Europeans who dominated migratory inflows at that time became subject to xenophobic charges of 'unassimilability', and in some cases deportation, during the economic depression of the 1930s. Although migratory inflows from Africa, Asia and the Caribbean outstripped those from Europe soon after the Second World War, it was not until the labour market turned sour in the second half of the 1970s that these new minorities became the subject of intense public debate.

The almost relentless rise in unemployment and job insecurity witnessed in France during the last twenty years has made the process of social incorporation correspondingly difficult for growing numbers of people. Prior to this period, first-generation members of minority ethnic groups experienced a relatively high degree of functional incorporation within the booming post-war labour market. Their children have been reaching adulthood in very different circumstances. Across the country as a whole, unemployment is particularly high among young people, and some (but not all) minority ethnic groups have been particularly badly hit. As was shown in Chapter 2, the high unemployment levels suffered by certain visible minorities cannot be accounted for solely by reference to below-average levels of certified skills, and still less in terms of cultural differences among those concerned. If young people of South-East Asian origin fare less badly than other minority groups, this may be due in part to better educational qualifications, but they appear also to be less vulnerable to discrimination by employers than young Maghrebis and others of African descent, whose unemployment rates far exceed the national average. Although the descendants of Portuguese immigrants are often as badly qualified as second-generation Maghrebis, their unemployment rate is well below the national average.

While the poor qualifications gained by many young people of immigrant origin are sometimes blamed on a school system which tends to perpetuate social inequalities from one generation to the next, the state educational system is nevertheless proving extremely effective as an institution of acculturation. The evidence reviewed in Chapter 3 demonstrates clearly that most of the descendants of immigrants identify more closely with the cultural codes dominant in France than with those prevailing in sending countries, and it is clear that the educational system (together with the mass media) has played a central role in this. The disorders which have broken out periodically in certain *banlieues* containing high concentrations of minority ethnic youths are not in any sense a mark of inadequate acculturation or ethnic separatism. On the contrary, it is precisely because they share to a large extent the values and aspirations common to the majority of young people in France, but are denied equal opportunities for the fulfilment of their ambitions, that immigrant-born youths have sometimes vented their frustration in violent attacks on property and the representatives of the state, most notably the police (Lapeyronnie 1987; Body-Gendrot 1993).

Schain (1994) has pointed out that through institutions such as the Fonds d'Action Sociale (FAS), the French state today deals directly with associations organized along ethnic lines to a far greater degree than was previously the case. It is important to note, however, that the official recognition of ethnically-based associations and the decline of other organizations of a more 'universal' nature as instruments in the social incorporation of immigrants and their descendants are rooted primarily in changes in the receiving society. French trade unions, for example, which are universal in character in the sense that they are open to all workers, irrespective of ethnic origins, have traditionally played a significant role in inducting immigrants into organizational structures alongside native members of the labour force. During the 1980s, economic restructuring saw the number of trade union members as a proportion of the total labour force fall from about one in five to one in ten; among 18–24-year-olds it is estimated to have plummeted from about one in ten to one in a hundred (SOFRES 1992: 39). High levels of youth unemployment, which are particularly severe among minority groups, mean that many people of immigrant origin now have little, if any, direct çontact with organized labour. This has inevitably weakened the role of trade unions in the social incorporation of minority groups.

As immigrants have generally been concentrated in manual occupations, they have in the past tended to affiliate with French organizations based in the working classes, particularly the French Communist Party (PCF) and its trade union ally, the Confédération Générale du Travail (CGT), which has traditionally served as recruiting-ground for the party. The PCF has always depended more than any other party on the support of blue-collar workers, particularly in manufacturing and other sectors with relatively high rates of unionization. The party has therefore been greatly weakened by the rapid contraction of these sectors in recent years. Until the late 1970s, the PCF was by far the most powerful party of the Left. Since then, it has been eclipsed by the Socialist Party (PS), which has been strongly influenced by a more pluralist vision of French society than was generally encountered in French politics until the near-revolutionary upheaval of 1968.

Ireland (1994) has shown, however, that where, at a local level, the PCF still retains organizational strength, it continues to play a major role in structuring the incorporation of first- and second-generation members of minority groups. Thus throughout the 1980s in the Paris suburb of La Courneuve, where the Communists retained control of the municipal council while losing power in many other localities, 'ethnic-based organizing remained tributary to the working-class movement' (Ireland 1994: 123). The fact that this became increasingly untypical of the national pattern of minority incorporation arises not from the influx of Maghrebi and other Third World immigrants (who are strongly represented in La Courneuve as in other parts of the country) but from the wave of economic restructuring which has cut through much of French industry, severely weakening the PCF in many of the urban areas where its strength was traditionally concentrated.

In the northern textile town of Roubaix, the PCF has always been weaker than the Socialists and Catholic centrists, who governed the city in coalition throughout the post-war period until 1977. The PS then took overall control with minority PCF support. Compared with the Communist municipality of La Courneuve, the Socialist-led administration in Roubaix adopted a much more pluralist approach towards people of immigrant origin. Typical of this was the creation in 1978 of a Commission Extra-Municipale aux Etrangers (Associate Municipal Commission for Foreigners – CEM), a consultative body made up of representatives of the town's immigrant population. Similar consultative bodies were established for other types of minority groups such as the old and the disabled (Ireland 1994: 123–4). These initiatives were undertaken in the spirit of 'participation', a rallying-cry from 1968 which inspired the PS to favour the greater democratization of French society.

The same spirit was at work when the Socialists came to power nationally, again with minority PCF support, in 1981. Decentralization was an early priority, with substantial powers being shifted from the national government in Paris to regional and local councils. The regionalization of the Fonds d'Action Sociale and the introduction of people of immigrant origin into its decision-making bodies in 1983 was part of the same process, as was the creation in 1984 of the Conseil National des Populations Immigrées. While this increased willingness formally to recognize people of immigrant origin within consultative or decision-making public institutions was welcomed by many of those concerned, it is important to note that it came about primarily as a consequence of changes among French political elites, rather than in response to new demands from minority groups.

Members of older-established European minorities in France, such as the Italians and Spanish, have taken advantage of the liberal rights of association granted to foreigners in 1981 no less than have more recent arrivals of African or Asian origin (Campani, Catani and Palidda 1987; *Tribune Fonda* 1991; Diantelli 1992). On a per capita basis, the Portuguese probably have a denser network of voluntary associations than any other minority ethnic group (Hily and Poinard 1987). The more vigorous presence of ethnically based organizations is in this respect unconnected with the increased weight of non-Europeans among the population of recent immigrant origin.

Central and local arms of the state have recently encouraged Muslims to become more involved in the organization of community life than has hitherto been the case. In Mantes-la-Jolie, for example, judicial and police authorities supported by the Socialist mayor, Paul Picard, and his centre-right rival, Pierre Bédier, arranged for local Muslims to hold widely based elections to the governing council of the town's mosque in December 1994, with the aim of ousting a small fundamentalist faction which had taken control of this institution (*Le Monde*, 20 December 1994).[1] National initiatives undertaken by the Interior Ministry since 1990 under governments of both Left and Right have had a similar objective: to encourage the establishment of representative institutions reflecting the aspirations of the broad mass of Muslims in France, thereby marginalizing the minority of fundamentalists among them.

An important element implicit in this strategy is the conviction that most Muslims understand and accept the norms governing religious practices within the French tradition of *laïcité*. Interior Minister Charles Pasqua said as much only a day after deporting an Algerian imam accused of inciting violence in November 1994. During a parliamentary debate Raoul Béteille, who, like Pasqua, is a member of the centre-right Rassemblement pour la République (RPR), called on the minister to confront what he called the single most important question facing France at the end of the twentieth century: was the country not in danger of losing its identity because of the settlement of Muslim immigrants? Pasqua replied that while he would be uncompromising in the repression of anti-French religious propaganda, the situation was far less worrying than many people thought, since the overwhelming majority of Muslims in

France were as opposed to intolerance as the rest of the population (*Le Monde*, 8 November 1994, 9 November 1994).

After a period of acute discord in the late 1970s and early 1980s, most of France's political elite has come to recognize that recent migratory inflows are now irreversible. The question is no longer whether, but how, immigrants and their descendants should best be incorporated into French society. The discourse of integration contains many ambiguities, and widespread acts of discrimination place many obstacles in the way of minority groups. Even a radical improvement in the economic climate may not entirely remove those obstacles, but behind the sound and fury generated by party-political rivalry, the position of minority ethnic groups now appears somewhat less insecure than when the 'end' of immigration was decreed in the mid-1970s.

Chronology of events

Year	French executive	French public policy	Other developments
	Changes of President, Prime Minister (PM), and principal ministers with responsibility for immigration and minority ethnic groups		
1968	31 May – centre-right government reshuffle under PM Georges Pompidou; Raymond Marcellin appointed Interior Minister	1 and 29 July – reassertion of control over migratory inflows by restricting 'regularization' procedures and imposing quotas on Algerians	May–June – France paralysed by student demonstrations and workers' strikes
	11 July – Maurice Couve de Murville appointed PM of centre-right government		23 and 30 June – Centre-right parties win landslide majority in parliamentary elections
1969	15 June – Georges Pompidou elected President following resignation of Charles de Gaulle		29 February – report to Conseil Economique et Social by Corentin Calvez recommends tighter immigration controls, ethnic selection and improved social provisions

Year	French executive	French public policy	Other developments
	22 June – Jacques Chaban-Delmas appointed PM of centre-right government; Joseph Fontanet appointed Labour Minister		
1970			
1971			March–May – nine die in anti-Algerian attacks
1972		January-February – Marcellin-Fontanet circulars further tighten immigration controls	
	5 July – Pierre Messmer appointed PM of centre-right government	1 July – Parliament passes law prohibiting racial discrimination and incitement to racial violence	
1973	5 April – Georges Gorse appointed Labour Minister		4 and 11 March – centre-right victory in parliamentary elections
			19 September – Algerian government halts emigration following further racist killings in France
			October – Middle East war, followed by oil crisis and fears of economic downturn in West
1974	1 March – Jacques Chirac appointed Interior Minister		

Year	French executive	French public policy	Other developments
	19 May – Valéry Giscard d'Estaing elected President		
	27 May – Jacques Chirac appointed PM of centre-right government; Michel Poniatowski appointed Interior Minister		
	8 June – André Postel-Vinay appointed Minister of State for Immigrant Workers	5 July – suspension of labour migration by non-EC nationals	
	22 July 1974 – Paul Dijoud replaces Postel-Vinay as Minister of State for Immigrant Workers	9 October – government adopts 25-point package for tighter immigration controls and improved social provisions	
1975			April – Communist victory over US-backed regime in South Vietnam prompts exodus of asylum-seekers from South-East Asia
1976	25 July – Raymond Barre appointed PM of centre-right government		
1977	29 March – Christian Bonnet appointed Interior Minister; Lionel Stoléru appointed Minister of State for Manual and Immigrant Workers	26 April – creation of *aide au retour* (repatriation assistance)	

Year	French executive	French public policy	Other developments
1978		Stoléru conducts inconclusive negotiations aimed at mass repatriation of non-EC immigrants	
1979		December – insufficient parliamentary support to carry legislation proposed by Stoléru to facilitate large-scale forcible repatriations	
1980		10 January – Bonnet Law tightens entry and residence regulations	24 December – Communist mayor of Vitry orders demolition of hostel for African workers
1981	10 May – François Mitterrand elected President		April – hunger strike in Lyon against administrative expulsions
	21 May – Pierre Mauroy appointed PM of Socialist–Communist government; Gaston Deferre appointed Interior Minister	29 May – most expulsions halted	14 and 21 June – Left wins large majority in parlimentary elections
	23 June – François Autain appointed Minister of State for Immigrants	August–November – family reunifications made easier; amnesty announced to permit 'regularization' of illegal immigrants; foreigners granted free right of association; *aide au retour* abolished	July–August – disorders in Lyon suburbs

Year	French executive	French public policy	Other developments
1982		June – end of amnesty for illegal immigrants, with a total of 132,000 regulized	
1983	22 March – Georgina Dufois appointed Minister of State for Family, Population and Immigrant Workers		6 and 13 March – Right makes gains in municipal elections after campaign marked by heavy emphasis on immigration Summer – young Maghrebis targeted in upsurge of racist killings 4 September – Front National scores 17 per cent of first-round vote in municipal by-election in Dreux October–December – march Against Racism from Marseille to Paris
1984		27 April – reintroduction of repatriation assistance, now called *aide à la réinsertion* 29 May – Creation of Conseil National des Populations Immigrées (CNPI), consultative body on immigration and minority ethnic groups	17 June – FN takes 11 per cent of national vote in European Parliament elections

Year	French executive	French public policy	Other developments
	19 July – Laurent Fabius appointed Prime Minister of Socialist government	17 July – ten-year combined work and residence permit for most immigrants approved by Parliament	
	23 July – Pierre Joxe appointed Interior Minister; Georgina Dufoix appointed Minister for National Solidarity and Social Affairs	4 December – new restrictions on family reunifications	
1985			15 June – SOS-Racisme's first rock concert in Paris attracts crowd of 300,000
1986	20 March – Jacques Chirac appointed Prime Minister of centre-right government; Charles Pasqua appointed Interior Minister; Philippe Seguin appointed Minster for Social Affairs	9 September – Pasqua Law toughens entry and residence regulations for foreigners

12 November – government agrees draft legislation for reform of French nationality laws (CNF) | 16 March – centre-right parties win narrow overall majority in parliamentary elections

December – student demonstrations against proposed university reforms |
| 1987 | | 17 January – government delays CNF reform

14 March – Government announces special Commission to examine CNF | |

Year	French executive	French public policy	Other developments
1988	8 May – François Mitterand re-elected President		
	10 May – Michel Rocard appointed PM of Socialist-led government		
	12 May – Pierre Joxe appointed Interior Minister; Claude Evin appointed Minister for Solidarity		5 and 12 June – Socialists win relative majority in parliamentary elections
1989		2 August – Joxe Law softens Pasqua Law	Autumn – Islamic headscarf affair in Creil
		19 December – creation of Haut Conseil à l'Intégration	3 December – FN candidate wins parliamentary by-election in Dreux
1990	19 December – Michel Delebarre appointed Minister of State for Urban Affairs		October – disorders in Vaulx-en-Velin
1991			January–March – Gulf War
	15 May – Edith Cresson appointed PM of Socialist-led government		March – disorders in Sartrouville
	16 May 1991 – Philippe Marchand appointed Interior Minister; Jean-Louis Bianco appointed Minister for Social Affairs and Integration		May – disorders in Mantes-la-Jolie

Year	French executive	French public policy	Other developments
	25 May – Kofi Yamgnane appointed Minister of State for Social Affairs and Integration	13 July – Parliament passes 'anti-ghetto' law, requiring balanced urban developments	
1992	2 April – Pierre Bérégovoy appointed PM of Socialist-led government; Paul Quilès appointed Interior Minister; René Teulade appointed Minister for Social Affairs and Integration; Bernard Tapie appointed Minister for Urban Affairs		20 September – referendum approves Maastricht Treaty
1993	29 March – Edouard Balladur appointed PM of centre-right government; Charles Pasqua appointed Interior Minister; Simone Veil appointed Minister for Social Affairs, Health and Urban Affairs	July–August – 'Pasqua' laws reform access to French nationality, facilitate easier identity checks by police and limit entry and residence rights of foreigners	21 and 28 March – RPR and UDF win sweeping majority in parliamentary elections
		19 November – Parliament approves constitutional revision tightening asylum laws	
1994			Autumn – Education Ministry circular sparks new school confrontations over Islamic headscarf

Resource and documentation centres

The following organizations hold specialist collections of material relating to minority ethnic groups in France. Except where otherwise stated, these collections may be consulted by members of the public without charge.

Agence pour le Développement des Relations Interculturelles (ADRI)

4 rue René-Villermé,
75011 Paris,
France.

Telephone: (1) 43.48.49.19
Fax: (1) 43.48.25.17

A wide variety of books, periodicals and thematic dossiers. Particularly good holdings of official reports. Open to researchers and professionals active in the field of ethnic relations.

Association des Trois Mondes (ATM)

63 bis rue Cardinal Lemoine,
75005 Paris,
France.

Telephone: (1) 43.54.78.69
Fax: (1) 46.34.70.19

Specializes in audio-visual materials dealing with issues relating to the Third World, including immigration in France. Holds extensive catalogues of film and video productions, press dossiers, etc. To consult these holdings, it is necessary to make an appointment in advance.

Centre d'Information et d'Etudes sur les Migrations Internationales (CIEMI)

46 rue de Montreuil,
75011 Paris,
France.

Telephone: (1) 43.72.49.34
Fax: (1) 43.72.06.42

Wide-ranging collections include extensive newspaper cuttings. A small charge is made for a reader's card.

CNDP-Migrants

91 rue Gabriel-Péri,
92120 Montrouge,
France.

Telephone: (1) 46.57.11.67
Fax: (1) 46.57.10.60

User-friendly collections of books, periodicals and newspaper cuttings amply repay the short bus ride (route number 68) from the centre of Paris. Strong interest in pedagogic materials.

Centre for Research in Ethnic Relations (CRER)

University of Warwick,
Coventry CV4 7AL,
United Kingdom.

Telephone: 01203 523605
Fax: 01203 524324

Open to all *bona fide* researchers. While initially concerned primarily with the UK, specialist holdings of periodicals and pamphlets now increasingly embrace continental Europe, with France well represented.

Institut de Recherches et d'Etudes sur le Monde Arabe et Musulman

3–5 avenue Pasteur,
13617 Aix-en-Provence,
France.

Telephone: 42.21.59.88
Fax: 42.21.52.75

Open to postgraduate researchers and full-time academic staff. Specializes in French relations with the Islamic world.

Institut de Monde Arabe

1 rue des Fossés Saint-Bernard,
75005 Paris,
France.

Telephone: (1) 40.51.38.38
Fax: (1) 43.54.76.45

Open access to a wide range of books, periodicals and specialist collections, including a substantial body of material on immigrants originating in the Arab world.

La Médiathèque des Trois Mondes

63 bis rue du Cardinal Lemoine,
75005 Paris,
France.

Telephone: (1) 43.54.33.38
Fax: (1) 46.34.70.19

Run in conjunction with the ATM. Holds a large stock of films and video cassettes, including many relating to immigration, available for hire or purchase.

Keeping up to date

Up-to-the-minute bibliographic information on immigration and ethnic relations in France can be obtained by consulting the electronic data-base REMISIS (Réseau d'Information sur les Migrations Internationales). Annual cumulations derived from this data-base are also available in hard-copy form. Details on access and charges are available from REMISIS, CNRS-Université de Paris VIII, 15 rue Catulienne, 93200 Saint-Denis, France. Telephone: (1) 42.43.48.71. Fax: (1) 42.43.43.52.

The following periodicals specialize in immigration and ethnic relations in France:

ADRI-Biblio

Bi-monthly bibliographic roundup covering a wide range of disciplines. Published by ADRI.

Hommes et migrations

Long-established monthly featuring articles, debates, book reviews, and a chronology of recent events. Address: 40 rue de la Duée, 75020 Paris, France. Telephone: (1) 47.97.26.05. Fax: (1) 47.97.99.77.

Images Nord–Sud

Quarterly magazine listing audio-visual productions dealing with the Third World, including immigration in France. Published by ATM.

Migrance

Bi-annual listing organizations, research in progress and recent publications dealing with the history of minority ethnic groups in France. Published by Génériques, 34 rue de Citeaux, 75012 Paris, France. Telephone: (1) 49.28.57.75. Fax: (1) 49.28.09.30.

Migrants-formation

Monthly collection of articles, usually dealing with a specific theme. Emphasis on social, cultural and educational issues. Produced by CNDP-Migrants.

Migrants-nouvelles

Monthly bibliographic survey covering books, periodicals, official reports and major events in the field of ethnic relations. Cheap and quite comprehensive. Produced by CNDP-Migrants.

Migrations études

Monthly digest of official reports and research findings. Published by ADRI.

Migrations société

Bi-monthly. In addition to articles on recent research, includes regular analyses of media coverage in the field of ethnic relations and a list of recent acquisitions in the Documentation Centre of CIEMI, which produces this journal.

Mouvements

Monthly digest of news and information, dealing particularly with administrative aspects of the immigration field. Published by the Office des Migrations Internationales (OMI), 44 rue Bargue, 75015 Paris, France. Telephone: (1) 45.66.26.00. Fax: (1) 47.34.88.57.

OMIclasseur

Annual round-up and analysis of administrative changes in the field of immigration. Published by OMI.

OMIstats

Annual statistical digest published by OMI.

Paris-Plus

Bi-monthly guide to current and forthcoming cultural activities by minority ethnic groups. Published by Agence de Promotion des Cultures et du Voyage, 18 impasse Picou, 93200 Saint-Denis, France. Telephone and fax: (1) 48.20.38.23.

Plein droit

Monthly specializing in current issues, particularly legal aspects. Published by Groupe de Soutien des Travailleurs Immigrés (GISTI), 30 rue des Petites Ecuries, 75010 Paris, France. Telephone: (1) 42.47.07.09.

Panorama de la presse

Weekly press-cuttings on minority ethnic groups in France, and French relations with Third World countries. Produced by ADRI. Subscription rates are high.

Revue européenne des migrations européennes

Scholarly journal focusing frequently but not uniquely on France. Published quarterly by Département de Géographie, Université de Poitiers, 95 avenue du Recteur Pineau, 86022 Poitiers Cedex, France. Telephone: (1) 49.45.32.86.

Notes

PREFACE

1 While there are many valuable essays in the volume edited by Horowitz and Noiriel (1992), they are divided in their focal points between France and the US. Contributions to the volume edited by Ogden and White (1989) are scattered across a much longer historical period than that dealt with here.
2 See also the special issue of *Ethnic and Racial Studies* (1991).
3 Miller (1981), Safran (1986, 1992) and Ireland (1994) are rare exceptions.
4 All translations from French into English are my own.
5 Safran (1991) argues a similar case. However, in a more recent publication, Safran (1992) recognizes that, compared with Latinos in the US, Maghrebis in France have been far less able to resist the erosion of their cultural heritage.

1 OVERVIEW

1 For a fuller discussion of the limitations of French census data for the study of immigrants and their descendants, see Silberman (1992).
2 An authoritative account of this transition is presented by Cross (1983).
3 For a convenient encyclopaedic-style guide to immigration in twentieth-century France, see Amar and Milza (1990). The essays edited by Ogden and White (1989) span the nineteenth and twentieth centuries. Surveys of the period since 1945 include Georges (1986); Mestiri (1990); Ogden (1991); Fitzpatrick (1993). On the period since 1974, see Gaspard and Servan-Schreiber (1985); Fuchs (1987); Voisard and Ducastelle (1990); Taguieff (1991); Bernard (1993).
4 In 1987 the name of this organization was changed to the Office des Migrations Internationales (OMI).
5 For a useful survey of the literature, see Yinger (1985).
6 For a defence of this approach, see Banton (1991); for a critique, see Miles (1993).
7 On the history of French perceptions of Islam and the marginal role of

this religion within French society prior to the post-war period, see Sellam 1987.

8 Cf. Rath 1993 on the related concept of 'minorization'.

2 SOCIO-ECONOMIC STRUCTURES

1 The notion of the ghetto as a place for outsiders has been present since the term was introduced into Europe in the sixteenth century, when it denoted a neighbourhood in which Jews were forced to live.

2 For an analysis of French perceptions of this kind, see Crowley (1992).

3 Cultural differences are, however, only part of the picture. Until the mid-1980s, Algerian and other African women legally resident in France were not uncommonly refused work permits, whereas Portuguese women enjoyed unrestricted access to the labour market (Costa-Lascoux 1989: 7).

4 For a literature review of this field, see Aldrich and Waldinger (1990).

3 ETHNIC IDENTIFICATION AND MOBILIZATION

1 For an incisive critique of the supposed opposition between ethnicity and modernization, see Safran (1987).

2 Through the codification and enforcement of laws governing kinship structures, the state does, of course, play a major role in shaping the broad parameters within which family relationships develop. Todd (1994) has argued that differences in family structures are an important factor in conditioning both the pace of acculturation among minority groups and the willingness of receiving societies to accommodate cultural differences.

3 A useful overview of French educational policy in relation to the children of immigrants is provided by Boyzon-Fradet (1992).

4 For a literature review of this concept, see Olzak (1983).

5 These ratios have been calculated by assuming that a total of approximately 125,000 girls from Muslim families were attending French state secondary schools in 1994 (data derived from Conseil Economique et Social 1994: 57). The figure of 350,000 quoted by Rocard in 1989 included Muslim girls of primary- as well as secondary-school age. Although at least one girl has been expelled from a primary school for wearing a headscarf (*Le Monde*, 26 November 1994) it is normally only girls of secondary-school age who might potentially be involved. If the ratios were calculated on the basis of the total given by Rocard, the proportion of Muslim girls wearing headscarves would be one in 23 on the higher estimate advanced by the Interior Ministry or one in 175 on the higher estimate given by the Education Ministry.

6 On the problematic nature of the concept of the 'home country' or 'homeland', see Safran (1990).

7 Citing a news magazine account of the 1990 French Defence Ministry report, Safran (1991: 229) says it 'revealed that only 25 per cent of Beurs ... fulfilled their military obligations in France (the remainder either

serving in Algeria or getting exemption)'. This highly selective account of the report – echoed in Fitzpatrick's assertion that three-quarters of Franco-Algerian conscripts have 'found ways of avoiding it [i.e. military service] or opted to do it in the Algerian army' (Fitzpatrick 1993: 113) – passes over the fact that no more than three in ten have been opting for Algeria, and as almost two-thirds of these have been declared unfit for service only about one in ten has actually served in the Algerian armed forces (Faivre 1990: 33). Under Algerian law, the age of majority is 21. The French Defence Ministry believes that some Algerian fathers have used their parental rights to enlist their sons in the Algerian armed forces prior to their reaching the age of majority; once this has been done, the young men concerned have been prevented from serving in France (Biville 1990: 10). A clear majority of Franco-Algerian bi-nationals have nevertheless been opting for France, where about half have been declared unfit for service (Faivre 1990: 33); hence the seemingly low participation rate quoted by Safran. Contrary to the gloss put on these figures by Fitzpatrick, rejection by the French authorities cannot in all fairness be described as a way of 'avoiding' military service.

4 NATIONAL IDENTITY, NATIONALITY AND CITIZENSHIP

1 On the wider context within which anxieties over French national identity have developed, see Safran (1991: 223–4).
2 In a perceptive essay, Silberman (1992: 118–21) has shown that despite the official silence on ethnic origins maintained by the census authorities, traces of this ethnic hierarchy are clearly visible just below the surface of seemingly technical aspects of French census data.
3 Maghrebis were referred to at this time as North Africans. In Mauco's pre-war survey, they appeared as Arabs.
4 Until 1993, the *Code de la Nationalité Française* (CNF) was formally separate from the main body of civil laws, which are collectively known as the *Code civil*. Besides revising the laws governing French nationality, the 1993 reform incorporated them within the *Code civil*. In this sense, the CNF no longer exists as a separate entity.
5 On the historical evolution of French nationality laws, see Masson (1985); Laacher (1987); Decouflé (1992). Prior to 1993, the acquisition of French nationality by second-generation foreigners was automatic in the sense that it was conferred upon them without their having to request it. Although certain conditions applied (see below, p. 169), an act of volition was not formally among them. To prove their citizenship, those concerned had to demonstrate that they were born in France and had lived there during the five years preceding the age of majority; in formal terms, the submission of the necessary documents did not constitute a request for citizenship but served to prove that it was already held.
6 The calculation of data on military service is made complex by a number of factors, one of which is the fact that, depending on their personal circumstances, draftees may enlist at any point between the ages of 18

and 29. A Defence Ministry report compiled in 1990, based on a longer run of data than that submitted to the Nationality Commission in 1987, indicated that up to three in ten Franco-Algerian bi-nationals were opting to serve in Algeria: see above, p. 136.

5 POLITICS AND PUBLIC POLICY

1   As Ogden (1991: 300) has observed, an important exception to this lay in the DOM-TOM, where the French government actively recruited migrant workers from the early 1960s onwards.

2   Contrasting assessments of the relationship between these twin policy pillars are offered by Freeman (1992) and by Silverman (1992: 82–8).

3   For an analysis of the FN's policy platform, see Taguieff (1989). On the party's organizational structures and electoral strategies, see Fysh and Wolfreys (1992). On its origins and development within the wider historical context of the extreme Right in France, see Hainsworth (1992).

4   Valuable analyses of the evidence available on sources of support for the FN include Mitra (1988); Husbands (1991); Perrineau (1991) and Mayer and Perrineau (1993).

5   These new measures – covering entry and residence rights, police identity checks, and access to French nationality – were popularly dubbed the 'Pasqua' laws (cf. Costa-Lascoux 1994a). Although Interior Minister Charles Pasqua was directly responsible for most of this legislation, the nationality reform did not technically fall within his ministerial brief, but was the formal responsibility of Justice Minister Pierre Méhaignerie.

6   On the French concept of 'public order', see HCI (1992b: 17–25).

7   These figures concern the number of foreigners residing legally in France expelled each year. In addition, several thousand illegal residents are deported each year because they lack residence permits: see Costa-Lascoux (1989: 62–3).

8   The French designation was Secrétaire d'Etat aux Travailleurs Immigrés. This is sometimes misleadingly translated as Secretary of State for Immigrant Workers. In Britain, the term Secretary of State applies only to very senior ministers, and in the US it denotes the minister responsible for foreign affairs, whereas a *Secrétaire d'Etat* is a junior French minister responsible for a particular sector of activities, usually within a larger government department. Postel-Vinay, for example, was a subordinate of the Minister of Labour, Michel Durafour. Verbunt (1985: 137) captures the technical sense of *Secrétaire d'Etat* by translating it as Vice-Minister. The nearest formal equivalent in Britain is Minister of State.

9   A similar signal was sent by placing the new Minister of State for Immigrants, François Autain, within the Ministry of National Solidarity (a new name for the Ministry of Social Affairs), rather than within the Ministry of Labour.

10 It should also be noted that, compared with similar institutions in Britain, which distinguish a range of minority ethnic groups, some of which are

more disadvantaged than others, the FAS formally operates on the basis of a very crude distinction between only two ethnic groups: 'immigrant workers and their families' on the one hand, and the rest of the population on the other. While the FAS tends in practice to prioritize minority groups which are believed to be particularly disadvantaged, its programmes are not formally structured or evaluated on that basis.

11 On the history and operational structures of the FAS, see Caron (1990): 11–12; Khellil (1991): 122–9; Lapeyronnie (1993): 177–85.

12 For a literature review dealing with cultural policy in the field of immigration, see ADRI (1994).

13 The first experimental programme of this kind, aimed at the children of Portuguese immigrants, began in 1973. The scheme was widened to include children of other nationalities from 1975 onwards. While initially conceived in response to the wishes of sending states anxious to ensure that the cultural heritage of their expatriates was maintained, the LCO programme soon came to be regarded by the French authorities as a valuable tool in preparing the ground for repatriation (Boyzon-Fradet 1992: 155–7).

14 Schain (1985: 177) incorrectly states that the government decrees instituting the LCO programme provided for the children of immigrants to receive one-third of their instruction in their native languages. These classes were in fact confined to a part of the school timetable known as *le tiers temps pédagogique* (the third teaching sector), accounting for just three hours (not one-third) of the total teaching week (Costa-Lascoux 1989: 88; Lorcerie 1994a: 8).

15 The drastic reform or even abolition of the LCO programme was called for in official reports such as those of the Haut Conseil à l'Intégration (HCI 1992b: 51–3) and the Conseil Economique et Social (1994: 124).

16 As Roy (1994: 64) has pointed out, this formally involves the state in recognizing *religious* – but not *ethnic* – minorities. Although this distinction is in some respects a fine one (most – but not all – Muslims in France are of immigrant origin), it is important from the perspective of French republicanism. Recognition of religious organizations is considered acceptable because their members choose freely to associate with each other; by contrast, state recognition of ethnic groups would be a denial of personal freedom, since the origins of individuals are, as a matter of biological fact, beyond their control. The objective of the French state is to separate Muslims as far as possible from their foreign origins, treating them as individuals exercising their freedom of conscience – albeit through organized forms of religious belief – within the overarching framework of France's republican tradition.

17 Jean-Claude Barreau, advisor to Charles Pasqua on matters relating to immigration, confirmed this in a television interview on F3, 13 October 1994.

18 Although the current *Recteur* (head) of the Grande Mosquée de Paris, Dalil Boubakeur, was appointed by the Algerian government in 1992, it is important to note that he is a French national and the son of an earlier *Recteur*, Si Hamza Boubakeur, who sided with the French during the Algerian war of independence (*Libération*, 13 April 1992). Complex

from the outset, the juridical status of the Grande Mosquée de Paris, inaugurated in 1926, became the subject of labyrinthine disputes after decolonization: see Kepel (1987: 61–94, 313–52); *The Independent*, 12 February 1992.

CONCLUSION

1 These hopes were vindicated by the results of the elections, held in January 1995 (*Le Monde*, 24 January 1995).

Bibliography

Abelkrim-Chikh, R. (1991) 'Les Femmes exogames: entre la loi de Dieu et les droits de l'homme', in B. Etienne (ed.),; *L'Islam en France: islam, état et société*, Paris: CNRS, pp. 235–54

Abou Sada, A. (1990) 'L'Avenir des travailleurs immigrés dans le contexte de la restructuration des entreprises', in A. Abou Sada *et al.* (eds), *L'Immigration au tournant*, Paris: CIEMI/L'Harmattan, pp. 157–68

ADRI (Agence de Développement des Relations Interculturelles) (1990) *Dossier de presse sur l'affaire du foulard*, 4 vols, Paris: ADRI

—— (1994) *Action culturelle et intégration: un bilan des connaissances*, Paris: ADRI

Aissou, A. (1987) *Les Beurs, l'école et la France*, Paris: CIEMI/L'Harmattan

Aldrich, H. E., and Waldinger, R. (1990) 'Ethnicity and entrepreneurship', *Annual Review of Sociology*, vol. 16, pp. 111–35

Amar, A., and Milza, A. (1990) *L'Immigration en France au xxe siècle*, Paris: Armand Colin

Anstett, S. (1992) 'Suspension de l'immigration et besoins de l'économie française', *Revue française des affaires sociales*, vol. 46 (December), pp. 105–26

Asiatiques en France, Les (1994) Colloque, 18, 19, 20 novembre 1993, Paris: Mairie du 13e arrondissement

Auvolat, M., and Benattig, R. (1988) 'Les Artisans étrangers en France', *Revue européenne des migrations internationales*, vol. 4, no. 3, pp. 37–55

Babadji, R. (1992) 'Le Mixte franco-algérien: remarques à partir des conventions sur le service national et les enfants de couples mixtes séparés', in K. Basfao and J.-R. Henry (eds), *Le Maghreb, l'Europe et la France*, Paris: CNRS, pp. 323–42

Babylone (1989) 'L'Immigration à l'Université et dans la recherche', *Babylone*, nos 6–7 (November)

Bachmann, C., and Basier, L. (1984) 'Le Verlan: argot d'école ou langue des Keums?', *Mots*, no. 8 (March) pp. 169–87

Balibar, E. (1988) 'Propositions sur la citoyenneté', in C. Wihtol de Wenden (ed.), *La Citoyenneté et les changements de structures sociale et nationale de la population française*, Paris: Edilig/Fondation Diderot, pp. 221–34

Banton, M. (1983) *Racial and Ethnic Competition*, Cambridge: Cambridge University Press

—— (1991) 'The Race Relations Problematic', *British Journal of Sociology*, vol. 42, no. 1, pp. 115–30

Barbara, A. (1986) 'Discriminants et jeunes "beurs"', in G. Abou-Aada and H. Milet (eds), *Générations issues de l'immigration: 'mémoires et devenirs'*, Paris: Arcantère, pp. 123–38

—— (1993) *Les Couples mixtes*, Paris: Bayard

Barbulesco, L. (1985) 'Les Radios arabes de la bande FM', *Esprit*, no. 102 (June), pp. 176–85

Barou, J. (1989) 'L'Insertion des immigrés passe par leurs conditions de logement', *Hommes et migrations*, no. 1118 (January), pp. 29–37

—— (1992a) *L'Immigration en France des ressortissants des pays d'Afrique noire*, Paris: Secrétariat Général à l'Intégration

—— (1992b) 'Des Chiffres en général et de ceux de l'INSEE en particulier', *Migrants-formation*, no. 91 (December), pp. 5–10

Barreau, J.-C. (1992) *De l'immigration en général et de la nation française en particulier*, Paris: Le Pré aux Clercs

Bastenier, A., and Dassetto, F. (1993) *Immigration et espace public: la controverse de l'intégration*, Paris: CIEMI/L'Harmattan

Battegay, A. (1992) 'L'Actualité de l'immigration dans les villes françaises: la question des territoires ethniques', *Revue européenne des migrations internationales*, vol. 8, no. 2, pp. 83–100

Bazin, C., and Vermes, G. (1990) 'L'Enseignement du portugais et de l'arabe dans le secteur associatif: premiers résultats d'une recherche-action', *Migrants-formation*, no. 83 (December), pp. 76–97

Beaud, S., and Noiriel, G. (1991) 'Penser l' "intégration" des immigrés', in P.-A. Taguieff (ed.), *Face au racisme*, vol. 2: *Analyses, hypothèses, perspectives*, Paris: La Découverte, pp. 261–82

Beaugé, G. L. (1990) 'Immigration et nouvelles formes de salariat dans la crise du BTP', in G. Abou Sada *et al.* (eds), *L'Immigration au tournant*, Paris: CIEMI/L'Harmattan, pp. 181–93

Begag, A. (1986) *Le Gone du Chaâba*, Paris: Seuil

—— (1989) *North African Immigrants in France: The Socio-Spatial Representation of 'Here' and 'There'*, Loughborough: European Research Centre

—— (1991) 'Voyage dans les quartiers chauds', *Les Temps modernes*, vol. 47, nos 545–6 (December), pp. 134–64

Begag, A., and Delorme, C. (1994) *Quartiers sensibles*, Paris: Seuil

Berger, S., and Piore, M. J. (1980) *Dualism and Discontinuity in Industrial Societies*, Cambridge: Cambridge University Press

Bernard, P. (1993) *L'Immigration*, Paris: Le Monde-Editions/Marabout

Berrier, R. J. (1985) 'The French Textile Industry: A Segmented Labour Market', in R. Rogers (ed.), *Guests Come to Stay: The Effects of European Labor Migration on Sending and Receiving Countries*, Boulder: Westview Press, pp. 51–68

Berris, D. (1990) 'Scarves, Schools and Segregation: The *Foulard* Affair', *French Politics and Society*, vol. 8, no. 1 (Winter), pp. 1–13

Betts, R. F. (1961) *Assimilation and Association in French Colonial Theory and Practice*, New York: Columbia University Press

Biville, Y. (1990) 'Les Jeunes d'origine maghrébine et le service national', *Hommes et migrations*, no. 1138 (December), pp. 7–18

Blanc, M. (1990) 'Les Politiques d'attribution de logements sociaux aux minorités ethniques en France, Grande-Bretagne et Allemagne fédérale', *Migration*, no. 7, pp. 69–91

—— (1992) 'From Substandard Housing to Devalorized Social Housing: Ethnic Minorities in France, Germany and the UK', *European Journal of Intercultural Studies*, vol. 3, no. 1, pp. 7–25

Body-Gendrot, S. (1993) *Ville et violence: l'irruption de nouveaux acteurs*, Paris: Presses Universitaires de France

Bonnafous, S. (1992) 'Le terme "intégration" dans *Le Monde*: sens et non-sens', *Hommes et migrations*, no. 1154 (May), pp. 24–6

Borella, F. (1991) 'Nationalité et citoyenneté', in D. Colas, C. Emeri and J. Zylberberg (eds), *Citoyenneté et nationalité: perspectives en France et au Québec*, Paris: Presses Universitaires de France, pp. 209–29

Borkowski, J.-L. (1990) 'L'Insertion sociale des immigrés et de leurs enfants', *Données sociales 1990*, Paris: INSEE, pp. 310–14

Bouamama, S. (1989) 'Elections municipales et immigration: essai de bilan', *Migrations société*, vol. 1, no. 3 (June), pp. 22–45

Bouamama, S., Cordeiro, A., and Roux, M. (1992) *La Citoyenneté dans tous ses états: de l'immigration à la nouvelle citoyenneté*, Paris: CIEMI/ L'Harmattan

Boulot, S., and Boyzon-Fradet, D. (1987) 'Un Siècle de réglementation à l'école', in G. Vermes and J. Boutet (eds), *France, pays multilingue*, vol. 1: *Les Langues en France, un enjeu historique et social*, Paris: L'Harmattan, pp. 163–204

—— (1988) *Les Immigrés et l'école: une course d'obstacles*, Paris: CIEMI/ L'Harmattan

Boumaza, N., Rudder, V. de, and Maria, M. F. de (1989) *Banlieues, immigration, gestion urbaine*, Grenoble: Institut de Géographie Alpine

Bourdin, M.-J. (1992) '"Tu ne couperas point"', in E. Rude-Antoine (ed.), *L'Immigration face aux lois de la République*, Paris: Karthala, pp. 165–75

Bourgeba-Dichy, M. (1990) 'Des Militants maghrébins de la deuxième génération en France', *Revue du Tiers Monde*, vol. 31, no. 123 (July–September), pp. 623–36

Boyzon-Fradet, D. (1992) 'The French Education System: Springboard or Obstacle to Integration?', in D. L. Horowitz and G. Noiriel (eds), *Immigrants in Two Democracies: French and American Experiences*, New York and London: New York University Press, pp. 148–66

Brubaker, R. (1992) *Citizenship and Nationhood in France and Germany*, Cambridge, Mass.: Harvard University Press

Brunel, E. (1992) 'Les Chinois à Marne-la-Vallée', *Revue européenne des migrations internationales*, vol. 8, no. 3, pp. 195–209

Bryson, S. S. (1987) 'France Through the Looking Glass: The November–December 1986 French Student Movement', *French Review*, vol. 61, no. 2 (December), pp. 247–60

Cahier de l'Observatoire de l'Intégration (1994) 'L'Apport de la migration espagnole: bibliographie analytique', no. 11 (May)

Caron, M. (1990) 'Immigration, intégration et solidarité', *Regards sur l'actualité*, no. 116 (December), pp. 3–45

Campani, G., Catani, M., and Palidda, S. (1987) 'Italian immigrant associations in France', in J. Rex, D. Joly and C. Wilpert (eds), *Immigrant Associations in Europe*, Aldershot: Gower, pp. 166–200

Castellan, M., Marpsat, M., and Goldberger, M. F. (1992) 'Les Quartiers prioritaires de la politique de la ville', *INSEE Première*, no. 234 (December), pp. 1–4

Castles, S., and Kosack, G. (1973) *Immigrant Workers and Class Structures in Western Europe*, London: Oxford University Press for the Institute of Race Relations

Catani, M., and Palidda, S. (1989) 'Devenir Français: pourquoi certains jeunes étrangers y renoncent?', *Revue européenne des migrations internationales*, vol. 5, no. 2, pp. 89–106

Centre des Cultures Méditerranéennes (1989) *Les Immigrés et la participation à la vie locale*, Paris: Adels/Syros

Cesari, J. (1989) 'Les Stratégies identitaires des musulmans à Marseille', *Migrations société*, vol. 1, nos 5–6 (October–December), pp. 59–71

—— (1992) 'L'Emergence d'une élite intermédiaire parmi les Franco-Maghrébins', in K. Basfao and J.-R. Henry (eds), *Le Maghreb, l'Europe et la France*, Paris: CNRS, pp. 401–13

—— (1993) 'Les Leaders associatifs issus de l'immigration maghrébine: intermédiaires ou clientèle?', *Horizons maghrébins*, nos 20–1, pp. 80–94

Chaabaoui, M. (1989) 'La Consommation médiatique des Maghrébins', *Migrations société*, vol.1, no. 4 (August), pp. 23–40

Chaïb, Y. (1994) 'Le Lieu d'enterrement comme repère migratoire', *Migrations société*, vol. 6, nos 33–4 (May–August), pp. 29–40

Chaker, S. (1988) 'Le Berbère: une langue occultée en exil', in G. Vermes (ed.), *Vingt-cinq communautés linguistiques en France*, vol. 2: *Les Langues immigrées*, Paris: L'Harmattan, pp. 145–64

Champion, J.-B., Goldberger, M.-F., and Marpsat, M. (1993) 'Les Quartiers "en convention"', *Regards sur l'actualité*, no. 196 (December), pp. 19–28

Chauviré, Y. (1993) 'Répartition spatiale des principales nationalités étrangères en France', *Espace, populations, sociétés*, no. 3, pp. 533–40

Citron, S. (1987) *Le Mythe national: l'histoire de France en question*, Paris: Editions ouvrières/Etudes et documentation internationales

Club de l'Horloge (1985) *L'Identité de la France*, Paris: Albin Michel

CNCDH (Commission Nationale Consultative des Droits de l'Homme) (1991) *1990. La Lutte contre le racisme et la xénophobie*, Paris: La Documentation Française

—— (1992) *1991. La Lutte contre le racisme et la xénophobie*, Paris: La Documentation Française

—— (1993) *1992. La Lutte contre le racisme et la xénophobie*, Paris: La Documentation Française

—— (1994) *1993. La Lutte contre le racisme et la xénophobie*, Paris: La Documentation Française

Condon, S. E., and Ogden, P. E. (1991) 'Afro-Caribbean migrants in France:

employment, state policy and the migration process', *Transactions of the Institute of British Geographers*, n.s. 16, pp. 440–57

Conseil Economique et Social (1994) *La Scolarisation des enfants d'immigrés*, Paris: Conseil Economique et Social

Costa-Lascoux, J. (1983) 'L'Immigration algérienne et la nationalité des enfants d'Algériens', in L. Talha *et al.*, *Maghrébins en France: émigrés ou immigrés?*, Paris: CNRS, pp. 299–320

—— (1989) *De l'immigré au citoyen*, Paris: La Documentation Française

—— (1994a) 'Les Lois "Pasqua": une nouvelle politique de l'immigration', *Regards sur l'actualité*, no. 199 (March), pp. 19–43

—— (1994b) 'French Legislation against Racism and Discrimination', *New Community*, vol. 20, no. 3 (April), pp. 371–9

Courault, B. A. (1990) 'Les Etrangers "catégorie" du marché dual ou "vecteur" de la flexibilité du travail', in G. Abou Sada *et al.* (eds), *L'Immigration au tournant*, Paris: CIEMI/L'Harmattan, pp. 109–22

Courtois, S. (1989) *Le Sang de l'étranger: les immigrés de la MOI dans la résistance*, Paris: Fayard

Cross, G. S. (1983) *Immigrant Workers in Industrial France: The Making of a New Laboring Class*, Philadelphia: Temple University Press

Cross, M. (1995) '"Race", Class Formation and Political Interests: A Comparison of Amsterdam and London', in A. G. Hargreaves and J. Leaman (eds), *Racism, Ethnicity and Politics in Contemporary Europe*, Aldershot: Edward Elgar, pp. 47–78

Crowley, J. (1992) 'Minorités ethniques et ghettos aux Etats-Unis: modèle ou anti-modèle pour la France?', *Esprit*, no. 182 (June), pp. 78–94

—— (1993) 'Paradoxes in the Politicisation of Race: A Comparison of the UK and France', *New Community*, vol. 19, no. 4 (July), pp. 627–43

Culture et immigration (1980) Rapport de la commission mixte 'Culture et immigration' installée le 21 novembre 1979 par le Président de la République, Paris: ICEI

Cunha, M. do C. (1988) *Portugais de France: essai sur une dynamique de double appartenance*, Paris: L'Harmattan

Dabène, L., and Billiez, J. (1987) 'Le Parler des jeunes issus de l'immigration', in G. Vermes and J. Boutet (eds), *France, pays multilingue*, vol. 2: *Pratiques des langues en France*, Paris: L'Harmattan, pp. 62–77

Decouflé, A.-C. (1992) 'Historic Elements of the Politics of Nationality in France', in D. L. Horowitz and G. Noiriel (eds), *Immigrants in Two Democracies: French and American Experiences*, New York and London: New York University Press, pp. 357–67

Decouflé, A.-C., and Tétaud, M. (1993) *La Politique de la nationalité en 1992: données chiffrées et commentaires*, Paris: Ministère des Affaires Sociales, Direction de la Population et des Migrations

Déjeux, J. (1989) *Image de l'étrangère: unions mixtes franco-maghrébins*, Paris: Boîte à documents

Désir, H. (1985) *Touche pas à mon pote*, Paris: Grasset

Desplanques, G. (1985) 'Nuptialité et fécondité des étrangères', in *Economie et statistique*, no. 179 (July–August), pp. 29–46

Desplanques, G., and Tabard, N. (1991) 'La Localisation de la population étrangère', *Economie et statistique*, no. 242 (April), pp. 51–62

Diantelli, E. (1992) 'L'Etat espagnol et les associations d'émigrés en France: une relation structurante', *Migrations société*, vol. 4, no. 19 (January–February), pp. 35–43

Dignan, D. (1981) 'Europe's Melting-Pot: A Century of Large-Scale Immigration into France', *Ethnic and Racial Studies*, vol. 4, no. 2 (April), pp. 137–52

Dreyfus, M., and Milza, P. (1987) *Un Siècle d'immigration italienne en France (1850–1950): Etat des travaux*, Paris: CEDEI/CHEVS

Droit de vivre (1981) Campaign statements by presidential candidates, May, pp. 15–17

Dubet, F. (1987) *La Galère: jeunes en survie*, Paris: Fayard, 1987

—— (1989) 'Immigrations: qu'en savons-nous?' (special issue of *Notes et études documentaires*, no. 4887)

Dubet, F., and Lapeyronnie, D. (1992) *Les Quartiers d'exil*, Paris: Seuil

Duhamel, O., and Jaffré, J. (1987) 'L'Opinion publique et le chômage: réflexions sur trois courbes', *Les Temps modernes*, vol. 42, nos 496–7 (November–December), pp. 305–18

Echardour, A., and Maurin, E. (1993) 'La Main-d'oeuvre étrangère', in *Données sociales*, Paris: INSEE, pp. 504–11

Economie et statistique (1991) 'Les Etrangers en France', no. 242, April

Espaces 89 (1985) *L'Identité française*, Paris: Tierce

Ethnic and Racial Studies (1991) 'Migration and Migrants in France', vol. 14, no. 3 (July)

Etienne, B. (1987) *L'Islamisme radical*, Paris: Hachette

—— (1989) *La France et l'islam*, Paris: Hachette

—— (ed.) (1991) *L'Islam en France: islam, état et société*, Paris: CNRS

Etre Français aujourd'hui et demain (1988) Rapport de la Commission de la nationalité présenté par M. Marceau Long, président, au Premier Ministre, 2 vols, Paris: Union Générale d'Editions

Faivre, M. (1990) 'Le Service militaire des binationaux', *Hommes et migrations*, no. 1138 (December), pp. 32–7

Feldblum, M. (1993) 'Paradoxes of Ethnic Politics: The Case of Franco-Maghrebis in France', *Ethnic and Racial Studies*, vol. 16, no. 3 (January), pp. 52–74

Fitzpatrick, B. (1993) 'Immigrants', in J. E. Flower (ed.), *France Today*, London: Hodder & Stoughton, pp. 99–125

Freeman, G. P. (1979) *Immigrant Labor and Racial Conflict in Industrial Societies: The French and British Experiences*, Princeton: Princeton University Press

—— (1992) 'The Consequences of Immigration Policies for Immigrant Status: A British and French Comparison', in A. M. Messina *et al.* (eds), *Ethnic and Racial Minorities in Advanced Industrial Democracies*, New York: Greenwood Press, pp. 17–32

Fuchs, G. (1987) *Ils resteront: le défi de l'immigration*, Paris: Syros

Fysh, P., and Wolfreys, J. (1992) 'Le Pen, the National Front and the Extreme Right in France', *Parliamentary Affairs*, vol. 45, no. 3 (July), pp. 309–26

Galap, J. (1993) 'Phénotypes et discriminations des Noirs en France: questions de méthode', *Migrants-formation*, no. 94 (September), pp. 39–54

Gallissot, R., Boumaza, N., and Clément, G. (1994) *Ces Migrants qui font le prolétariat*, Paris: Méridiens Klincksieck

Garson, J.-P., and Mouhoud, E. M. (1989) 'Sous-traitance et désalarisation formelle de la main-d'oeuvre dans le BTP', *La Note de l'IRES*, no. 19, pp. 36–47

Garson, J.-P., and Tapinos, G. (eds) (1981) *L'Argent des immigrés: revenus, épargne et transferts de huits nationalités immigrées en France*, Paris: Presses Universitaires de France

Gaspard, F. (1990) *Une Petite Ville en France*, Paris: Gallimard

Gaspard, F., and Servan-Schreiber, C. (1985) *La Fin des immigrés*, revised edition, Paris: Seuil

Gastaut, Y. (1994) 'Les Mutations du thème de l'immigration dans le journal *Le Monde* (1958–1992)', *Migrations société*, vol. 6, no. 31 (January–February), pp. 40–51

Geertz, C. (ed.) (1963) *Old Societies and New States: The Quest for Modernity in Asia and Africa*, New York: Free Press

Geisser, V. (1992) 'Les Elites politiques issues de l'immigration maghrébine: l'impossible médiation', *Migrations société*, vol. 4, nos 22–3 (July–October), pp. 129–38

Georges, P. (1986) *L'Immigration en France: faits et problèmes*, Paris: Armand Colin

Gillette, A., and Sayad, A. (1984) *L'Immigration algérienne en France*, 2nd edition, Paris: Entente

Gilroy, P. (1993) *The Black Atlantic: Modernity and Double Consciousness*, London: Verso

Ginesy-Galano, M. (1984) *Les Immigrés hors la cité: le système d'encadrement dans les foyers (1973–1982)*, Paris: L'Harmattan/CIEM

Girard, A., and Stoetzel, J. (1953) *Français et immigrés*, vol. 1: *L'Attitude française. L'adaptation des Italiens et des Polonais*, Paris: Presses Universitaires de France/Institut National d'Etudes Démographiques

Giudice, F. (1992) *Arabicides: une chronique française 1970–1991*, Paris: La Découverte

Gokalp, A. (1992) 'L'Immigration turque: repères communautaires et transition générationnelle', *Migrations société*, vol. 4, no. 20 (March–April), pp. 41–6.

Gonzales-Quijano, Y. (1988) 'Les "Nouvelles" Générations issues de l'immigration maghrébine et la question de l'islam', in R. Leveau and G. Kepel (eds), *Les Musulmans dans la société française*, Paris: Presses de la Fondation Nationale des Sciences Politiques, pp. 65–76

Gordon, M. M. (1964) *Assimilation in American Life: The Role of Race, Religion and National Origins*, New York: Oxford University Press

Green, N. (1991) 'L'Immigration en France et aux Etats-Unis: historiographie comparée', *Vingtième siècle*, no. 29 (January–February), pp. 67–82

Grillo, R. D. (1985) *Ideologies and Institutions in Urban France*, Cambridge: Cambridge University Press

Guillaume, S. (1991) 'Citoyenneté et colonisation', in D. Colas, C. Emeri and J. Zylberberg (eds) (1991) *Citoyenneté et nationalité: perspectives en France et au Québec*, Paris: Presses Universitaires de France, pp. 123–36

Guillon, M., and Taboada-Leonetti, I. (1986) *Le Triangle de Choisy: un quartier chinois à Paris*, Paris: CIEMI/L'Harmattan

Hainsworth, P. (1992) 'The Extreme Right in Post-War France: The Emergence and Success of the Front National', in P. Hainsworth (ed.), *The Extreme Right in Europe and the USA*, London: Pinter, pp. 29–60

Hall, S. (1992) 'The Question of Cultural Identity', in S. Hall, D. Held and T. McGrew (eds), *Modernity and its Futures*, Cambridge: Polity Press in association with the Open University, pp. 273–325

Hames, C. (1989) 'La Construction de l'islam en France', *Archives en sciences sociales des religions*, vol. 68, pp. 79–82

Hamoumou, M. (1993) *Et ils sont devenus harkis*, Paris: Fayard

Hargreaves, A. G. (1988) 'The French Nationality Code Hearings', in *Modern and Contemporary France*, no. 34 (July), pp. 1–11

—— (1990) 'Algerians in France: The End of the Line?', *Contemporary French Civilization*, vol. 14, no. 2 (Summer–Fall), pp. 292–306

—— (1991a) *Voices from the North African Immigrant Community in France: Immigration and Identity in Beur Fiction*, Oxford and New York: Berg

—— (1991b) 'The Political Mobilization of the North African Immigrant Community in France', *Ethnic and Racial Studies*, vol. 14, no. 3 (July), pp. 350–67

—— (1992a) 'L'Europe, les pays anglo-saxons et le Tiers-Monde chez les jeunes issus de l'immigration maghrébine en France', in K. Basfao and J.-R. Henry (eds), *Le Maghreb, l'Europe et la France*, Paris: CNRS, pp. 379–89

—— (1992b) 'Ethnic Minorities and the Mass Media in France', in R. Chapman and N. Hewitt (eds), *Popular Culture and Mass Communication in Twentieth Century France*, Lewiston, Queenston and Lampeter: Edwin Mellen Press, pp. 165–80

—— (1993a) 'Figuring Out Their Place: Post-Colonial Writers of Algerian Origin in France', in *Forum for Modern Language Studies*, vol. 29, no. 4 (October), pp. 335–45

—— (1993b) 'Télévision et intégration: la politique audiovisuelle du FAS', *Migrations société*, vol. 5, no. 30 (November–December), pp. 7–22

—— (1995) 'Perceptions of Place among Writers of Algerian Immigrant Origin in France', in R. King and P. White (eds), *Migration and Literature*, London: Routledge, pp. 89–100

—— (forthcoming) 'A Deviant Construction: The French Media and the *Banlieues*', in M. Cross (ed.), *Split Cities: Migrants, Minorities and Social Exclusion in Europe*, London: UCL Press

Hargreaves, A. G., and Perotti, A. (1993) 'The Representation on French Television of Immigrants and Ethnic Minorities of Third World Origin', *New Community*, vol. 19, no. 2 (January), pp. 251–61

Hargreaves, A. G., and Stenhouse, T. S. (1991) 'Islamic Beliefs Among Youths of North African Origin in France', *Modern and Contemporary France*, no. 45 (April), pp. 27–35.

—— (1992) 'The Gulf War and the Maghrebian Community in France', *Maghreb Review*, vol. 17, nos 1–2, pp. 42–54.

Harris, N. (1991) 'La "Loi Joxe" et son substrat politique et symbolique', *Contemporary French Civilization*, vol. 15, no. 1 (Winter–Spring), pp. 18–34

HCI (Haut Conseil à l'Intégration) (1991) *Pour un modèle français de l'intégration*, Paris: La Documentation Française

—— (1992a) *La Connaissance de l'immigration et de l'intégration, novembre 1991*, Paris: La Documentation Française

—— (1992b) *Conditions juridiques et culturelles de l'intégration*, Paris: La Documentation Française

—— (1993a) *La Connaissance de l'immigration et de l'intégration, décembre 1992*, Paris: La Documentation Française

—— (1993b) *Les Etrangers et l'emploi: décembre 1992*, Paris: La Documentation Française

—— (1993c) *L'Emploi illégal des étrangers*, Paris: La Documentation Française

Hechter, M., *et al.* (1982) 'A Theory of Ethnic Collective Action', *International Migration Review*, vol. 16, no. 2, pp. 412–34

Heisler, M. D. and Schmitter Heisler, B. (1986) 'Transnational Migration and the Modern Democratic State: Familiar Problems in New Form, or a New Problem?', *Annals of the American Academy of Political and Social Science*, vol. 485 (May), pp. 12–22

Héran, F. (1993) 'L'Unification linguistique de la France', *Population et sociétés*, no. 285 (December), pp. 1–4

Hessel, S. (ed.) (1988) *Immigrations: le devoir d'insertion*, 2 vols, Paris: La Documentation Française

Hily, M.-A., and Poinard, M. (1987) 'Portuguese Associations in France', in J. Rex, D. Joly and C. Wilpert (eds), *Immigrant Associations in Europe*, Aldershot: Gower, pp. 126–65

Hollifield, J. F. (1992) *Immigrants, Markets and States: The Political Economy of Postwar Europe*, Cambridge, Mass.: Harvard University Press

Hommes et migrations (1991a) 'Elles . . . Femmes en mouvement(s)', no. 1141 (March)

—— (1991b) 'Aux soldats méconnus: étrangers, immigrés, colonisés au service de la France (1914–1918 et 1939–1945)', no. 1148 (November)

—— (1993) 'Le Bouddhisme en France', no. 1171 (December)

Horowitz, D. L., and Noiriel, G. (eds) (1992) *Immigrants in Two Democracies: French and American Experiences*, New York and London: New York University Press

Humblot, C. (1989) 'Les Émissions spécifiques: de "Mosaïque" à "Rencontre"', *Migrations-société*, vol. 1, no. 4 (1989), pp. 7–14

Husbands, C. T. (1991) 'The Support for the *Front National*: Analyses and Findings', *Ethnic and Racial Studies*, vol. 14, no. 3 (July), pp. 382–416

IGAS (Inspection Générale des Affaires Sociales) (1992) 'Enquête sur l'insertion des jeunes immigrés dans l'entreprise', 2 vols, Paris: IGAS

INSEE (Institut National de la Statistique de des Etudes Economiques) (1986) *Les Etrangers en France*, Contours et caractères, Paris: INSEE

—— (1992a) *Recensement de la population de 1990: nationalités, résultats du sondage au quart*, Paris: INSEE

—— (1992b) 'La Fécondité des étrangères en France se rapproche de celle des Françaises', *INSEE Première*, no. 231 (November)

—— (1994) *Les Etrangers en France*, Contours et caractères, Paris: INSEE

Ireland, P. (1994) *The Policy Challenge of Ethnic Diversity: Immigrant Politics in France and Switzerland*, Cambridge, Mass.: Harvard University Press

Jazouli, A. (1986) *L'Action collective des jeunes maghrébins de France*, Paris: CIEMI/L'Harmattan

—— (1992) *Les Années banlieues*, Paris: Seuil

Jerab, A. (1988) 'L'Arabe des maghrébins: une langue, des langues', in G. Vermes (ed.), *Vingt-cinq communautés linguistiques en France*, vol. 2: *Les Langues immigrées*, Paris: L'Harmattan, pp. 31–59

Jones, T. (1993) *Britain's Ethnic Minorities*, London: Policy Studies Institute

Kastoryano, R. (1986) *Etre Turc en France: réflexions sur familles et communauté*, Paris: CIEMI/L'Harmattan

Kepel, G. (1987) *Les Banlieues de l'islam: naissance d'une religion en France*, Paris: Seuil

Kessas, F. (1990) *Beur's Story*, Paris: L'Harmattan

Khellil, M. (1991) *L'Intégration des Maghrébins en France*, Paris: Presses Universitaires de France

Kokoreff, M. (1991) 'Tags et zoulous: une nouvelle violence urbaine', *Esprit*, no. 169 (February), pp. 23–36

Laacher, S. (ed.) (1987) *Questions de nationalité: histoire et enjeux d'un code*, Paris: CIEMI/L'Harmattan

Lallaoui, M. (1993) *Du bidonville aux HLM*, Paris: Syros

Lapeyronnie, D. (1987) 'Assimilation, mobilisation et action collective chez les jeunes de la seconde génération de l'immigration maghrébine', *Revue française de sociologie*, vol. 28, no. 2 (April–June), pp. 287–318

—— (1993) *L'Individu et les minorités: la France et la Grande-Bretagne face à leurs immigrés*, Paris: Presses Universitaires de France

Lebon, A. (1987) 'Attribution, acquisition et perte de la nationalité française: un bilan (1973–1986)', *Revue européenne des migrations internationales*, vol. 3, nos 1–2, pp. 7–34

—— (1993) *Immigration et présence étrangère en France: le bilan d'une année 1992–1993*, Paris: Ministère des Affaires Sociales, Direction de la Population

Lee, S. M. (1993) 'Racial Classifications in the US Census, 1890–1990', *Ethnic and Racial Studies*, vol. 16, no. 1 (January), pp. 75–94

Lefort, F., and Néry, M. (1985) *Emigré dans mon pays*, Paris: CIEM/L'Harmattan

Le Gallou, J.-Y., and Jalkh, J. F. (1987) *Etre Français, cela se mérite*, Paris: Albatros

Lehembre, B. (1984) 'L'Immigration sur la bande FM', *Im'média magazine*, no. 1 (Autumn), pp. 30–3

Le Huu Khoa (1985) *Les Vietnamiens en France: insertion et identité*, Paris: CIEM/L'Harmattan

—— (1987) *Les Jeunes Vietnamiens de la deuxième génération: la semi-rupture au quotidien*, Paris: CIEMI/L'Harmattan

Lemoine, M. (1992) 'Les Difficultés d'intégration professionnelle des jeunes étrangers ou d'origine étrangère', *Revue française des affaires sociales*, vol. 46 (December), pp. 173–80

Le Pen, J.-M. (1984) *Les Français d'abord*, Paris: Editions Carrère-Michel Lafon

Le Pors, A. (1977) *Immigration et développement économique et social*, Paris: La Documentation Française

Lequin, Y. (ed.) (1988) *La Mosaïque France: histoire des étrangers et de l'immigration en France*, Paris: Larousse

Leveau, R. (1988) 'The Islamic Presence in France', in T. Gerholm and Y. G. Lithman (eds), *The New Islamic Presence in Western Europe*, London: Mansell, pp. 107–22

Leveau, R., and Wihtol de Wenden, C. (1991) *Modes d'insertion des populations de culture islamique dans le système politique français*, Paris: Mission Interministérielle Recherche Expérimentation

Liebkind, K. (ed.) (1989) *New Identities in Europe: Immigrant Ancestry and the Ethnic Identity of Youth*, Aldershot: Gower

Lloyd, C. (1991) 'Concepts, Models and Anti-Racist Strategies in Britain and France', *New Community*, vol. 18, no. 1, pp. 63–73

Lochak, D. (1992) 'Discrimination against Foreigners under French Law', in D. L. Horowitz and G. Noiriel (eds), *Immigrants in Two Democracies: French and American Experiences*, New York and London: New York University Press, pp. 391–410

Lorcerie, F. (1994a) 'Les Sciences sociales au service de l'identité nationale: le débat sur l'intégration en France au début des années 1990', in D.-C. Martin (ed.), *Cartes d'identité: comment dit-on 'nous' en politique?*, Paris: FNSP, pp. 245–81

—— (1994b) 'L'Islam dans les cours de "langue et culture d'origine": le procès', *Revue européenne des migrations internationales*, vol. 10, no. 2, pp. 5–43

—— (1994c) 'Les ZEP 1990–1993 pour mémoire', *Migrants-formation*, no. 97 (June), pp. 30–48

McKesson, J. A. (1994) 'Concepts and Realities in a Multiethnic France', *French Politics and Society*, vol. 12, no. 1 (Winter), pp. 16–38

Malik, S. (1990) *Histoire secrète de SOS-Racisme*, Paris: Albin Michel

Ma Mung, E. (1992) 'L'expansion du commerce ethnique: Asiatiques et Maghrébins dans la région parisienne', *Revue européenne des migrations internationales*,vol. 8, no. 1, pp. 39–59

Ma Mung, E., and Guillon, M. (1986) 'Les commerçants étrangers dans l'agglomération parisienne', *Revue européenne des migrations internationales*, vol. 2, no. 3 (December), pp. 106–34

Marangé, J., and Lebon, A. (1982) *L'Insertion des jeunes d'origine étrangère dans la société française*, Paris: La Documentation Française

Marie, C.-V. (1988) 'L'Immigration clandestine et l'emploi des travailleurs étrangers en situation irrégulière', in S. Hessel (ed.), *Immigrations: le devoir d'insertion. Analyses et annexes*, Paris: La Documentation Française, pp. 331–74

—— (1992) 'Les Etrangers non-salariés en France, symbole de la mutation économique des années 80', *Revue européenne des migrations internationales*, vol. 8, no.1, pp. 27–38

—— (1993a) *Les Populations des DOM-TOM, nées et originaires, résidant en France métropolitaine*, Paris: INSEE

—— (1993b) 'Les Antillais en France: histoire et réalités d'une migration ambiguë', *Migrants-formation*, no. 94 (September), pp. 5–14

Marseille–Paris, je marche, moi non plus (1984), Paris: Sans frontière

Marshall, T. H. (1950) *Citizenship and Social Class, and Other Essays*, Cambridge: Cambridge University Press

Martiniello, M. (1994) 'La Citoyenneté à l'aube du 21ième siècle: questions et enjeux majeurs', rapport de recherche préparé à la demande et pour la Fondation Roi Baudouin, Brussels

Mason, D. (1990), '"A Rose by Any Other Name . . ."? Categorisation, Identity and Social Science', *New Community*, vol. 17, no. 1 (October), pp. 123–33

—— (1991) 'The Concept of Ethnic Minority: Conceptual Dilemmas and Policy Implications', *Innovation*, vol. 4, no. 2, pp. 191–209.

Masson, J. (1985) 'Français par le sang, Français par la loi, Français par le sang', *Revue européenne des migrations internationales*, vol. 1, no. 2 (December), pp. 9–19

Maurin, E. (1991) 'Les Etrangers: une main-d'oeuvre à part?', *Economie et statistique*, no. 242 (April), pp. 39–50

Mayer, N. (1987) 'De Passy à Barbès: deux visages du vote Le Pen à Paris', *Revue française de science politique*, vol. 37, no. 6 (December), pp. 891–906

—— (1995) 'Ethnocentrism and the Front National Vote in the 1988 French Presidential Elections', in A. G. Hargreaves and J. Leaman (eds), *Racism, Ethnicity and Politics in Contemporary Europe*, Aldershot: Edward Elgar, pp. 96–111

Mayer, N., and Perrineau, P. (1993) 'La Puissance et le rejet ou le lepénisme dans l'opinion', in SOFRES, *L'Etat de l'opinion 1993*, Paris: Seuil, pp. 63–78

M'Barga, J.-P. (1992) 'Excision, fonctions et conséquences de sa répression en milieu migrant en France', in E. Rude-Antoine (ed.), *L'Immigration face aux lois de la République*, Paris: Karthala, pp. 165–75

Mela, V. (1988) 'Parler verlan: règles et usages', in *Langage et société*, no. 45 (September), pp. 47–70

Merckling, O. (1987) 'Nouvelles politiques d'emploi et substitution de la main-d'oeuvre immigrée dans les entreprises françaises', *Revue européenne des migrations internationales*, vol. 3, nos 1–2, pp. 73–95

Mestiri, E. (1988) 'Le Souffle d'une jeunesse: jeunes d'origine étrangère dans le mouvement étudiant de l'automne de 1986', *Tribune immigrée*, nos 24–5 (January–March), pp. 118–19

—— (1990) *L'Immigration*, Paris: La Découverte

Migrants-formation (1990) 'Religions et intégration', *Migrants-formation*, no. 82 (September)

Migrations société (1992) 'Immigrés de Turquie', *Migrations société*, vol. 4, no. 20 (March–April)

—— (1994) 'Intermédiaires culturels: le champ religieux', vol. 6, nos 33–4 (May–August)

Miles, R. (1989) *Racism*, London: Routledge

―――― (1993) *Racism after 'Race Relations'*, London: Routledge

Miles, R., and Phizacklea, A. (1977) 'Class, Race, Ethnicity and Political Action', *Political Studies*, vol. 25, no. 4 (December), pp. 491–507

Miller, M. J. (1981) *Foreign Workers in Western Europe: An Emerging Political Force*, New York: Praeger

Milza, P. (1985) 'Un Siècle d'immigration étrangère en France', *Vingtième siècle*, no. 7 (July–September), pp. 3–18

Ministère de l'Education Nationale (1989) 'L'Enseignement des langues et cultures d'origine dans le premier degré en 1988–1989', *Note d'information*, 89–53

Mitra, S. (1988) 'The National Front in France – A Single-Issue Movement?', *West European Politics*, vol. 11, no. 2 (April), pp. 47–64

Moreau-Desportes, A. (1990) 'Les Emissions des radios locales privées', *Hommes et migrations*, no. 1136, pp. 46–8

Moreira, P. (1987) *Rock métis en France*, Paris: Souffles, 1987

Morokvasic, M. (1990) 'Le Comportement économique des immigrés dans le secteur de la confection', in G. Abou Sada, B. Courault and Z. Zeroulou (eds), *L'Immigration au tournant*, Paris: CIEMI/L'Harmattan, pp. 237–48

Morokvasic, M., Phizacklea, A., and Rudolph, H. (1986) 'Small Firms and Minority Groups: Contradictory Trends in the French, German and British Clothing Industries', *International Sociology*, vol. 1, no. 4 (December), pp. 397–419

MRAP (Mouvement contre le Racisme et pour l'Amitié entre les Peuples) (1984) *Vivre ensemble avec nos différences*, Paris: Editions Différences

Muller, M. (1987) *Couscous pommes frites: le couple franco-maghrébin, d'hier à aujourd'hui*, Paris: Ramsay

Muñoz-Perez, F., and Tribalat, M. (1984) 'Mariages d'étrangers et mariages mixtes en France: évolution depuis la Première Guerre', *Population*, no. 3 (May–June), pp. 427–62

Muxel, A. (1988) 'Les Attitudes socio-politiques des jeunes issus de l'immigration maghrébine en région parisienne', *Revue française de science politique*, vol. 38, no. 6 (December), pp. 925–40

Naïr, S. (1988) 'L'Immigration maghrébine: quelle intégration? Quelles citoyenneté?', in C. Wihtol de Wenden (ed.), *La Citoyenneté et les changements de structures sociale et nationale de la population française*, Paris: Edilig/Fondation Diderot, pp. 257–79

Nielsen, J. S. (1992) *Muslims in Western Europe*, Edinburgh: Edinburgh University Press

Nini, S. (1993) *Ils disent que je suis une Beurette . . .*, Paris: Fixot

Noiriel, G. (1988) *Le Creuset français: histoire de l'immigration, xixᵉ–xxᵉ siècles*, Paris: Seuil

―――― (1991) *La Tyrannie du national: le droit d'asile en Europe (1793–1993)*, Paris: Calmann-Lévy

―――― (1992a) 'Difficulties in French Historical Research on Immigration', in D. L. Horowitz and G. Noiriel (eds), *Immigrants in Two Democracies: French and American Experiences*, New York and London: New York University Press, pp. 66–79

―――― (1992b) 'Français et étrangers', in P. Nora (ed.), *Les Lieux de mémoire*, III: *Les France*, vol. 1: *Conflits et partages*, Paris: Gallimard, pp. 275–319

OFPRA (Office Français de Protection des Réfugiés et Apatrides) (1994) *Bilan de trieze années de fonctionnement de l'OFPRA (1981–1993)*, Fontenay-sous-Bois: OFPRA

Ogden, P. E. (1991) 'Immigration to France since 1945: Myth and Reality', *Ethnic and Racial Studies*, vol. 14, no. 3 (July), pp. 294–318

Ogden, P. E., and White, P. E. (eds) (1989) *Migrants in Modern France: Population Mobility in the Later 19th and 20th Centuries*, London: Unwin Hyman

Olzak, S. (1983) 'Contemporary Ethnic Mobilization', *Annual Review of Sociology*, vol. 9, pp. 355–74

Oriol, P. (1992) *Les Immigrés devant les urnes*, Paris: CIEMI/L'Harmattan

Palidda, S., and Muñoz, M.-C. (1988) 'The Condition of Young People of Foreign Origin in France', in C. Wilpert (ed.), *Entering the Working World: Following the Descendants of Europe's Immigrant Workforce*, Aldershot: Gower, pp. 89–110

Panoramiques (1991) 'Islam, France et laïcité: une nouvelle donne?', *Panoramiques*, no.1 (June–August)

Passages (1989) 'Immigration business: l'état, la politique, les immigrés et l'argent', September, pp. 21–30

Pellegrini, C. (1992) *Le FIS en France, mythe ou réalité*, Paris: Edition°1

Perotti, A., and Thépaut, F. (1990) 'L'Affaire du foulard islamique: d'un fait divers à un fait de société', *Migrations société*, vol. 2, no. 7 (January–February), pp. 61–82

Perotti, A., and Toulat P. (1990) 'Immigration et médias: le "foulard" surmédiatisé?', *Migrations société*, vol. 2, no. 12 (November–December), pp. 9–45.

Perrineau, P. (1991) 'Le Front National: du désert à l'enracinement', in P.-A. Taguieff (ed.), *Face au racisme*, vol. 2: *Analyses, hypothèses, perspectives*, Paris: La Découverte, pp. 83–104

Piet, E. (1992) 'Excision et prévention', in E. Rude-Antoine (ed.), *L'Immigration face aux lois de la République*, Paris: Karthala, pp. 189–203

Piore, M. (1979) *Birds of Passage: Migrant Labor and Industrial Societies*, Cambridge, Cambridge University Press

Platone, F., and Rey, H. (1989) 'Le FN en terre communiste', in N. Mayer and P. Perrineau (eds), *Le Front National à découvert*, Paris: FNSP, pp. 268–83

Poinsot, M. (1993) 'Competition for Political Legitimacy at Local and National Levels among Young North Africans in France', *New Community*, vol. 20, no. 1 (October), pp. 79–92

Poiret, C. (1992) 'Le Phénomène polygamique en France', *Migrants-formation*, no. 91 (December), pp. 24–42

Poiret, C., and Guégan, C. (1992) 'L'Habitat des familles polygames en région Ile-de-France'. Etude réalisée pour le compte du FAS, du Plan Architecture Construction et du GIAPP, Paris: Vivre la Ville

Ponty, J. (1988) *Polonais méconnus: histoire des travailleurs immigrés en France dans l'entre-deux-guerres*, Paris: Publications de la Sorbonne

Population (1971) 'Attitudes des Français à l'égard de l'immigration étrangère: enquête d'opinion publique', no. 5, pp. 827–75

—— (1974) 'Attitudes des Français à l'égard de l'immigration étrangère. Nouvelle enquête d'opinion', no. 6, pp. 1015–69

Portes, A. (1981) 'Modes of Structural Incorporation and Present Theories of Immigration', in M. M. Kritz, C. B. Keely and S. M. Tomasi (eds), *Global Trends in Migration*, New York: Center for Migration Studies, pp. 179–298

Presse et mémoire (1990) *France des étrangers, France des libertés*, Paris: Mémoire Génériques Editions/Editions Ouvrières

Quemener, H. (1991) *Kofi, histoire d'une intégration*, Paris: Payot

Questions clefs (1982) 'Jeunes immigrés hors le murs', *Questions clefs*, no. 2 (March)

Rachedi, N. (1994) 'Elites of Maghrebian Extraction in France', in B. Lewis and D. Schnapper (eds), *Muslims in Europe*, London and New York: Pinter, pp. 67–78

Rath, J. (1993) 'The Ideological Representation of Migrant Workers in Europe: A Matter of Racialisation?', in J. Wrench and J. Solomos (eds), *Racism and Migration in Western Europe*, Oxford: Berg, pp. 215–232

Raulin, A. (1990) 'La Consommation médiatique: une passion des minorités urbaines?', *Mediaspouvoirs*, no. 17 (January–March), pp. 19–28

Revue de linguistique et de didactique des langues (1990) 'Les Langues et cultures des populations migrantes: un défi à l'école française', no. 2

Rex, J. (1986a) *Race and Ethnicity*, Milton Keynes: Open University Press

—— (1986b) 'Preface', in J. Rex and D. Mason (eds), *Theories of Race and Ethnic Relations*, Cambridge: Cambridge University Press

—— (1988) *The Ghetto and the Underclass: Essays on Race and Social Policy*, Aldershot: Avebury

Rex, J., and Tomlinson, S. (1979) *Colonial Immigrants in a British City*, London: Routledge & Kegan Paul

Rimani, S. (1988) *Les Tunisiens de France: une forte concentration parisienne*, Paris: CIEMI/L'Harmattan

Rodrigues, N., *et al.* (1985) *La Ruée vers l'égalité*, Paris: Mélanges

Rogers, R. (1986) 'The Transnational Nexus of Migration', *Annals of the American Academy of Political and Social Science*, vol. 485 (May), pp. 34–50

Roux, M. (1991) *Les Harkis: les oubliés de l'histoire*, Paris: La Découverte

Roy, O. (1990) 'Dreux: de l'immigration au ghetto ethnique', *Esprit*, no. 159 (February), pp. 5–10

—— (1991) 'Ethnicité, bandes et communautarisme', *Esprit*, no. 169 (February), pp. 37–47

—— (1993) 'Les Immigrés dans la ville: peut-on parler de tensions "ethniques"?', *Esprit*, no. 191 (May), pp. 41–53

—— (1994) 'Islam in France: Religion, Ethnic Community or Ethnic Ghetto?', in B. Lewis and D. Schnapper (eds), *Muslims in Europe*, London and New York: Pinter, pp. 54–66

Rudder, V. de (1990) 'Notes à propos de l'évolution des recherches françaises sur "l'étranger dans la ville"', in I. Simon-Barouh and P.-J. Simon (eds), *Les Etrangers dans la ville: le regard des sciences sociales*, Paris: L'Harmattan, pp. 60–80

—— (1992) 'Immigrant Housing and Integration in French Cities', in D. L. Horowitz and G. Noiriel (eds), *Immigrants in Two Democracies: French and American Experiences*, New York and London: New York University Press, pp. 247–67

Rudder, V. de, and Goodwin, P. (1993) 'Théories et débats sur le racisme en Grande-Bretagne', *L'homme et la société*, no. 110 (October–December), pp. 5–19

Rudder, V. de, and Guillon, M. (1987) *Du marché d'Aligre à l'îlot Chalon*, Paris: L'Harmattan

Rude-Antoine, E. (1991) 'La Polygamie et le droit français', *Regards sur l'actualité*, no. 176 (December), pp. 38–49

Safran, W. (1985) 'The Mitterrand Regime and its Policies of Ethnocultural Accommodation', *Comparative Politics*, vol. 18, no. 1 (October), pp. 41–63

—— (1986) 'Islamicization in Western Europe: Political Consequences and Historical Parallels', *Annals of the American Academy of Political and Social Science*, vol. 485 (May), pp. 98–112

—— (1987) 'Ethnic Mobilization, Modernization, and Ideology: Jacobinism, Marxism, Organicism and Functionalism', *Journal of Ethnic Studies*, vol. 15, no.1 (Spring), pp. 1–32

—— (1990) 'Ethnic Diasporas in Industrial Societies: A Comparative Study of the Political Implications of the "Homeland" Myth', in I. Simon-Barouh and P.-J. Simon (eds), *Les Etrangers dans la ville: le regard des sciences sociales*, Paris: L'Harmattan, pp. 163–77

—— (1991) 'State, Nation, National Identity and Citizenship: France as a Test Case', *International Political Science Review*, vol. 12, no. 3, pp. 219–38

—— (1992) 'Sociopolitical Context and Ethnic Consciousness in France and the United States: Maghrebis and Latinos', in A. M. Messina *et al.* (eds), *Ethnic and Racial Minorities in Advanced Industrial Democracies*, New York: Greenwood, pp. 67–87

Salgues, B. (1988) 'Les Flux financiers des travailleurs immigrés', in S. Hessel (ed.), *Immigrations: le devoir d'insertion. Analyses et annexes*, Paris: La Documentation Française, pp. 393–5

Sayad, A. (1975) 'El Ghorba: le mécanisme de reproduction de l'émigration', *Actes de la recherche en sciences sociales*, no. 2 (March), pp. 50–66

—— (1978) *Les Usages sociaux de la culture des immigrés*, Paris: CIEMI

—— (1979) 'Qu'est-ce qu'un immigré?', *Peuples méditerranéens*, no. 7 (April–June), pp. 3–23

—— (1987) 'Les Immigrés algériens et la nationalité française', in S. Laacher (ed.), *Questions de nationalité: histoire et enjeux d'un code*, Paris: L'Harmattan, pp. 125–203

Schain, M. (1985) 'Immigrants and Politics in France', in J. S. Ambler (ed.), *The French Socialist Experiment*, Philadelphia: Institute for the Study of Human Issues, pp. 166–90

—— (1987) 'The National Front in France and the Construction of Political Legitimacy', *West European Politics*, vol. 10, no. 2 (April), pp. 229–52

—— (1988) 'Immigration and Changes in the French Party System', *European Journal of Political Research*, vol. 16, no. 6 (November) pp. 597–621

—— (1993) 'Policy-Making and Defining Ethnic Minorities: The Case of Immigration in France', *New Community*, vol. 20, no. 1 (October), pp. 59–77

—— (1994) 'Policy and Policy-Making in France and the United States: Models of Incorporation and the Dynamics of Change', paper presented to the conference of the Association for the Study of Modern and Contemporary France, Portsmouth, England, 16–18 September

Schmitter Heisler, B. (1986) 'Immigrant Settlement and the Structure of Emergent Immigrant Communities in Western Europe', *Annals of the American Academy of Political and Social Science*, vol. 485 (May), pp. 76–86

Schnapper, D. (1988) 'La Commission de la Nationalité, une instance singulière', *Revue européenne des migrations internationales*, vol. 4, nos 1–2, pp. 9–28

—— (1990) *La France de l'intégration: sociologie de la nation en 1990*, Paris: Gallimard

—— (1992) *L'Europe des immigrés: essai sur les politiques d'immigration*, Paris: François Bourin

Schor, R. (1985) *L'Opinion française et les étrangers en France, 1919–1939*, Paris: Publications de la Sorbonne

Sellam, S. (1987) *L'Islam et les musulmans en France*, Paris: Tougui

Shields, J. S. (1991) 'The Politics of Disaffection: France in the 1980s', in J. Gaffney and E. Kolinsky (eds), *Political Culture in France and Germany*, London and New York: Routledge, pp. 69–90

Siblot, P. (1992) 'Ah! Qu'en termes voilés ces choses-là sont mises', *Mots*, no. 30 (March), pp. 5–17

Silberman, R. (1992) 'French Immigration Statistics', in D. L. Horowitz and G. Noiriel (eds), *Immigrants in Two Democracies: French and American Experiences*, New York and London: New York University Press, pp. 112–23

Silverman, M. (1992) *Deconstructing the Nation: Immigration, Racism and Citizenship in Modern France*, London and New York: Routledge

Simon, P. (1992) 'Belleville, un quartier d'intégration', *Migrations société*, vol. 4, no. 19 (January–February), pp. 45–68

Sindonino, P. (1993) 'Les Africains de Vincennes', *Migrations société*, vol. 5, no. 25 (January–February), pp. 58–67

Smaïn (1990) *Sur la vie de ma mère*, Paris: Flammarion

SOFRES (1984) *Opinion publique. Enquêtes et commentaires: 1984*, Paris: Gallimard

—— (1990) *L'Etat de l'opinion 1990*, Paris: Seuil

—— (1991) *L'Etat de l'opinion 1991*, Paris: Seuil

—— (1992) *L'Etat de l'opinion 1992*, Paris: Seuil

—— (1993) *L'Etat de l'opinion 1993*, Paris: Seuil

—— (1994) *L'Etat de l'opinion 1994*, Paris: Seuil

Souida, A. (1990) 'Roubaix, les "RONA" dans la cité', *Hommes et migrations*, no. 1135 (September), pp. 59–64

Stora, B. (1990) '1789–1989: Nationalité et citoyenneté (histoire d'un couple, histoire d'une crise'), in *1789–1989: Actes du colloque organisé à la Maison de la Culture d'Amiens les 27, 28 et 29 octobre dans le cadre de la commémoration du bicentenaire de la révolution française*, Amiens: Association de Soutien à l'Expression des Communautés d'Amiens, pp. 20–41

—— (1991) *La Gangrène et l'oubli*, Paris: La Découverte

Streiff-Fenart, J. (1989) *Les Couples franco-maghrébins en France*, Paris: L'Harmattan

—— (1993) 'The Making of Family Identities among Franco-Algerian Couples', in A. G. Hargreaves and M. J. Heffernan (eds), *French and Algerian Identities from Colonial Times to the Present: A Century of Interaction*, Lewiston and Lampeter: Edwin Mellen, pp. 225–37

Taboada-Leonetti, I. (1982) 'Identité nationale et liens avec le pays d'origine', in H. Malewska-Peyre *et al.* (eds), *Crise d'identité et déviance chez les jeunes immigrés*, Paris: La Documentation Française, pp. 205–47

—— (1987) *Les Immigrés dans les beaux quartiers: la communauté espagnole dans le XVIᵉ*, Paris: CIEMI/L'Harmattan

—— (1989) 'Cohabitation pluri-ethnique dans la ville: stratégies d'insertion locale et phénomènes identitaires', *Revue européenne des migrations internationales*, vol. 5, no. 2, pp. 51–70

Taguieff, P.-A. (1989) 'The Doctrine of the National Front in France (1972–1989): A "Revolutionary" Programme?', *New Political Science*, nos 16–17 (Fall–Winter), pp. 29–70

—— (1990) 'The New Cultural Racism in France', *Telos*, no. 83, pp. 109–22

Taguieff, P.-A. (ed.) (1991) *Face au racisme*, 2 vols, Paris: La Découverte

Talha, L. (1989) *Le Salariat immigré dans la crise*, Paris: CNRS

Tapinos, G. (1975) *L'Immigration étrangère en France, 1946–1973*, Paris: Presses Universitaires de France

—— (1992) 'Immigration féminine et statut des femmes étrangères en France', *Revue française des affaires sociales*, vol. 46 (December), pp. 29–60

Todd, E. (1994) *Les Destins des immigrés: assimilation et ségrégation dans les démocraties occidentales*, Paris: Seuil

Toubon, J.-C., and Kessamah, K. (1990) *Centralité immigrée: le quartier de la Goutte d'or. Dynamique d'un espace pluriethnique: succession, compétition, cohabitation*, Paris: CIEMI/L'Harmattan

Tribalat, M. (1993) 'Les Immigrés au recensement de 1990 et les populations liées à leur installation en France', *Population*, no. 6, pp. 1911–46

—— (ed.) (1991) *Cent ans d'immigration: Etrangers d'hier, Français d'aujourd'hui*, Paris: Presses Universitaires de France/INED

Tribune Fonda, La (1991) 'Associations et immigration: 10 ans de liberté associative pour les étrangers en France', nos 82–3, November

Tripier, M. (1990) *L'Immigration dans la classe ouvrière en France*, Paris: CIEMI/L'Harmattan

UNESCO (1986) *Mass Media and the Minorities*, Bangkok: UNESCO Regional Office for Education in Asia and the Pacific

Varro, G., and Lesbet, D. (1986) 'Le Prénom révélateur', in G. Abou-Aada and H. Milet (eds), *Générations issues de l'immigration: 'mémoires et devenirs'*, Paris: Arcantère, pp. 139–53

Verbunt, G. (1985) 'France', in T. Hammar, *European Immigration Policy: A Comparative Analysis*, Cambridge: Cambridge University Press, pp. 127–64

Verhaeren, R.-E. (1990) 'Avenir de l'immigration face aux mutations du marché du travail', in G. Abou Sada, B. Courault and Z. Zeroulou (eds), *L'Immigration au tournant*, Paris: CIEMI/L'Harmattan, pp. 123–36

Vichniac, J. E. (1991) 'French Socialists and the *droit à la différence*: A Changing Dynamic', *French Politics and Society*, vol. 9, no. 1 (Winter), pp. 40–56

Villanova, R., and Bekkar, R. (1994) *Immigration et espaces habités*, Paris: CIEMI/L'Harmattan

Voisard, J., and Ducastelle, C. (1990) *La Question immigrée*, revised edition, Paris: Seuil

Vuddamalay, V., White, P., and Sporton, D. (1991) 'The Evolution of the Goutte d'or as an Ethnic Minority District of Paris', *New Community*, vol. 17, no. 2, pp. 245–58

Wacquant, L. J. D. (1992) 'Banlieues françaises et ghetto noir américain: de l'amalgame à la comparaison', *French Politics and Society*, vol. 10, no. 4 (Autumn), pp. 81–103

Wayland, S. (1993) 'Mobilising to Defend Nationality Law in France', *New Community*, vol. 20, no. 1 (October), pp. 93–110.

Weil, P. (1988) 'La Politique française d'immigration (entre 1974 et 1986) et la citoyenneté', in C. Wihtol de Wenden (ed.), *La Citoyenneté et les changements de structures sociale et nationale de la population française*, Paris: Edilig/Fondation Diderot, pp. 189–200

—— (1991) *La France et ses étrangers: l'aventure d'une politique de l'immigration, 1938–1991*, Paris: Calmann-Lévy

—— (1994) 'La Politique française de l'immigration depuis 1945', in B. Falga, C. Wihtol de Wenden and C. Leggewie (eds), *Au miroir de l'autre: de l'immigration à l'intégration en France et en Allemagne*, Paris: Editions du Cerf, pp. 251–69

Weil, P., and Crowley, J. (1994) 'Integration in Theory and Practice: A Comparison of France and Britain', *West European Politics*, vol. 17, no. 2 (April), pp. 110–26

White, P. E. (1989) 'Immigrants, Immigrant Areas and Immigrant Communities in Postwar Paris', in P. E. Ogden and P. E. White (eds), *Migrants in Modern France: Population Mobility in the Later 19th and 20th Centuries*, London: Unwin Hyman, pp. 195–211

Wieviorka, M. (1990) 'La Crise du modèle français d'intégration', *Regards sur l'actualité*, no. 161 (May), pp. 3–15

Wihtol de Wenden, C. (1987) *Citoyenneté, nationalité et immigration*, Paris: Arcantère

—— (1988) *Les Immigrés et la politique*, Paris: Presses de la Fondation Nationale des Sciences Politiques

—— (1994a) 'Le Cas français', in B. Falga, C. Wihtol de Wenden and C. Leggewie (eds), *Au miroir de l'autre: de l'immigration à l'intégration en France et en Allemagne*, Paris: Editions du Cerf, pp. 41–59

—— (1994b) 'The French Response to the Asylum Seeker Influx, 1980–93', *Annals of the American Academy of Political and Social Science*, vol. 534 (July), pp. 81–90.

Wilson, W. J. (1987) *The Truly Disadvantaged*, Chicago: Chicago University Press

—— (ed.) (1989) 'The Ghetto Underclass: Social Science Perspectives' (special issue of *Annals of the American Academy of Political and Social Science*, vol. 501)

Yinger, J. M. (1985) 'Ethnicity', *Annual Review of Sociology*, vol. 11, pp. 151–80

Yok-Soon, N. G. (ed.) (1991) *Guide de la communauté chinoise en France, 1991–1992*, Paris: Editions les Cent Fleurs

Zaleska, M. (1982) 'Identité culturelle des adolescents issus des familles de travailleurs immigrés', in H. Malewska-Peyre *et al.* (eds), *Crise d'identité et déviance chez les jeunes immigrés*, Paris: La Documentation Française, pp. 177–204

Zamora, F., and Lebon, A. (1985) 'Combien d'étrangers ont quitté la France entre 1975 et 1982?', *Revue européenne des migrations internationales*, vol. 1, no. 1, pp. 67–80

Index